Zapotec Wome

Texas Press Sourcebooks in Anthropology, No. 16

ZAPOTEC WOMEN

LYNN STEPHEN

UNIVERSITY OF TEXAS PRESS, AUSTIN

First Edition, 1991

Requests for permission to reproduce material from this work
should be sent to Permissions, University of Texas Press, Box 7819,
Austin, Texas 78713-7819.

∞ The paper used in this publication meets the minimum requirements of American
National Standard for Information Sciences—Permanence of Paper for Printed Library Materials, ANSI Z39.48-1984.

Library of Congress Cataloging-in-Publication Data
Stephen, Lynn.
    Zapotec women / by Lynn Stephen. — 1st ed.
        p.   cm. — (Texas Press sourcebooks in anthropology ; no. 16)
    Includes bibliographical references and index.
    ISBN 0-292-79064-3. — ISBN 0-292-79065-1 (pbk.)
    1. Zapotec Indians—Women.   2. Zapotec Indians—Social conditions.   3. Zapo-
tec Indians—Economic conditions.   4. Women—Mexico—Teotitlán de Valle—Economic conditions.   5.   Women—Mexico—Teotitlán de Valle—Social conditions.
6. Textile industry—Mexico—Teotitlán de Valle.   7. Social structure—Mexico—
Teotitlán de Valle.   8. Teotitlán de Valle (Mexico)—Social life and customs.
I. Title.   II. Series.
FI221.Z3S74   1991
305.48'8976—dc20   91-8904
                                                                             CIP

I DEDICATE THIS BOOK TO THE PEOPLE OF TEOTITLÁN DEL
VALLE AND TO MY NEPHEW, BENJAMIN GOLDMAN STEPHEN,
IN THE HOPES THAT HE MAY SHARE THE WONDERS AND
KNOWLEDGE THAT THE PEOPLE OF TEOTITLÁN SHARED WITH ME.

Contents

Photographs

Maps

Figures

Tables

Acknowledgments

THIS BOOK represents a seven-year period of my life beginning as a second-year graduate student at Brandeis University. In the seven years that I have dedicated to this project, family, friends, mentors, and colleagues both in the United States and in Mexico have contributed immensely and provided me with a rich and supportive context.

When I was a graduate student in the anthropology department at Brandeis University, Robert Hunt provided inspiration, support, and encouragement for this project from its very beginning until its completion as a book. The careful attention of Sutti Ortiz in the conceptualization and analysis of the larger effort this book represents was also invaluable. Judith Zeitlin was the first person to open the doors of ethnohistory to me and I thank her for her example and her encouragement in better integrating local and regional history into the project.

While I was teaching at MIT, Martin Diskin and James Howe provided intellectual and collegial support, spending many hours discussing various aspects of the book. They have remained important colleagues.

While working in Mexico during the past seven years, I have been fortunate to have shared my fieldwork, graduate school, and "new faculty" status with Jonathan Fox, who has provided unending support, encouragement, and intellectual inspiration, resulting in exciting collaborative research. Jeffrey Rubin has also been an invaluable Mexicanist colleague.

Since I began teaching at Northeastern University in 1987, my colleagues have shown tremendous support and encouragement. Christine Gailey, in particular, has provided me with inspiration, challenges, friendship, and critical feedback on several sections of this book. Debra Kaufman, Michael Blim, Alan Klein, Carol Owen, and Pat Golden have provided intellectual and collegial support for this project. My students have also provided challenges and encouragement. The Women's Studies Program and its executive board members at Northeastern have also provided support.

Other scholars in the United States have provided encouragement, criticism, and inspiration, including Stefano Varese, Karen Sacks, and Art Murphy. June Nash has provided critical intellectual and editorial feedback and suggestions. Friends and colleagues who have proven invaluable in supporting this project include Carol Zabin, Sylvia Maxfield, Nicole Sault, and Helen Clements.

I would like to thank Judith Hellman, Fran Rothstein, Michael Kearney, and anonymous reviewers from the University of Arizona Press and the University of Texas Press for their careful comments and suggestions, which helped to make this a better book.

Funding for field research was provided by the Inter-American Foundation, the Wenner-Gren Foundation for Anthropological Research, and the Damon Fellowship of Brandeis University. Additional research and writing time was funded by the Center for U.S.-Mexican Studies, University of California, San Diego.

My six months at the Center for U.S.-Mexican Studies resulted in a wonderful intellectual experience in a superb physical and academic environment. I wish to thank Wayne Cornelius and my colleagues Teresa Korack, Neil Harvey, María Cook, Ilan Semo, and Enrique Semo for making this a particularly interesting and productive time.

In Mexico, I have many people to thank for their contributions to this work. In Oaxaca I would like to thank Cecil Welte, resident anthropologist and director of the Oficina de Estudios de Humanidad del Valle de Oaxaca for advice and use of his wonderful library. The Oaxaca office of the Instituto Nacional de Anthropología e Historia was extremely generous in assisting me to secure permission to work in Oaxaca, particularly Lic. María de la Luz Topete, Dra. Alicia Barabas, and Dr. Miguel Bartolomé. Colleagues at GADE (Grupo al Apoyo del Desarrollo Etnico), including Gary Martin, Alejandro de Avila, Teresa Pardo, and Pedro Lewin, were particularly helpful. Jorge Hernández and Josefina Aranda of the Instituto de Investigaciones Sociológicas de la Universidad Autónoma Benito Juárez de Oaxaca provided great assistance in making the resources and data available and offering opportunities for intellectual interchange with students. Dr. Manuel Esparza, director of the Archivos del Estado de Oaxaca, was very helpful in locating historical information. Kate Raisz provided critical support and encouragement during the longest stretch of fieldwork for this project.

In Oaxaca, my ten years of personal and intellectual friendship with Margarita Dalton and Guadalupe Musalem have been invaluable. They were the first people to open their homes to me there. Michael Higgins, whom I associate more with Mexico than with the United States, has also been an important friend and colleague.

My family has provided me with comfort, support, and inspiration throughout this project, often visiting me in the field and encouraging me through the more difficult parts of writing. Suzanne Brown, Bruce Stephen, and Rachel Goldman have backed me through the entire process. Ellen Herman has provided unending daily support, encouragement, and critical intellectual feedback throughout the writing of this book and the dissertation that preceded it.

A special group of friends in Boston always made it a wonderful place to come back to after being in the field.

More than anyone, the people of Teotitlán are to be thanked for opening their homes, hearts, and minds to me for over seven years. I would like to thank the González family for sharing their home with me, my family, and friends for so many years, particularly Paco, who has served as one of my primary teachers, guides, and friends, along with Cristina. To Petra I owe many wonderful insights into local culture and history. María Chávez has also been a valuable friend and research assistant. Many other people in the community who prefer to remain unnamed have been important friends and collaborators in this research.

Zapotec Women

Chapter 1. Introduction

We really like speaking Zapotec. We speak it because it is our language—the language that our parents and their parents spoke. Even though they teach us another language in school and other kinds of customs and traditions, we like being Zapotec. We can be modern and Zapotec at the same time. (Carlota, age 17)

Scene 1: Soledad sits surrounded by the four oldest women at the wedding fiesta. Before them are the cooked carcasses of four pigs. The older women and Soledad work quickly to divide up the meat, putting large chunks into bowls to be served to the guests. They make sure that the largest portions are given to the most important people. This is the second meal of the day. A more elaborate meal will be served tomorrow to the 200 men and women assembled in the courtyard. Outside, groups of younger women, some unmarried and others married with small children, are making tortillas. They comment on the recent improvements in Soledad's house. Soledad's family has six good-sized looms and a new pickup truck. They completed a new wing of construction, which doubled the size of their house. And, just in time for the wedding, they built a bathroom, complete with a flush toilet. Some of the women comment about how they would like to have additional rooms in their one-room homes. Others describe beds, refrigerators, and new dishes they hope to buy in the future.

Scene 2: Petra steps inside as her neighbor opens the door. She solemnly enters the house, crossing over to the altar at the center of the main room. She kisses the altar, greeting the saints, and then turns to Pedro and Gloria, whom she has come to see. She formally greets them and explains that she and her family are going to sponsor a *posada,* a three-day celebration involving several large meals and drinking in conjunction with the visit of the local Christ-child saint to their home at Christmas. She requests that they return the turkey she loaned to them two years ago when their youngest son was married. Pedro and Gloria pull out a small blue notebook and find the entry recording the loan of Petra's turkey. They nod and agree to deliver a turkey of equal or greater weight one week before the Christmas *posada*.

Scene 3: fourteen-year-old María is alone in the house. Her parents are across town celebrating the baptism of the new son of their *compadres*. Outside, an American in a white Volkswagen Rabbit has pulled up to María's house. The driver gets out and knocks at the door. María lets in the American, Susan, who owns an importing business in Dallas. She has come to pick up an order of 200 weavings. She tells María that she hopes they are ready because she is flying back to the United States in two days. Perplexed, María gives her a hot tortilla, explaining that her parents are not home. She knows they have not completed the order because of the baptismal invitation. She also knows, however, that Susan is a very important client. She quickly sends her younger brother to give a message to her parents. Half an hour later, María's father returns, after explaining to his *compadre* that he has to meet with a client. María's mother remains at the *compadre*'s house to help with the cooking.

These scenes are descriptions of common events in the Zapotec-speaking community of Teotitlán del Valle, Oaxaca, Mexico. Known internationally for its wool textiles, Teotitlán has become an economic success story in a state that is distinguished by having the lowest per capita gross domestic product in all of Mexico.

In conjunction with this successful weaving industry, people continue to devote a significant amount of time and energy to ritual activity. Looking at the impact of textile commercialization on Teotitlán, we might expect to find a community that is rapidly abandoning its links to the past and being absorbed into the international capitalist economy. We might also predict a rapid advancement of class differentiation and an increase in women's status as they begin to work as weavers paid at rates equal to those of men. These were the predictions I made during my first two months of fieldwork during the summer of 1983.

I settled into my first stretch of summer fieldwork in Teotitlán after looking at several Zapotec communities in the central valleys of Oaxaca as possible fieldsites. I was initially attracted to Teotitlán because of three factors. First, upon visiting for several days I discovered that—contrary to everything I had ever read about treadle loom weaving and about Teotitlán in particular—a significant number of the weavers were women. This seemed to signal an important change in the gendered division of labor, which could have major consequences for the status of women not only in production, but in other areas as well. Second, it was abundantly clear that economic development was taking place in the community. New homes were being constructed and everyone was busy producing or selling wool textiles. English signs to attract tourists were frequent. During my first days, most of the people I met tried to sell me a *serape* or inquired about whether or not I had an importing business in the United States. Finally, in spite of obvious evidence of rapid economic development and direct connections to U.S. marketing outlets, including Pier 1, Bloomingdale's, Filene's, and private import stores, there was a strain of traditionalism in the community. Everyone spoke Zapotec and every day someone, somewhere, was having a ritual ceremony, which completely disrupted the rhythm of weaving production. I decided to stay in Teotitlán precisely because what I saw happening was not what was predicted. It seemed to be a place caught between a rapidly advancing future in export production and a long-entrenched past of ethnic uniqueness anchored in ongoing institutions, setting out on an orbit I wanted to become part of, temporarily.

Most of my first two-month fieldwork stint was spent trying to understand the basic social structure of the community, the daily routine of households, the agricultural cycle, and the gendered division of labor. Because I knew very few people, like most anthropologists I became an expert in initiating conversations on any pretext. One of my most successful techniques was to inquire about fine-looking cows, pigs, and chickens. Most women and men were willing and interested in talking about animal production—when I was able to communicate with them.

While well prepared to speak Spanish, I soon discovered that life in Teotitlán went on exclusively in Zapotec. Because my first place of residence was with a largely monolingual Zapotec-speaking family, my first efforts at conversation, while painful, came quickly out of necessity. My first friends turned out to be either monolingual elderly Zapotec women or younger married men who were interested in talking about agriculture and politics. Because I wanted to include gender as a major category of my research, it became clear that my monolingual elderly female friends were critical in helping me to gain an understanding of women's lives in Teotitlán. As my first and most consistent teachers, I credit them with providing many of the insights I gained with more time. Another way of learning more Zapotec was to exchange Zapotec lessons for English lessons appropriate for selling textiles. I finally got so many requests for English terms of color, size, design, counting, and description (the basics of making a sale) that I produced a small document that I gave to people as a study aid. Eventually I also began to work consis-

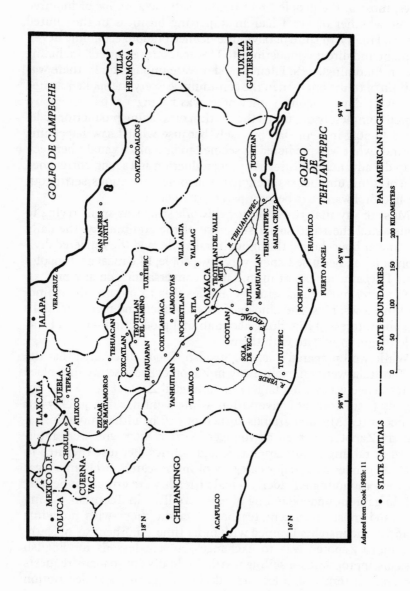

Adapted from Cook 1982b: 11

● STATE CAPITALS   — ·· — STATE BOUNDARIES   —— PAN AMERICAN HIGHWAY

Map 1. State of Oaxaca and Surroundings

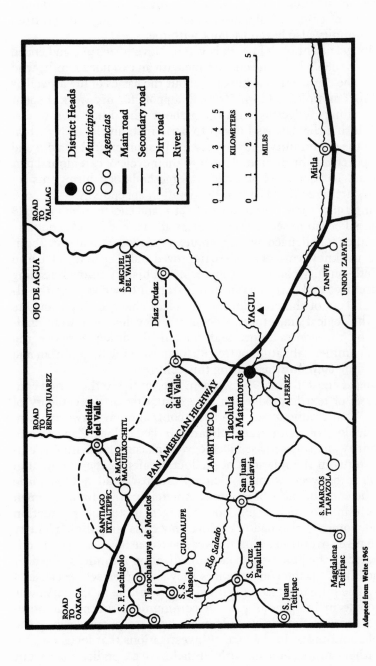

Map 2. Teotitlán and Surrounding Communities

Adapted from Welte 1965

tently with one young man, who became my Zapotec tutor and most consistent research collaborator. Later several young women from the community also began to work with me.

My longest stint of fieldwork began in November 1984 and ended in January 1986. I lived the entire time with an extended family, who proved to be critical in teaching me about the basics of life as well as providing emotional and intellectual support for my work. I spent many evenings reflecting with them about what I had seen or discussed during the day. As I began to participate in the heavy ritual cycle of the community, they trained me in appropriate behavior and ritual speech and incorporated me into their cycle of ceremonial participation. The details of my fieldwork methodology during this period and later are described in more detail in appendix A.

During 1985, 1986, the summer of 1987, and shorter visits in 1988 and 1989, I began to see my initial ideas about gender and economic development challenged by the complexity of recent history in Teotitlán. As my knowledge of Zapotec improved and I began to delve into twentieth-century community and regional history through reading local archives and carrying out oral history interviews with the eldest members of the community, my ideas changed. My thoughts about the logical trajectory of economic development were challenged by the contradictory and dialectical consequences of the gradual commercialization of treadle loom weaving in Teotitlán and surrounding communities during this century.

Because I chose to focus on women, I began to see the varied consequences of textile production for export first in the category of gender. What I came to see as a basic contradiction between a kin-based ideology of community solidarity linked to local Zapotec ethnic identity and a class-based ideology emphasizing wealth and employer status in the relations of production alerted me to potential differences between women. Generalizations could not be made about the consequences of textile commercialization for *all* women in Teotitlán. To understand how changes in textile production affected women, I also had to explore how class and ethnic identity have changed over time. This allowed me to see how women are differentiated in the process of commercialization regardless of gender and shed light on the consequences they share precisely because of gender. The primary lesson I learned from working in Teotitlán was that people in indigenous peasant communities are not homogeneous. There are significant differences between people even at the level of community. In the case of investigations that focus on gender, neither can we come up with all-inclusive generalizations about all men and all women.

One more scene is offered to illustrate the differences between women as well as some of the common roles they share. The rest of the book elaborates on this theme, focusing on gender relations in ritual, weaving, production, and politics.

Scene 4: ritual space is segregated by gender, with men eating, drinking, lounging, and sitting apart from women. Within this segregation by gender, a ritual order of respect and prestige is evident, based on ritual experience and age. Those men and women with the most ritual experience have leadership roles. In this context an elderly woman, Gloria, discusses how the dance should be structured with the male host *mayordomo*. Later she instructs a young merchant woman to serve shots of *mescal* to all of the women present. The next week, outside of the ritual event, Gloria comes into contact with the young merchant woman in a different context. She visits the woman's house in order to pick up yarn for several wall hangings she has agreed to weave on a piecework basis. Gloria is told by the young woman, who is probably acting in accordance with her husband's specifications, what size to make the weavings, what colors to use, what design to copy, and when they should be ready. Gloria will be paid when the weavings are completed. That evening Gloria is at home finishing up a day of weaving. She talks with her husband, who is preparing to go to the town hall for a community assembly. Gloria gives her opinion on how difficult negotiations with the state-run yarn factory have been and urges him to push for community control. When he leaves, she continues to weave. Gloria does not go to community meetings because it is not the custom for women to attend.

As this example illustrates, an elderly woman who holds the highest authority in a ritual event may have little or no control over the style, color, and dimensions of what she weaves. In contrast, a young merchant woman who has little authority in a ritual event has some authority in production relations, particularly in comparison to women who are working for her and her husband. Neither woman has much of a voice in formal community assemblies. Their political participation comes through discussions with other women in the market, at ritual events, and at community water sites, through subtle protest actions, and through efforts to influence their husbands, who do attend community assemblies.

For women in Teotitlán and other indigenous communities, the shifting dynamics of ethnicity and class frame and define their daily world as well as their possibilities for changing it. Because of this, gender does not function as a separate analytical category. Rather than simply being about "women" as a group opposed to "men," this book attempts to clarify the way in which gender takes on specific meaning in relation to particular economic and cultural arrangements—in this case, in relation to commercial capitalism, the class system it engenders, and formulations of ethnic identity influenced by traditional aspects of indigenous Zapotec culture and state-promoted images of "Mexican Indians." In trying to reassess the idea that world markets determine local social and economic relations, the book tries to show that the changed positions of women in Zapotec society are not simply the products of increased demand for woven goods. Rather, the lives of Zapotec women have been shaped by the intersection of regional, national, and international markets with education, local and national gender ideology, changes in the local and national gender ideology, migration, changes in the local and national political system, and local and national processes of ethnic labeling. The chapters that follow emphasize the multiple representations of gender, class, and ethnicity and how they are used, particularly by women, to achieve goals and agendas.

Chapter 2 provides a discussion of key concepts used in the book (including ethnicity, class, and kin-based institutions of solidarity and exchange such as ritual kinship and reciprocal goods and labor exchanges) and outlines how these institutions function in relation to social reproduction. The concept of social reproduction is proposed as a model for understanding gender relations.

Chapter 3 uses the life-histories of five Zapotec women—merchants and weavers, young and old—to explore on a personal level the arenas of weaving production, ritual, and politics. These life-histories provide concrete illustrations of many of the analytical and descriptive points made in the book.

Chapter 4 provides an introduction to the Zapotecs and to the community of Teotitlán, offering background information on agriculture, the division of agricultural labor, occupations, land distribution, geography and climate, political ties, markets, religious institutions, education, and health.

Chapter 5 documents Teotitlán's transition from a community of subsistence farmers and part-time weavers laboring under a system of mercantile capitalism to a town of artisans producing for export under a system of commercial capitalism. It contrasts local constructions of economic history to those of the state, focusing on women's role in the labor force, state constructions of indigenous women, and the impact on women of large-scale male migration to the United States.

Chapter 6 continues this discussion, covering the more recent transformation of weaving production under commercial capital.

It explores how class differentiation distinguishes between merchant and weaver women in the arena of weaving production and marketing.

Chapter 7 lays the historical basis for a discussion of women's changing participation in ritual and political life in Teotitlán. Focusing on the divorce of civil from religious offices in local government beginning in the 1930s and the phasing out of *mayordomías*, this chapter examines the changing structural conditions that have decreased women's role in politics.

Chapter 8 documents how the ritual content and form of *mayordomías* have been transferred to life-cycle rituals and how women use these rituals and the traditional notion of *respet* to continue to influence the community.

Chapter 9 explores the current dimensions of women's political participation, documenting how they are shut out of most formal political institutions and how their age and class status influence their ideas about themselves as political actors and their strategies for political participation.

Chapter 10 applies the lessons learned about the limitations on women's political participation by comparing the Teotitlán ethnographic material with three other cases where indigenous peasant women were able to establish an autonomous presence in communities and/or in peasant organizations in Mexico.

The final chapter looks at the implications of this historical and ethnographic material for the political, economic, and ritual participation of peasant women in other areas of Mexico, particularly in relation to grassroots popular movements in which women play a major part.

Chapter 2. Ethnicity, Class, and Social Reproduction: The Frames of Women's Daily Lives

We are all united here. This is a very quiet town where no one causes any problems. We aren't like other towns where people are divided. We are all just one community. No one is better than anyone else. (Jorge, age 50)

Of course some women have more status than others. The ones who are older, who have given a lot of fiestas, they are always the most distinguished. (Marina, age 25)

THIS BOOK focuses on changes in women's roles and authority in production, ritual, and local politics from 1920 to 1989, a period in which the economic base of Teotitlán changed from mercantile to commercial or circulation capital. Of particular interest is the question of how the dynamics of ethnicity and class formation work to create differences between women and to promote or discourage solidarity within the context of community activity. At a larger level, the case of Zapotec women is compared with that of other Mexican women in the rural sector in an effort to determine if there are common economic, cultural, or historical factors that produce specific forms of women's networking and organizing and have marginalized them from political institutions. By way of clarifying key concepts used in the book and placing them in the context of a larger literature on Mexico and Latin America, the following topics are covered in this chapter: the concept of ethnicity and its definition in Teotitlán; ethnicity in Mexico; the concept of class and class relations in Teotitlán; class relations in mercantile and commercial capitalism in Oaxaca; kin-based institutions of solidarity and exchange, including *respet* (ritually based authority), *compadrazgo* (ritual kinship), and *guelaguetza* (reciprocal goods and labor exchanges); and how these institutions function in relation to the social reproduction of laborers and social actors. The concept of social reproduction is proposed here as an alternate framework to the public/private model of gender relations.

The Concept of Ethnicity

In an ongoing battle to determine the analytical primacy of class or ethnicity as the major motor of social relations in rural communities, both Mexican and North American anthropologists have often reduced ethnicity to class, or class to ethnicity, without really looking at the ways in which the two intersect. This reflects a larger problem in anthropology that emerges when the concept of culture is used to analyze social class formation and transition, usually in the guise of acculturation. Culture is most often defined as a set of shared values or rules for organizing social life. Precisely because culture is usually assumed to be equally shared by all and passed on intact from one generation to another, it is seldom used in analyses of change. Culture either becomes derivative, "an attachment of more basic political-economic processes," or becomes "independent of the realities of social class" (Sider 1986 : 5).

Anthropologists' attempts to define ethnicity or specific ethnic groups have suffered from some of the same problems Sider cites for models of culture. All too often ethnic identities are assumed to be constituted in the same way for all who hold them and to be identifiable according to a set of objective characteristics. Historically, anthropologists divided people into discrete units such as cultures, tribes, or ethnic groups based on the fact that they spoke a particular language, shared common ceremonies and material artifacts, and lived in similar areas. This time-honored approach was taken by anthropologists in Mexico in relation to particular ethnic groups as well as by the government census office. Bilingualism and migration, among other things, have led most anthropologists to conclude that ethnic groups cannot necessarily be distinguished by objective empirical traits such as the language they speak or the territory they occupy. Instead, ethnicity has become a subjective, dynamic concept through which groups of people determine their own distinct identities by creating boundaries between themselves and other groups through interaction (Adams 1988; Barth 1969).

Ethnicity is a concept used by a group of people in particular situations where they are trying to assert their status vis-à-vis another group of people, often for political, economic, or social reasons. A self-chosen ethnic identity is usually based on a claim to historical autonomy and perceived cultural or physical traits that are emphasized as a primary source of identity and recognized internally as well as externally (Stephen and Dow 1990). Steve Stern (1987: 15–16) has pointed out that presumed physical and cultural traits draw social boundaries that may or may not coincide with economic class boundaries. Depending on the context in which a specific ethnic identity is used, by whom, and toward what end, ethnicity may be used to link classes together in opposition to a perceived common threat or to reinforce the dominant position of one class over another. Ethnicity is an identity that is used in different ways by people in various situations, usually to stake a particular claim.

The above discussion is meant to clarify the way in which ethnicity is framed as an analytical concept, which is distinct from the particular way in which Teotitecos and non-Teotitecos culturally construct ethnicity for themselves. I argue below, and in greater detail in chapter 8, that Teotitecos' construction of ethnicity has two dimensions to it: an ethnic identity for outside consumption that emphasizes community solidarity and a common claim to being the originators of treadle loom weaving in the Oaxaca Valley and an internal version of ethnic identity that, although it emphasizes common language, participation in local social and cultural institutions, and weaving production, also allows the contradictions of class differentiation, age, and gender to slip through in subtle ways. These different dimensions are part of one cultural construction, but demonstrate the ways in which indigenous peoples have consciously built ethnic identities to serve their needs in different contexts.

The specific construction of Teotitlán ethnic identity also has important historical and processual aspects. Rather than proposing that the specific content of Teotiteco ethnic identity be characterized as a protective defense of "traditional" local institutions from outside intervention, I try to demonstrate that Teotitecos, particularly merchants, were actively engaged with the discourses of state officials on "Indian tradition" and incorporated pieces of hegemonic national culture into their own construction of what it means to be from Teotitlán. William Roseberry (1989:75–76) notes in his discussion of images of the Venezuelan peasant, following Raymond Williams (1977), that tradition is *selective* tradition. Alternative, oppositional cultural forms are created out of dominant culture, as Teotiteco merchants have done with official versions of Mexican "Indian tradition." Because the process of Teotiteco ethnic identity construction takes place within a community that is neither homogeneous nor egalitarian, differentiation that has existed within the community during this century (according to wealth, gender, and relative ritual and economic status) is reflected in the ways in which ethnic identity is formulated and expressed within Teotitlán.

The notion of resistance is important here in understanding the ways in which Teotiteco ethnic identity has been constructed and manifested during this century. Resistance does not imply complete isolation from and rejection of the dominant culture. In the case of the Zapotecs, this is discussed in relation to the ways Teotitecos addressed postrevolutionary ideology emphasizing the creation of a national subject incorporating both Spanish and "Indian" heritage as *la raza cósmica*. Resistance to cultural domination is a dialectical project in which ongoing local processes of identity creation along several dimensions (class and gender in particular) produce alternate realities to hegemonic ideology precisely because of their local specificity and content. For example, the fact that Teotiteco weavers have continued to produce textiles in a local economic system that included reciprocal labor and goods exchanges as well as commoditized labor has affected the way in which they have formulated their identity as indigenous craft producers. They have not simply absorbed outside designations of them as weavers unchanged by time using the same technology, but have developed an identity commensurate with their place in both international capitalism and local reciprocal exchange.

The notion of resistance has been discussed in various contexts in relation to ethnicity and culture. One of the key questions in contemporary anthropological studies of ethnicity concerns the role of what Spicer (1971) calls "the oppositional process" in the establishment of persistent ethnic identities. Spicer and others maintain that persistent ethnic identities are the result of efforts to incorporate or assimilate groups into the larger whole, whether culturally, economically, socially, or religiously (Castile 1981; Peterson Royce 1982; Spicer 1971). They argue that resistance to incorporation has varied from silence to violence, but that, without some form of antagonism, persistent identity systems would fail to develop (Peterson Royce 1982 : 46). This oppositional process produces intense collective consciousness and a high degree of internal solidarity. Spicer has used this analysis to explain the persistent ethnic identity of the Maya, Yaqui, and Navajo groups in Mexico and the U.S. Southwest.

Taking a more political perspective, Gerald Sider (1976) has also examined the conditions that foster ethnic solidarity in the face of national racial and cultural oppression, distinguishing between what he calls cultural nationalism and political nationalism. Drawing on the example of the Lumbee in the United States, he defines political nationalism as a call for autonomy and fundamental economic and political changes within a group, particularly with regard to material inequalities. Cultural nationalism is based on symbolic issues that internally colonized groups use to distinguish themselves from dominant ethnic groups that are the prime benefactors of state policy (Sider 1976 : 163). What is useful about Sider's formulation is his description of how a historically marginalized people can simultaneously develop a collective identity based on a place outside of the state and a class structure dependent upon, but separate from, the class structure of the dominant state. In the same way, while the changing Zapotec class structure caused by a transition from mercantile to commercial capitalism is related to changes in the larger political economy of Mexico after the Revolution, the Zapotecs of Teotitlán have created their own locally defined ethnic identity in opposition to, *and* incorporating elements of, the commoditized Indian identity promoted first by the postrevolutionary Mexican state and later by U.S. and Mexican textile entrepreneurs.

The incorporation and reinterpretation of elements of imposed culture is also raised in Edward Sapir's (1956) notion of genuine and spurious culture. In a seminal essay, Sapir (1956 : 93) distinguishes between the creation of an oppositional, internally generated culture that may exist within the confines of larger oppressive social relations and an external or spurious culture that does not "build itself out of the central interests and desires of its bearers" (see also Gailey 1987b : 36– 37). Stanley Diamond (1951) points out that genuine culture includes the creation of new cultural forms that combine the structure and content of older forms with new social and political reality.

Sider's later work, incorporating the Gramscian concept of hegemony and the problematic notion of culture, provides further insight into the larger processes at work in the forging of indigenous ethnic identities in postrevolutionary Mexico. His work in Newfoundland emphasizes the possibility of creating an assertive and autonomous life for one class out of the cultural hegemony of another (1986 : 119). As used by Sider, William Roseberry (1989), Stefano Varese (1988), Raymond Williams (1977), and others, the concepts of hegemony and counterhegemony suggest that cultural and economic patterns of expression and consumption involve a dialectical dynamic in which the marginalized sectors of a national population absorb and rework material conditions, ideology, and culture imposed on them by dominant classes. "Hegemony, I suggest, is not opposed by protesting elite values in the abstract—simply as values—but by opposing the conjunction of these values with appropriations. . . . Rather, opposition to hegemonic domination advances values that are, or become, rooted in the ties people have to one another in daily life and in production. The fragmentation of these ties in Newfoundland shaped both the hegemonic assertions and the capacity of fisherfolk to resist" (Sider 1986:122). This reworking of dominant culture is one step in a process of resistance that may or may not reach a level of violent confrontation.

The dominant culture that is reworked by marginalized groups in the routines of daily life and through social reproduction can emanate from the state as well as from dominant economic classes. While Antonio Gramsci initially separated the "state" from "civil society," he later argued that the two were inseparable (Harvey 1989). Power is expressed by the state as government and carried out through coercive means. But power is also diffused through state ideology in institutions linked to civil society, meaning that the state is integrated with and not separate from civil society (Nagengast 1990). Gramsci (1971:242) identified the characteristic institutions of civil society as newspapers, schools, public buildings and spaces, national symbols, and churches.[1] As such, these institutions were the medium of hegemony through which the state and dominant classes delivered their cultural messages. Such institutions serve the educational interests of the state through helping to create new types of civilization that link the national productive system to a shared sense of morality.

Ethnicity in Mexico

Gramsci's model of the integral state is certainly an appropriate one for examining the creation and dissemination of dominant ideology concerning what it means to be "Indian" in Mexico.[2] Through a battery of state-linked institutions including schools, cultural missions, newspapers, development projects, and local systems of government, Mexico's ruling political party (Partido Revolucionario Institucional, PRI) and its precursors made "Indian" an identity to which all Mexicans could lay claim as they sought to build a nationalist consciousness to support continued domination of the political system. Promoting Indianness as part of Mexican national identity was a political strategy for incorporating indigenous communities into the political system and also provided a national racial distinction to separate Mexico from its dominant northern neighbor. In the 1988 presidential election, this strategy backfired when many indigenous Mexicans voted for the opposition candidate because he was *mexicano,* meaning of mixed (mestizo, i.e., half Indian) descent, rather than for the *español* candidate of the PRI, who was white.

While general Indianness became acceptable, chic, and even de-sired in some social circles in urban capitals (Friedlander 1975 : 165 – 188), local ethnic identity was encouraged by the Mexican govern-ment as a marketing strategy for tourism. In many Latin countries indigenous ethnic groups have been encouraged to maintain and re-produce certain outwardly picturesque characteristics, in particular dress, ritual, and craft production, which make them identifiable as Indians to tourists (see Cook 1984a; García Canclini 1982; Graburn 1982). Such external characteristics stand in contrast to internally defined characteristics and social relations used by a particular eth-nic group to distinguish itself from others.

The basic distinction between a self-chosen ethnic identity and that of an imposed Indian identity is discussed by Richard Chase Smith (1985) in his analysis of ethnic federations, peasant unions, and Indianist movements in the Andean republics. While he is speak-ing largely of foreign colonial powers, his characterization of Indian identity as a "political and racial label imposed on the indigenous population irrespective of tribal identity marking a hierarchical rela-tionship" (1985:9) could also be applied to outside appropriation and definition of specific ethnic identities. When the state and pri-vate business market "Indian culture," whether it is a specific cul-ture or not, they invoke the same relationship as the colonial desig-nation of *indio*, indicating the subordinate position of indigenous peoples (Bonfil Batalla 1981; Smith 1985).

It is interesting to note, however, that most discussions of eth-nicity in Mexico, while they are critical of the colonial meaning at-tached to *indio*, nevertheless indirectly embrace a similar paradigm by keeping discussions at the level of two large racial/ethnic groups in Mexico, mestizos and *indios*. For example, Judith Friedlander (1975) concludes that ethnicity is not a significant form of identity because the Nahuatl-speaking people she studied in a community in Morelos do not have a shared sense of culture with other "Indians" and exhibit very few traits that are unquestionably prehispanic. She concludes that Indian identity is meaningful only in terms of a low socioeconomic position in the national stratification system. It is just another way of saying "poor."

Descriptions of ethnicity in Mexico that either focus on the mes-tizo/*indio* dichotomy or deny the existence of any type of meaning-ful ethnic identity ignore the ways in which indigenous peoples have reappropriated dominant concepts about themselves. Reappro-priation and reworking of indigenous ethnicity have served to main-tain local autonomy and functioned as a basis for grassroots political movements, such as the Movimiento de Unificación y Lucha Triqui (Movement for the Unification and Struggle of the Triquis). In Oaxaca, the Triquis have built a movement of over 10,000 people in several communities that focuses on a confrontation involving more than 13,000 acres of disputed woodlands and communal land (Amnesty International 1986). Denial of the importance of their specific ethnicity rooted in a historical claim to resources relegates groups such as the Triquis to passive Indian masses.

While the situation of the Teotiteco Zapotecs explored here is certainly less dramatic than that of the Triquis, Teotitecos' specific claim to local Zapotec ethnicity and a right to control weaving production and distribution has been critical to the community's struggle for autonomy in relation to the larger political economy of Mexico. Evidence of a desire for autonomy is found first as the community circumvented documentation of its growing textile industry by the state and later avoided involvement in craft development programs that put the state in the role of middleman peddling Indian crafts.

The phenomenon of both state and commercial appropriation of ethnic identity for the purposes of tourism and craft production for export makes it necessary to amend Edward Spicer's (1971) model of opposition slightly in the context of Teotiteco ethnic identity. In the case considered here, local indigenous identity has been maintained and perhaps strengthened by an indirect opposition to pressures of assimilation. This opposition has taken the form of a multidimensional ethnic identity—one face is shown to consumers of indigenous culture (such as tourists, importers, state agencies, and foreigners who purchase indigenous crafts), and another operates within Teotitlán and is accessible to those who are members of the community by virtue of their participation in local networks and institutions. This internal dimension not only emphasizes the common heritage of Teotitecos as weavers, but also subtly accommodates the tensions that threaten community solidarity. Thus we might modify Spicer's model for situations of outside appropriation or imposition of ethnicity. Here the dynamic of opposition comes through a local redefinition of ethnicity as an alternative to the commoditized version of ethnic identity promoted by the state and textile importers and tourists.

Local Teotitlán Zapotec Identity

In addition to articulating the oppositional nature of the ethnic identity constructed by Teotitecos, we must also address its local orientation. Critical to understanding the specific identity of people such as Teotitecos is the relative autonomy maintained by indigenous populations in Oaxaca and the political atomization of the area, prehispanically, colonially, and thereafter. The growth of Teotitlán and other valley communities as population centers is closely linked with the rise and fall of Monte Albán.

Located about 38 kilometers from Teotitlán, Monte Albán was the prehispanic capital of a valley-wide Zapotec political state that had broad regional influence in matters of religion and military offense and defense, but did not seem to interfere directly in production and trade. Unlike the great civilization at Teotihuacán that thrived during the same period (A.D. 200–700), Monte Albán appears never to have distorted the Oaxaca Valley's existing central place hierarchy (Blanton 1978:108). Local populations continued to play important administrative and economic roles.

The population of Monte Albán reached an apex of 30,000–60,000 (Blanton 1978:108; Flannery and Marcus 1983:183) between A.D. 400 and 600 and probably exerted its greatest influence on surrounding communities at this time. Monte Albán was largely abandoned after A.D. 700. Richard Blanton (1978) speculates that the downfall of Monte Albán is related to the collapse of Teotithuacán during the same period. With the decline of Monte Albán, local ceremonial centers seem to have taken over the political leadership of the Zapotecs and perhaps some of the population lost fom Monte Albán (Flannery and Marcus 1983:184). This is often referred to as the "Balkanization of Oaxaca." During Monte Albán Period V (A.D. 950–1500), the Oaxaca Valley was divided into numerous small states that were hostile to one another.

The archaeological record is supplemented by sixteenth-century historical sources such as the *Relaciones geográficas* and Fray Francisco de Burgoa's *Geográfica descripción*, written in 1674. The *Relaciones geográficas* are a survey of political, economic, and social conditions of New Spain conducted between 1579 and 1585 at the command of Philip II. According to historical information presented in the Oaxaca *Relaciones*, the political situation of the late prehispanic era was one in which small city-states were warring with one another and alliances changed rapidly.

Teotitlán, Macuilxóchitl, Mitla, and Tlacolula all came under Spanish control in 1521. Teotitlán and other communities were put in varying combinations of local administrative units called first *corregimientos* and then later *alcaldes mayores* (regional administrative offices of the crown). In 1531, Teotitlán and Macuilxóchitl were formally delegated to the Spanish crown and became a *corregimiento*, as did Mitla and Tlacolula. These two *corregimientos* were under the *alcalde mayor* of Antequera (Gerhard 1972:190–191). In 1680, the two jurisdictions of Teotitlán del Valle/Macuilxóchitl and Mitla/Tlacolula were combined to make one administrative unit, an *alcaldía mayor* administered from Teotitlán (Gay 1881:23; Gerhard 1972:191).

From 1680 until Mexican independence, Teotitlán was head of a large administrative unit as a district seat. After independence it reverted to being a *municipio* (municipal seat), one of 570 in the state of Oaxaca. Almost half of the municipal seats in all of Mexico are located in Oaxaca. Through the continued colonial and postindependence actions of the state, the political atomization of Oaxaca probably resulted in a high level of very localized allegiance and sense of ethnic identity tied to notions of community. A tendency toward anarchy and intercommunity conflict is often seen between communities that may share a language and be defined by the state as belonging to the same ethnic group (Barabas and Bartolomé 1986:29; Dennis 1987). While this pattern is not generalizable to all of Oaxaca's linguistic groups such as the Triquis, Mixe, and Chatinos, who all have extracommunity levels of political organization, it does apply to most communities.

In this century, the notion of community has been reinforced by Mexican anthropologists and bureaucrats who structured programs aimed at integrating the indigenous population with the national polity at the level of the community. Colonial and modern state policy of isolating communities and reinforcing the importance of locality has limited the possibilities for regional movements of ethnic autonomy (Medina Hernández 1983). The result in places such as Teotitlán is a high level of ethnic identification with the community. This strong sense of locality operates not only in relation to the state and outside textile entrepreneurs, but also in relation to surrounding Zapotec communities from which Teotitlán seeks to distinguish itself on the basis of producing high-quality weavings, maintaining an elaborate ceremonial system, and speaking a unique form of Zapotec. The strong locality of Teotiteco identity also operates as an ongoing dynamic of resistance to incorporation by dominant national ideologies that homogenize Oaxaca's fourteen distinct ethnic groups into Indians.

The Multiple Faces of Teotiteco Identity

According to people from different sectors of Teotitlán, some common elements of being from *šxia* (Zapotec for Teotitlán, meaning below the rock) involve speaking Teotitlán Zapotec, participating in

the social and cultural institutions that reproduce kinship relationships, and being the first people in Oaxaca to produce wool weavings. Because of the various levels through which Teotiteco identity
is manipulated, the common heritage of a united community of
weavers bonded together by kinship has been used by various sectors
of the population in different ways throughout history.

Critical to an understanding of Teotiteco ethnic identity is the
way in which the dimensions of its construction work in different
contexts. The version of Teotiteco identity projected to those outside of the community emphasizes community solidarity, particularly in laying claim to the fruits of Zapotec weaving. An important
piece of the current Teotiteco claim on textiles is a continuous link
to the past as the originators of treadle loom weaving in Oaxaca.

This claim is validated by people from other indigenous communities in the Oaxaca valleys. It is irrelevant to Teotitecos that the
technology and materials that they used to produce the first weavings were brought by the Spaniards. Those who penned the official
correspondence for Teotitlán in this century worked self-consciously
to maintain an aura of mystique about the community, reproducing
stereotypes of indigenous artisans and protecting the interests of
merchants by deemphasizing their activities. They created and recreated a picture of simple precapitalist relations of production,
describing "humble weavers working at simple looms," creating
unique blankets "adorned with designs and idols that signify the
history of Mitla and Monte Albán" (Archivo Municipal de Teotitlán
del Valle 1938).

While the commercial version of their identity that Teotitecos
maintain for outsiders emphasizes a united community of kin producing unique textiles and participating in an elaborate and important ceremonial life, internal representations of that same identity
are more contradictory. Riddled with subtle tensions, the picture of
local history and identity painted by older men and women suggests
a more complex reality. According to them, while community members did have a common history of weaving production and a rich
ceremonial life, there were also differences between people in terms
of what they wore, what they ate, the kind of houses they lived in,
how many godchildren they had, how many fiestas they were able to
sponsor, and the material conditions of their lives. On the one hand,
these histories offer a strong image of community identity and emphasize the importance of how things were done by *'be:n(i) lo'getš*
(Teotiteco Zapotec for people of the town). On the other hand, they
also focus on the diverse realities of that history for a population

with varied levels of wealth, ritual status, and distinct gender roles. Today Teotitecos still use the language of kinship and solidarity to manipulate each other toward specific ends. For example, merchants use the language of kinship and *compadrazgo* to recruit their god-children as pieceworkers. Merchant women may use the same language and the implication of equal relations in order to leave early from a ritual commitment. Weaver women use the same language to pressure a ritually superior *comadre* to purchase some clothing for a child's school graduation. This internal expression of Teotiteco identity in daily productive, ceremonial, and political relations provides a complex and sometimes conflicting reality for Zapotec women.

On the Concept of Class

An issue of major concern to students of Latin American peasantry is socioeconomic stratification. Macroeconomic theories of development and underdevelopment (see Cardoso and Faletto 1969; Frank 1967; Furtado 1970; Griffin 1969; and Kay 1975) tend to ignore the process of local economic differentiation and describe the economic position of peasants only in relation to their dependency on big capital. Refinements of underdevelopment theory focus on factors in the process of local and regional class formation. Discussion by Marxist-oriented scholars has centered on the relative importance of demographic factors, position in the labor force, and access to productive resources in the process of class formation (see Cook 1984a, 1984b; Deere and de Janvry 1979, 1981; de Janvry 1981; Greenberg 1981; Munck 1985; Roseberry 1989; Smith 1984). Anthropologists and others concerned with the symbolic and ideological elements of peasant cultures have been more drawn to a Weberian approach to stratification, differentiating among class, prestige, and power, often focusing on individual advancement (Cancian 1965; Mathews 1985; Vogt 1969).

The model of economic class used here describes Teotitecos in relation to one another vis-à-vis the relations of production. Ritual authority or *respet* is examined in the next section in relation to kin-based notions of status, which, although they coexist with class differences, are not the same. They are part of a distinct system of differentiation that interacts with class and is affected by it under different conditions of capitalist development.

As discussed below, the way in which class relations are manifested in the community has changed in conjunction with a shift from merchant to commercial capital. Therefore, one typology cannot be used to describe the ways in which class relations looked empirically throughout this century. Since many of the data in the book on class, ethnic, and gender relations focus on the past twenty years, however, I propose a general typology for current divisions in the population along class and gender lines—focusing on the categories of merchant and weaver.

The issue of class has been dealt with either directly or indirectly by many ethnographers of the Zapotecs. Those who have made class analysis a central part of their argument have usually aligned themselves with an explicitly Marxist framework (discussed below) or a more understated Weberian approach that outlines social class in terms of an interplay among wealth, social status or prestige, and lifestyle (Mathews 1985; Peterson Royce 1975). Other ethnographers such as Henry Selby (1974) have touched on social class in relation to specific topics such as deviance behavior. Since this book uses a concept of class that is economic and rooted in the relations of production, the contributions of other ethnographers in this area are relevant here.

In their book on the Oaxaca market structure, Scott Cook and Martin Diskin (1976:22) take a Marxist approach to class: "Accordingly, Valley of Oaxaca society would be viewed as a dual class (bourgeoise/proletariat) structure of multiple levels (medium and small bourgeoise, proletariat proper, semiproletariat, subproletariat, and lumpenproletariat) and sectors (e.g., industrial, commercial, agricultural, artisan)." Following this line of inquiry in a later book on Zapotec metate production, Cook cites Lenin's description of socioeconomic strata identified by their relation to the means of production, by their role in the division of labor, and consequently "by the dimensions of the share of social wealth of which they dispose and the mode of acquiring it" (Lenin 1967:213–214 as cited in Cook 1982b:71). Cook's 1982 book concludes with a discussion of the primacy of class versus ethnicity as a tool of social analysis in Oaxaca. His later work (1984b, 1988) takes on the issues raised by a Chayanovian (1966) analysis of social differentiation and looks at the complex process by which petty commodity producers become petty capitalists. This is discussed in greater detail in chapter 6. Cook's later work that focuses on the dynamic processes of class formation provides insight into the dynamics of local capital accumulation in Zapotec communities and suggests the importance of flexible, relational models of class rather than dualistic typologies.

Perhaps the most insightful general discussion of class in Oaxaca comes from James Greenberg (1981). Pointing out the differences between social status and economic class positions, Greenberg (1981:184) observes following Rodolfo Stavenhagen (1975) that, while multiple stratification systems can coexist in one society, only one class structure exists within a given socioeconomic system. Like Cook, he cites Lenin's relational definition of class, but he states that a strict definition of a two-class system is too general. Following the observations of Carmen Diana Deere (1986:59) and Edward Robbins (1975), he notes that a dualistic model does not specify the intermediate positions in the social structure that lie between the classic capitalist/labor split. In a two-class model, he believes that peasants may occupy an intermediate position. As stated by Robbins (1975:291), "modern political economy offers a range of roles neither clearly worker nor clearly owner."

Rather than engage in the debate about the actual class position(s) of the Zapotecs as proletarians/bourgeoise, or a class apart (i.e., peasants), I suggest an amendment to a class model based on the work of Erik Olin Wright that focuses on the relational aspect of class found in the sphere of work. In the case of Zapotec weaving production, which forms the basis for contemporary class relations in Teotitlán, class divisions rest not solely on forms of property ownership, but also on relations of domination and control in the labor process. In his model of contemporary class relations in industrial society, Wright (1979, 1985) distinguishes between basic class positions that reflect the dichotomy between bourgeoisie and proletariat and contradictory class locations that are positions within the productive process that are characterized by some elements of a two-class system. Households in Teotitlán can and do occupy intermediate positions in the class structure related to the transition from weaver to petty capitalist merchant. Both merchant households and weaving households could also be said to occupy somewhat contradictory class locations because their structural position is not strictly tied to property relations. Currently, ownership of the means of production is not a primary means for measuring class position among the weaving population since most weavers own their own looms. In the earlier part of this century, when land was the primary means of production, large landholdings were important in assessing class divisions.

Current class relations in Teotitlán are manifested more directly in domination and control over the labor process. This includes who gives orders and sets the parameters for how, when, and at what price textile production takes place. In particular, the difference between selling one's labor or hiring the labor of others, either directly or indirectly, is important. Class relations are also based on the extraction of surplus value from the labor of workers.

Merchants and Weavers as Class Groups

This book focuses on two class-based groups in Teotitlán: merchants and weavers. In relation to changes in gender roles, these two groups were found to be the most significant. While women in the community share common social roles based on their gendered positions as wives, mothers, and daughters, these roles are modified by the class position of their household. In their discussions of differences between themselves, women particularly emphasized merchant or weaving status, specifically in the role of each in local labor relations. As indicated in the next chapter, these are not the only occupations that operate in the local class system. They are the two that affect the largest portion of the population, however, and are the focus of my discussions of women in rituals, economics, and politics. As used throughout the text, and by Teotitecos themselves, the occupational terms "merchant" and "weaver" are also class labels that imply one's position in the relation of production.

While it is difficult to make absolute distinctions between merchant and weaver households,[3] for the purposes of discussion here, I have separated households into two types: merchants and weavers (both self-employed weavers who sell their own goods and piecework weaving households who are contracted by merchants). In Teotitlán, the linguistic categories of merchant and weaver have both political and economic significance. A weaver is called *rúnčilàt(ši)* (maker of weavings). A merchant or *hurešlat(ši)* (seller of weavings) is identified by Teotitecos as a person who purchases textiles and, through these textiles, the labor of others. Merchants are viewed, in the words of one weaver, as "buying what someone else labored to make. They didn't sweat for it." "A merchant is someone who makes more money than a weaver. Merchants are those who buy from other weavers. Half of what they make comes from other people; they earn money without working. A weaver only lives from his own work" (Salomón, age 40).

The class position of merchant households is based on the fact that the primary source of income for its members comes from either direct purchase of woven goods or payment of piece-wages to contracted weavers for textiles produced. While many merchant households continue to produce textiles, they have all reached a level of capital accumulation where they purchase the labor of others and thereby extract surplus value from weavers, which is then reinvested in their businesses.

The class position of weaver is based on the fact that weavers either produce independently and then sell to local merchants at a low price, not receiving the full value for their work reflected in the price the merchant will charge to tourists or importers, or are contracted as laborers by merchants and paid at a piece-rate, also resulting in an extraction of surplus value. While there are intermediate positions between merchant and weaver, all Teotitecos participating in weaving production are labeled by their peers as holding either a merchant or a weaver position. Such distinctions reflect real differences in control and domination in the labor process and in the distribution of profits and are also reflected in the cognitive classifications Teotitecos make. When viewed in relation to gender, distinctions between merchant women and weaver women, as well as between merchant men and weaver men, become important in understanding the dynamics of gendered participation in weaving production, ritual, and politics.

The Changing Nature of Class Relations under Mercantile and Commercial Capitalism

While the above explanation of class positions structured around the merchant/weaver distinction holds for the past fifteen years, this typology is tied to the current structure of weaving production for export. Earlier class relations were not manifested in the same way and involved a more subtle extraction of labor as mediated through the ritual system of forced *mayordomías.* The interaction of class and relations of ritual authority have changed through time. Here these dynamics are explored in the period from 1920 to 1989, a time characterized by a transition from mercantile to commercial capital intervention in Teotitlán. The following discussion on the changing nature of class provides a necessary context for understanding the ways in which women have experienced the intersection of class and ethnicity in this century.

As documented by Kate Young (1976, 1978), indigenous peasant economies in the Oaxaca Sierra region are characterized by the intervention of two kinds of capital during the late nineteenth and twentieth centuries. The period from 1870 to 1930 was marked by economic activities dominated by independent merchant capital— local capital not directly tied to a larger systemic process of industrialization. This domination was broken, and a new inflow of capital—commercial or circulation capital—resulted in the monetization of the economy and increasing social and economic differentiation after 1930 (Young 1978 : 135). While the timing and structural alignments of this transition were somewhat different in Teotitlán than in the higher sierra communities Young analyzes, her general description is also applicable to Teotitlán.

The concepts of merchant capital and commercial capital are important not only for understanding how Teotitlán fits into the wider political economy of Mexico after the Mexican Revolution, but also for understanding the changing nature of class relations from 1920 to 1989. As the economic base of Teotitlán changed from subsistence farming and part-time craft production in conjunction with merchant capital to migration and then full-time craft production in relation to commercial capital, the meaning, content, and form of class relations and ethnic identity shifted. Relating the changing nature of class relations to different types of capitalist development helps to clarify the way in which gendered production roles and the labor of women facilitated this transition.

Prior to 1931, Teotitlán was characterized by a shifting group of six to seven merchant/trader households who dominated economic relations through trade and an indirect hold on labor through debt connected to obligatory *mayordomías*. Because of continued poor economic conditions during and after the Mexican Revolution, cult sponsorship of *mayordomías* was obligatory, with future sponsors named, often against their will, by ritual elders. Unable to pay up front for their sponsorship, many men and women had to sell their land and their own and/or their children's labor to local merchants in order to cover ritual expenses.

As exemplified by Teotitlán in the late 1920s, merchant capitalism does not produce a system of differentiation that corresponds to categories of labor and capital. Rather, labor relations of dominance and subordination are indirect and often mediated by local cultural forms that are controlled by local leaders and may also provide mediums of community solidarity (Sider 1986 : 34). In Teotitlán, the *mayordomía* system, which sometimes resulted in debt peonage and cheap land for merchants, also pulled together large sectors of the community in celebrations that triggered reciprocal exchanges and symbolically united everyone with protective saints.

Two of the outstanding features of class relations under merchant capitalism are that capital does not directly appropriate labor through buying and selling labor, but rather through other mechanisms that may be political or cultural, and that internal stratification (within communities) does not occur in relation to permanent wealth differences and private appropriation of land and wage labor (Young 1976: 127, 133).

The class system in Teotitlán under conditions of mercantile capitalism was not characterized by direct and overt exploitation of labor by merchant/traders. Instead, labor was indirectly appropriated through the *mayordomía* system. Community elders who had already served as *mayordomos* sanctioned the desperate behavior of men and women who sold whatever was necessary to merchants and others to finance their ritual obligations. Because the *mayordomía* system was intertwined with the civil cargo system, the authority of elders was also political. While many elders had been poor themselves and were victims of the same system of obligatory *mayordomía*, they indirectly supported the interests of merchants, who in return gave them their political support and legitimized their ritual and political authority in the civil-religious hierarchy.

The hold that merchant/traders had over the population began to change in the 1930s as a consequence of both state intervention and the penetration of commercial capital into the community. While Mexico's industrial sector received a boost as it produced for the U.S. market during World War II, with peace, commercial capital made major inroads into the internal areas of states such as Oaxaca in search of new markets (Young 1978: 139). The completion of the Pan American Highway in Oaxaca in 1948 facilitated the further integration of Oaxaca's periodic markets with the Mexican national economy.

The inauguration of the second U.S.-Mexican *bracero* program in 1942 was a major factor in the penetration of commercial capital (industrial capital) into communities such as Teotitlán. While large numbers of men from Teotitlán migrated to the United States to work for wages during the late 1940s and 1950s, women supported themselves and their children by taking on additional chores, often labor performed by men. When the men returned home, they invested their savings in land, animals, and in several cases the means of production for weaving (looms and wool). The labor of women thus facilitated capital accumulation by men, which was later used by some households to move into merchant activity. As the tourist and U.S. market for Teotiteco weavings opened up in the 1960s, local entrepreneurs began to reinvest in weaving production and to employ nonhousehold laborers, paying them initially with money earned in the United States. Local wage labor relations were initiated first by men who paid others to do their farm labor while they were in the United States and then through piecework weaving production. As U.S. demand for Teotiteco textiles expanded, the labor of women was used to meet a shortage of weaving labor. Beginning in the 1970s, women and girls began to weave in large numbers.

In contrast to earlier labor relations, which were mediated by the civil-religious hierarchy until the 1930s, current labor relations are characterized by the direct appropriation of surplus labor through sale and purchase. Some people are obliged by economic necessity to sell labor and others are obliged by their need to accumulate capital for reinvestment to buy it (Young 1978:128). Under commercial capitalism, the dynamics of class have altered significantly in Teotitlán. Currently a semipermanent division between merchants and weavers appears to be developing. By 1989, a few merchant households who had achieved petty capitalist employer status in the 1970s were reproducing themselves by passing wealth on to children, who then used it to start their own businesses.

In contrast to class relations under mercantile capitalism, class relations today are characterized by a direct appropriation of labor by merchants through buying up finished textiles at a piece-wage below the value of labor embodied in the weavings (Cook 1988:11); the apparent reproduction of a petty capitalist merchant class through inherited wealth; and the presence of multiple classes, including those of merchant and weaver, but also one or more intermediary and overlapping classes (such as independent producers who sell to tourists but do not employ nonhousehold wage laborers).

The sharper reality of contemporary class relations in Teotitlán under commercial capitalism has created a challenge to the unified community-based ethnic identity that Teotitecos have projected to outsiders since the 1930s and to themselves as well. As the basis of the economy shifted to commercial capitalism and the merchant/ weaver dichotomy became more clearly and permanently articulated, the unity of a community of weavers bound by kinship and ceremonial ties has been challenged. In the center of this challenge are women, *benguna*, who throughout the history of the community have been an integral part of its productive, ritual, and political relations. Before moving on to the historical specifics of the changing roles of women in these relations, the concept of social reproduction is defined in order to provide a framework for the analytical integration of class, ethnicity, and gender in the context of Teotitlán. The specific institutions of *respet*, *compadrazgo*, and *guelaguetza* that form the backbone of women's roles in social reproduction are briefly defined here and discussed in detail in later chapters.

Kin-based Institutions of Solidarity and Social Reproduction

While the changing system of class relations in Teotitlán has provided individual Teotitecos with different identities in relation to production, the community's complex ceremonial system has provided another set of identities and statuses that are related to local constructions of ethnicity as well as to the reproduction of legitimate social actors. As argued later in this book, women's roles in three of these institutions (*respet, compadrazgo,* and *guelaguetza*) are a primary source of prestige, leadership, and access to labor and resources both within their households and in the community at large. While the benefits of superior class position as merchants have been contradictory for women, these three institutions continue to provide a basis of power and resources for all women in the community, although relations between women in these institutions are not untainted by their relative class positions.

Respect—Ritual Authority

Zapotec ethnographers who have not focused on economic differentiation have often emphasized individual status and the notions of respect, responsibility, and cooperation, deemphasizing the significance of class stratification in Zapotec communities and focusing on shared cultural concepts. *Respet* (Zapotec adoption of Spanish term *respeto* or respect) has been discussed by ethnographers as a characteristic of social relationships in which "individuals merit respect because of the kinds of relationships they develop and because of the ways they behave toward others in these relationships" (O'Nell 1979:184). Henry Selby (1974), Carl O'Nell (1979, 1986), and Douglas Fry (1988) have suggested that, while respect relationships are reciprocal, there are also dimensions of asymmetry. These ethnographic accounts signal the multiple meanings of the word *respet.* While all members of a community are accorded respect based on the fact that they are born into and participate in the community, respect is also something that exists in specific quantities and is allocated to people in relation to certain criteria. Thus, while it implies equality because everyone has it, it is not given in equal amounts to all people in a community. Selby (1974:27) notes the difficulties in the use of the term for a wealthy villager:

> It is very difficult to show respect for such a man, because respect is based on the subtle manipulation of the symbols of status as to indicate to the other that you feel he deserves a

higher status than he actually has. For another villager to say to Joaquín that "every man is equal; we are all poor humble souls" would be effrontery, because it would suggest that the former was "equal" with Joaquín and he would resent this. On the other hand, for Joaquín to say that "all men are equal; we are all poor humble souls" is a mark of great respect, because he has brought the other villager up to his level, and therefore obliterated the status difference.

In Teotitlán, where contemporary economic class differences do exist, the existence of *respet* does not signal a substitute for class differences, but the presence of criteria for social ranking that are rooted in relations of kinship and ritual participation. As suggested in chapter 7, the quantity of respect allotted to specific people because of their ritual participation and kinship ties is now beginning to be fused with class position and the amount of material wealth they display.

The concept of *respet* is an emic one that first surfaced in my research when I asked six informants, three male and three female of varying ages, including both merchants and weavers, to rank slips of paper with the names of forty household heads on them. At first they divided people by whether or not they were merchants or weavers and how much wealth they had, but they then mentioned that people could also be ranked according to the amount of respect they had. They discussed in detail what they meant by *respet* and specifically how it was measured. The concept was discussed at length with one hundred other people and later worked into a ranking exercise carried out by an additional six people. The outcome of this exercise and its relation to wealth and class-based occupational rankings are described in detail in chapter 9 and in appendix A.

In Teotitlán, the amount of *respet* accorded to an individual is based on several criteria. These include age, number of godchildren sponsored, number and type of civil cargos the household male head has completed with the support of all household numbers, and the number of fiestas (*mayordomías, posadas,* and life-cycle rituals) sponsored.[4] These are strikingly similar to the criteria for accumulating prestige that Beverly Chiñas (1973) documents for the Isthmus Zapotecs. She, like Holly Mathews (1985), notes that prestige received for ceremonial activities and sponsorship of godchildren transfers to both men and women as heads of households or co-sponsors. The transference of *respet* to women for ritual participation and *compadrazgo* sponsorship is discussed in chapter 7. Hugo

Nutini and Betty Bell also describe in detail the relationship between respect and sponsorship of godchildren (Nutini 1984).

Respect is reflected in deference behavior activated when two people meet and express their assessments of the respect owed to the other (see O'Nell 1981; Selby 1974). Respect also determines a person's ability to hold authority and to have an influential opinion. While respect is positively associated with fulfilling community and family ritual and social obligations, disruptive behavior can limit the amount of respect a household has. Disruptive behavior also tends to reflect more on the individual than on the household. Because the positive indicators of respect such as ritual participation, civil cargo participation, and fictive kinship ties are established on the basis of the household unit, the respect and prestige accrued from accomplishments within these institutions is returned at the household level. Disruptive social behavior such as drinking, gossiping, fighting, or being rude on the street is engaged in by individuals. But because the basic indexes of respect are tied to the household, extremely disruptive behavior on the part of one spouse can eventually cause the entire household to lose its respect position. Others feel sorry for household members affected by the deviant member, but comment that because of that person the household cannot function well in important social institutions. Because respect continues to be a major avenue of influence and access to resources for women, they often engage in extensive damage control to repair harm caused by deviant household members.

Compadrazgo—*Ritual Kinship*

In contrast to current class divisions in Teotitlán that differentiate the community, ritual kinship ties of *compadrazgo* bind together extended families from both merchant and weaving sectors in lifelong relationships and ritual commitments. As discussed in chapter 8, women are central actors in the *compadrazgo* system. In Teotitlán, *compadrazgo* refers to ritual kinship ties that are initiated when an individual female or a male/female couple acts as godmother and/or godfather to a child who is not biological or adopted offspring in relation to particular life-cycle events, usually associated with ceremonial milestones in the Catholic church such as baptism, confirmation, and marriage.

While the word *compadrazgo* is a Spanish import, this system of ritual kinship is also similar in form to elaborate sponsorship ceremonies that existed among the Aztec and Maya before the conquest.

Compadrazgo today reflects the Spanish system imposed on pre-existing indigenous systems of ceremonial sponsorship (see Sault 1985a). *Compadrazgo* remains a distinctive feature of Latin American social structure, particularly in Mexico, where many studies of it have been made (Foster 1953, 1969; Kemper 1982; Mintz and Wolf 1950; Nutini and Bell 1980; Nutini 1984; Sault 1985a). As pointed out by Nutini and Bell (Nutini 1984), while many ethnographers have documented *compadrazgo* systems, there is no standardized framework for study. Their insistence on treating *compadrazgo* as kinship and on focusing on the importance of *compadrazgo* networks is applicable to Teotitlán.

The importance of *compadrazgo* in Teotitlán stems from links that are created not only between sponsoring godparents and their godchildren, but in the relationship of *compadres*—the social ties that emerge between the biological parents and family of a child and the sponsoring godparents. In addition to kinship determined by marriage and descent, *compadrazgo* greatly increases the number of people any particular individual can count on as kin. Because kinship relations are built around a series of reciprocal obligations and responsibilities, the greater the number of kin a particular individual has, the greater access he or she has to labor and resources. In his exhaustive study of *compadrazgo* in the Tlaxcalan community of Belén, Nutini (1984:403) states that it is critical to transcend the dyadic, egocentric bias that has permeated the analysis of *compadrazgo*. Instead, he proposes that *compadrazgo* networks exhibit the permanence, structure, and behavior patterns associated with real kinship units.

As discussed by Christine Ward Gailey (1987a:x), what is important about kinship is the content of the relationship, rather than its source or how it is phrased: "kinship relations are many-faceted and encompass functions that would be housed in separate religious, economic, and political institutions in our own society." Through ritual kinship ties, Teotiteco women are able to extend the range of kin they can count on for aid in relation to specific economic, ritual, and political projects (see El Guindi 1986 for extensive descriptions of specific Zapotec rituals and women's role as godmothers in them).

Guelaguetza
The institution of *guelaguetza* is another extension of kin ties; although more limited than *compadrazgo* in terms of the kinds of obligations it entails (particularly in the exchange of goods), it offers an additional institutional setting for reciprocal exchanges of labor and goods. Often referred to as reciprocal exchange, the institution of

guelaguetza is well documented in Zapotec ethnographies.[5] *Guelaguetza* has been found in agricultural labor exchanges (Cook 1982b; Martínez Ríos 1964; as *gozona* in de la Fuenta 1949) and in reciprocal exchanges of goods and labor for ceremonial purposes (Beals 1970; Cook and Diskin 1976; Diskin 1986).

In Teotitlán *guelaguetza*, a Spanish conversion of the Zapotec word *xelgez*, is a system of economic exchanges in which interest-free loans of goods, cash, and labor are made from one household to another over long periods. Transactions are usually documented in notebooks, although they are also committed to memory by many women who are illiterate. Many cases were found in Teotitlán of people who either owed or could collect *guelaguetza* loans made by their parents up to fifty years ago. As Diskin (1986) found in San Sebastián Teitipac, *guelaguetza* debts can be inherited. As a rule, *guelaguetza* of money and goods is used exclusively for ritual consumption. Labor *guelaguetza* can be used interchangeably for either ritual or production activities. Agricultural *guelaguetza* in Teotitlán is detailed in chapter 5.

The primary purpose of in-kind *guelaguetza* is to allow a household, and women in particular, to prepare in advance for future ritual responsibilities. The principle of *guelaguetza* is to plant debts slowly and to recall them all at once to help finance major ritual events. The system allows women carefully to stock what they will need for a particular event by having loans planted with other people for particular items such as corn, beans, tortillas, bread, cacao, sugar, chiles, pigs, turkeys, and chickens, which they can recall as needed in conjunction with a specific event.

The place of *guelaguetza* exchanges in local economic systems has been debated. As pointed out by Cook (1982b: 115), scholars such as Charles Leslie (1960) have argued that the reciprocal exchange relations of *guelaguetza* are part of a different economic system than one that operates in relation to a profit motive. Cook suggests (1982b: 116) that *guelaguetza* transactions function as a part of the general production and circulation of commodities in a community and that an individual's decision making about participation in *guelaguetza* reflects the total economic situation of the domestic unit he or she represents. Diskin (1986: 288–289) argues that, economically, participating in *guelaguetza* transactions necessitates thinking about setting aside one portion of what one produces for fiestas. He suggests that the ceremonial systems of Zapotec communities, along with reciprocal labor exchanges and services, constitute an ethnic mechanism that can slow the formation of capital. While this process does not preclude the existence of capitalist activities, for Diskin the existence of *guelaguetza* suggests that there are ethnic communities where social reproduction is not exclusively capitalist or determined entirely by a capitalist dynamic.

In Teotitlán, *guelaguetza* does result in the reproduction of some social relations that are not exclusively capitalist in nature, but coexist with the accumulation of capital. It also clearly operates in relation to the larger political economy. Mexican inflation has had an interesting effect on *guelaguetza* in Teotitlán. Before the late 1970s, most *guelaguetza* books show many entries for loans made in cash. By the time women got their money back, however, its purchasing power had greatly diminished. Now Teotiteco women prefer to make loans of animals and food. By making in-kind loans, they have kept up with inflation because they reclaim the original value of the loan. This signals a basic flexibility in the exchange system. *Guelaguetza* is described in greater detail in chapters 4 and 8, particularly in relation to the pivotal role played by women, which has remained largely undocumented.

Social Reproduction: The Intersection of Class, Ethnicity, and Gender

The examination of women's roles in weaving production, ritual, *respet, compadrazgo,* and *guelaguetza* allows us to move beyond the public/private dichotomy for understanding gender relations. In its place, social reproduction is used as an alternative framework for understanding the complex nature of gender roles in contemporary indigenous peasant societies. As formulated below, social reproduction allows us to address not only women's roles in the reproduction of the labor force, but also their importance in the reproduction of social adults, incorporating both the class-based and kin- and ethnically based dimensions of their identity.

The study of Latin indigenous women, the Zapotecs in particular, has been informed by a critical dialogue with the public/private model initially proposed by Rosaldo (1974). A brief review of that work allows us to see how research has moved beyond that model to a more dynamic and historical understanding of women's daily lives. Rosaldo's (1974) initial explanation of the cross-cultural subordination of women was based on the existence of two distinct social spheres: a private or domestic sphere associated with institutions and activities organized around mothers and their children and a public sphere of activities, institutions, and forms of association that link, rank, organize, or subsume mother-child groups.

The first explicit study of Zapotec women by Chiñas (1973) at-

tempted to find hidden sources of female power through the introduction of a concept involving two sets of parallel male-female roles,
formalized and nonformalized, that she proposed as existing within
a public/private dichotomy. As pointed out by Mathews (1982),
while Chiñas concludes that "where formalized roles occur in complementary pairs by sex, the male role of the pair is normally accorded higher status than the female role" (1973:96), her own data
and later work suggest that the Isthmus Zapotecs do not necessarily
view female ritual roles as subordinate to those of males. A more
recent article (Chiñas 1987) provides important information on a
current trend among Isthmus Zapotecs: the ritual participation of
women appears to be increasing, while that of men seems to be de-
clining. Like the Zapotec women of Teotitlán, they are the primary
participants in reciprocal labor and goods exchanges. While Chiñas'
early material lacks an analytical framework consistent with her
data, her ground-breaking ethnographic work has drawn attention to
the roles of Zapotec women in social reproduction and how women
fit into community prestige systems.

A more recent use of Chiñas' analytical framework is found in the
work of Laurel Herbenar Bossen (1984), who compares women's
status in four Guatemalan communities, including a rural Maya village, an urban squatter settlement, a middle-class neighborhood in
Guatemala City, and a plantation. While her work documents important differences among women in the four communities in terms
of "formal public organizations, informal public networks, and the
domestic sphere," her reliance on the public/private dichotomy
as an explanatory mechanism prevents her from addressing the
subtleties of how ethnicity and class are manifested in the spheres
she analyzes. Her comparative approach in conjunction with her
well-grounded description of capitalist development in Guatemala
works best at showing the differing degrees to which capitalism has
brought about a "redivision of labor which has relatively penalized
women" (1984:320).

Working in a Oaxaca community of mixed Zapotec and Mixtec descent that ethnically identifies itself as mestizo, Mathews (1985:298)
rejects the public/private dichotomy, concluding that what appears
to be a division between the domestic roles of women and the public
roles of men is really a division between the community-oriented
religious sphere and the extra-community-oriented political sphere.
Mathews' theoretical orientation leads her to correct earlier views
on the institution of *mayordomía* and to provide new information
on women's political participation. She demonstrates that ritual
sponsorship of *mayordomías* is shared by both men and women and

that both perform important functions and receive equal social status for their participation. She has also found that women's political authority erodes as individual skills more likely to be possessed by men become more important in community decision making, a finding echoed in the work of Young (1978).

While Mathews does not frame her conclusions in terms of economic class and ethnicity, her findings suggest a similar situation to that found in Teotitlán. Her innovative analysis could be strengthened by a definition of class that examines local production relations more closely and explores how these have changed historically. As it stands, her work provides a bridge between studies using the public/private duality and those that emphasize the Marxist-feminist framework of production and social reproduction.

Mathews' work also resonates with the recent symbolic response of Jane Fishburne Collier and Sylvia Junko Yanagisako (1987), who strive to avoid analytical dualisms such as the public/private dichotomy through studying gender institutions as social wholes. Emphasizing the cultural meanings of gender relations, they focus on ways in which individual men and women in different social positions act out their relationships. While they stress the inevitability of systems of inequality in all societies, because they do not situate ideological inequalities historically, their model does not clarify why inequalities exist or persist in radically different settings through time.

The historical dimensions of systems of inequality (including gender) in Latin America have been best explained by dialectical Marxists who attempt not only to bridge the public/private dichotomy, but also to explore how cultural ideology and material circumstances interact. The exemplary ethnohistorical work of Irene Silverblatt (1987) does this by looking at the changing relationship among culture, class, and gender during ongoing colonial conflict in the Andes. She states (1987 : xix) that "the problem of power and its insinuation into cultural forms is central to historical process. Accordingly, gender systems—metaphors as well as conduits for the expression of power—stand out as pivotal to the creation of, and challenge to, social class." In her exploration of the interplay between political hierarchy and gender in the Andes under Inca and Spanish rule, Silverblatt unravels gendered cultural ideology and symbols to reveal how they are used to assert dominance by rulers and how they are reclaimed and manipulated by women as forms of cultural defiance. Her description of how women designated as "witches" by the Spanish fled to the *puna* and maintained their native religion provides direct evidence of the importance of gendered ritual institutions in indigenous responses to colonialism. Her emphasis on how religious and cultural forms are inherently political eliminates the necessity to deal with material/ideological dualism.

Kate Young (1976, 1978), in her work on women in the Sierra Juárez of Oaxaca, was one of the first to explore the historical dynamics of inequality in relation to changing gender roles in Mexico. Her ethnographic work in Oaxaca is organized around the notion of production and reproduction as articulated in a theoretical discussion she coauthored with Felicity Edholm and Olivia Harris (1977). These three Latin Americanists have tried to confront Engels, whose proclamation on a "world historical defeat of the female sex" virtually ended his discussion on women (Engels 1972, as cited in Edholm, Harris, and Young 1977:101). Operating from a theoretical framework stressing the articulation of modes of production, they have attempted to unravel the Marxist concept of reproduction. They suggest (1977:105–116) that the subordination of women and the nature of their participation in the labor force cannot be understood unless distinctions are made among biological reproduction, reproduction of the labor force, and social reproduction. Biological or human reproduction refers to child-bearing or procreation. Reproduction of the labor force refers to both the maintenance of the labor force here and now and the allocation of individuals to positions within the labor process over time. Social reproduction refers to the reproduction of conditions necessary for the continued existence of a particular mode of production.

Lourdes Benería (1979:205) broadens the definition of social reproduction, moving it out of a mode of production orientation and rephrasing it as "the reproduction of conditions sustaining a social system."[6] Both in her 1979 article and in a recent book coauthored with Martha Roldán (1987) focusing on women's response to the economic crisis in Mexico, she sees the reproductive sphere of the household as the primary locus for relations of subordination/domination between the sexes. She proposes (Benería and Roldán 1987: 110–113) that social scientists decompose the "monolithic household" in order to understand power relations between men and women that stem from control of money and resources, domestic exchanges, and marital relations.

A broader representation of "reproduction" is also found in Florence Babb's (1989) analysis of market women in Peru, where she points out that, just as housework is essential to the reproduction of a family, the distributive trades and service occupations in which so many women engage also maintain and reproduce society. Through work done both in the home and in the so-called informal sector, women ensure the continuity of society (Babb 1989:198). Cultural reproduction, however, is not a part of her discussion.

Here the production/reproduction model is used to analyze gender relations in Teotitlán, but the concept of social reproduction is expanded following the lead of Benería (1979) and a recent definition proposed by Gailey (1987a) in her ethnohistorical work on Tonga. While Benería conceptualizes social reproduction somewhat vaguely in relation to the conditions sustaining a social system, Gailey (1985a:76, 1987a) provides a more detailed definition. She points out that a limited notion of reproduction such as that proposed by Edholm, Harris, and Young (1977) does not discuss means of worker acquisition, which is nonbiological (adoption, fosterage, migration, and slavery), and leaves out the reproduction of social groups that function outside of strict production activities. Social reproduction "refers to the recreation of an entire set of social relations, including a division of labor, means of socialization and preparation for production, means of recruiting or creating future group members, maintenance of nonproducing members, beliefs and customary behaviors. . . . The concept includes, but is not restricted to, reproduction in the biological sense" (1987a:271). In her analysis of the changing nature of gender and kinship relations in conjunction with state formation and capitalist development, Gailey formulates a concept of social reproduction that integrates the cultural/ethnic dimensions of social reproduction with changing material conditions.

Following Gailey's definition, the expanded concept of social reproduction used here includes not only the maintenance of material relations of production, but also the maintenance and replication of institutions and relationships that define individuals as social actors in their specific ethnic context (see also Parrish 1982). These institutions and relationships often include noncapitalistic economic and social relations such as reciprocal exchanges made through extended kin-*compadrazgo* networks, frequently in the context of ceremonial activity. These kin-based institutions are the backbone of local ethnicity and are also crucial in the reproduction of the labor relations of class. Here the concept of social reproduction specifically includes reproduction and socialization of the labor force, including relationships linked to biological kinship, *compadrazgo* or ritual kinship, and apprenticeships; and institutions, events, and relationships tied to the socialization and status of individuals—primarily though *mayordomías* and life-cycle ceremonies and the reciprocal goods and labor exchanges that support them.

The case study of Teotiteco women advanced here suggests that the concept of social reproduction can link cultural and economic spheres to illuminate the way in which people operate simultaneously in the multiple arenas of their daily life. As explored in Teotitlán, women's and men's self-identities, motivations, and behavior as social actors are informed by the whole of social reproduction, not just part of it. While the first advocates of the Engels notion of reproduction focused primarily on the material and biological aspects of reproduction of the labor force, the past twenty years of research on the anthropology of women have clearly demonstrated that women's lives are equally influenced by cultural and social reproduction. Among the Teotiteco Zapotecs this includes the maintenance and cultivation of social institutions such as *guelaguetza*, kin-*compadrazgo* networks, *respet*, civil and religious cargos, and ritual events as well as the physical nurturing of future workers and the economic production of weavings. A focus on the social reproduction of people as both laborers and social actors and the institutions that support this process offers anthropologists a way out of the problematic polarities of the public/private model.

Conclusions

The ethnographic material included here demands an understanding of reproduction that goes far beyond reproduction of the labor force. The model of social reproduction used here focuses on how institutions associated with local ethnic identity, kinship, and changing class relations operate in the daily lives of Zapotec women. Rather than focus on the objective categories of ethnicity and class, the chapters that follow emphasize the multiple representations of each and how they are used, particularly by women, to achieve their own goals and agendas.

Chapter 3. Julia, Cristina, Angela, Alicia, and Imelda: Five Women's Stories

If I tell you my story, it is very sad. Maybe you want to talk to someone with an easier life. A lot of hard things have happened. . . . Even now when things are good I worry. Now my son is gone and when he leaves his children suffer a lot because there isn't any money to buy them food and the things they need. There is always something to worry about. (Julia, age 60)

LIKE WOMEN anywhere, Zapotec women share many common experiences yet are also distinguished by important differences. For the women of Teotitlán, these differences are most strongly related to age or generation and to the class position of their households. On the generational scale, women often describe themselves as divided into two groups: largely uneducated, monolingual Zapotec speakers over thirty who still wear traditional dress and strictly follow local customs and modern, bilingual, better-educated women under thirty who have economic aspirations for themselves and their families. In terms of class, they readily distinguish between merchants and weavers, but these differences are relative to the life experiences of individual women.

In reality, of course, individual women do not fit neatly into these categories. Women in their thirties and early forties seem to be a bridge generation, reflecting ideas of both younger and older generations. In terms of the class position of their households, many women, particularly merchant women, have experienced important changes in their standard of living in the past fifteen years. Older merchant women (such as Julia) spent the first forty years of their lives in extreme poverty, working from dawn to dusk, seven days a week, as weavers. Even as the economic status of their households has improved, women who are now part of merchant households do not feel that their individual workloads have lightened. While they certainly pursue the business agendas of their households, as individuals they still see their lives as full of hard work. The most optimistic women are those (such as Imelda) who are younger and feel that they are able to run a business and maintain some degree of independence from their families. Education, or a lack of it, has been critical to the abilities of all these women to control and improve their lives.

I collected these narratives over a three-year period in the process of developing ongoing relationships with these women. The stories of Julia, Cristina, and Angela are taken from transcripts of various interviews. Because Julia and Angela would not agree to be tape recorded, some parts of their narratives are not verbatim quotes, but are based on copious notes taken during the interviews and immediately transcribed. In the first three narratives the notation "[. . .]" indicates fragments that came from two different conversations, not omissions.

The narratives of Cristina, Alicia, and Imelda are direct transcriptions. Those of Alicia and Imelda are based on single interviews. The names of these five women and their family members have been changed at their request to maintain anonymity. Together their stories represent the range of experiences found among Teotiteco women today and provide a personal context for the historical material covered in the rest of the book.

Julia

Julia is sixty years old, born in 1929, just as the effects of the Mexican Revolution were winding down in Teotitlán. She has lived through times of great poverty in the community as well as recent prosperity. She never went to school, yet has learned some Spanish by teaching herself and opening a small general store. She prefers, however, to speak Zapotec. She wears her hair on top of her head in two braids wrapped with ribbons and wears a long piece of wool fabric called a *manta* wrapped around her waist and held in place with a bright pink woven sash.

Since the early 1980s, her living situation has improved considerably as the household textile business developed. Recently she was able to expand her tiny storefront and installed a gleaming glass display case that is her pride and joy. She enthusiastically supports her son's efforts to build up their merchant business, yet has also undertaken the organization of a large and seldom-sponsored *mayordomía*. With this effort she has devoted untold energy over the last year to organizing three large parties stretching for three to five days each. Julia enjoys being in charge and strongly believes that sponsorship of rituals for the local saints and virgins is extremely important. She has done it twice before and knows how hard the work is. She has been rewarded with a high degree of respect and is a very influential woman in the community. Recently this has been reinforced by her merchant status.

She has not had an easy domestic life. Her husband beat her often throughout their long marriage and she had to support her children alone for many years. She bore twelve children. Four of them died in their infancy, and one was shot and killed in an urban area of Mexico. Three others have lived near Los Angeles for over six years. She has never seen several of her grandchildren, and her voice becomes melancholy when she speaks of her lost children and those who have moved north. Her one act of self-indulgence is to take an hour-long bath every few days and wash out her long black hair, which still falls to her knees. She seems happiest when she is walking around her yard with her hair down, calling out to her chickens, turkeys, and pigs. Likewise, when sitting at the head of a long line of women calling out orders during a fiesta, she seems content and assured of her importance in the life of her family and the community.

When I was a little girl we could buy everything with centavos. You could get half a centavo's worth of coffee or hard brown sugar and it was plenty. Pesos used to be like dollars. Even when we used to take the serapes to sell them to the rich men we only got a peso or so. I remember that on my street there was a man who was very rich and people sold their serapes there.

[. . .] I was married in the church in 1949 when I was twenty years old. Only three couples came to my wedding. Each of our godparents from when we were baptized came to the wedding along with my husband's sister. I didn't get any presents at all. I remember that I cried a lot after my wedding because I didn't get any presents. Not even my mother gave me a present. No one had any money.

When I first moved in with Juan, before we were married, the lot was divided in half between Juan's father and his uncle. Well, actually, the uncle was dead, but the aunt was still living there. Eventually we bought the land, but at first it wasn't ours. We had nothing. Even the mats we slept on weren't ours.

When we were first living together I worked carding wool. Juan would go get the uncleaned wool in Oaxaca. There was no money around then. He would weave and I spun and he would go to the houses of two merchants and sell the blankets.

When I was first married I never left the house. Never. My husband would go alone to Oaxaca. He sold the blankets and kept the money. At first, I didn't even leave the house to buy food. I was too scared. I had never been out alone. He would give the money to his aunt and she would go to the market. I never left. I didn't know how to buy anything and we only ate tortillas. We didn't eat bread and meat. We didn't go to many fiestas then and there weren't any. Because we lived with the aunt I didn't get to say anything. A lot of women who were my age didn't go on the street. You know when we were first living together we just worked all of the time. I just worked in the house. Sometimes I would card wool and spin all night long.

After the aunt died, then I started to do more. Even before she died, my husband went to the United States to work. He went to the U.S. on and off all of the time. . . . You know this whole time I worked like a burro. I would card and spin two kilos of yarn in two days as well as doing other work. First I would get up and make tortillas for Laura and another woman who was a neighbor. I also made *tejate* [a corn drink] for her. Miguel, her husband, had a lot of money. I got paid 2 centavos [*mexicanos*] for making an *almud* [two kilos of corn]. It was a hard life.

My husband hit me ever since we were married. Once he went to jail for hitting a boy from here with a rock. We got a lawyer then. Maybe I will go talk with that lawyer. Before, when he was in the U.S., he was never here. And when he had all of his cargos it was me and the children who worked. I don't see why he has a right to get so mad when we all work so hard. He's like a lot of men who beat their wives here.

A woman's work is never done they say. That of men, yes. Men just do one thing for most of the day. Women have to run around and do a lot of different jobs. It was easier for me when I had both of my daughters at home. One would make *atole* [morning corn drink] and the other would make tortillas. Both of them know how to weave. My daughter María would start weaving and weave most of the day. When my husband had his cargo of being in charge of communal lands María worked really hard because my husband wasn't weaving.

[. . .] my husband had a lot of cargos and I had to work too. Even when he was a *šruɛz* [servant to the mayor] I had to work when the *presidente* [mayor] was leaving. I had to make tortillas at the *presidente*'s house for a week. When Juan went to the U.S., he paid someone to do his cargos. In 1957 we were *mayordomos* for the Virgen de Guadalupe. Like many things then, my husband didn't tell me he had made a *promesa* to be a *mayordomo*. Now I decide these things. But I wasn't afraid then because I had some turkeys ready that I had already given as *guelaguetza*. I had six years to get ready. I began to get more animals and to make *guelaguetza* with a lot of people. Men worry about how to get money and women worry about things for the kitchen and animals. I planted forty-five turkeys with people and some cacao too. There were three fiestas for this *mayordomía* and we were ready for them.

We didn't really have any *mozos* [contracted on-site piece-workers] until two years ago. All the looms we had were being used by our children. I would sell an animal each time we wanted to buy a loom. We would buy a loom for each child when they were big enough. . . . We bought our first loom in 1958 for Eduardo. I sold a pig to pay for it. In 1970 we bought a second loom for Carlos. Then in 1974 we bought a loom for Jorge and in 1976 one for María. In 1980 we bought the last loom. Now we have *mozos* working for us because none of our children are around anymore.

When my husband came back from the U.S. he bought about three blankets. He went to Oaxaca to sell them. Since then he always kept the money and had the key. I never knew how much money he made in Oaxaca or what he did. He used to go there all the time to try to sell blankets. He didn't work much and was hardly ever here. About fifteen years ago he started to go to Mexico City and sold the blankets our children made. One year in 1975 when he had another cargo, I started to run the business more. My children were weaving and the youngest was taking care of our oxen. I also started my little store. I learned more about money by running the store. Then my husband stopped controlling the key to the money and now all three of us share it—me, him, and my youngest son.

I don't know how to read and write and I need it to run the store. There are a lot of people who don't know how to read and write. You know last year I went to the school for adults that they had for one day. When I got home, my husband said, "Why do you want to learn? You are too old." I do want to learn, and I need to know for my family. My daughter doesn't know how to read, she didn't go to school either.

[. . .] my husband doesn't care about my granddaughter going to school either. I told you my husband wouldn't let me go to the school for adults. I think that a lot of men are jealous when women learn to read and write and that's why they don't like it when their wives are educated. I need to learn for the business and to go to Oaxaca and Tlacolula. I can't read the street signs.

Julia's story offers us insight into several themes that are explored later. Her household is a case study of the transition from weaver to merchant status. By using the household labor of children, Julia and her husband were able to accumulate a small amount of capital and using that, along with money earned in the United States and by Julia's sale of animals, were able to invest in a small inventory of textiles to begin business. Later they were able to contract other kin and neighbors as pieceworkers as well.

Julia's labor was important in the creation of the business, but for the first two years she was denied any participation in business transactions. This highlights the contradiction of merchant women, who may have control of household labor and resources for fiesta sponsorship, but who are denied active roles in business decision making. Her discussion of fiestas and *guelaguetza* suggests the importance of these activities in her life. Finally, her story reveals the presence of domestic violence, which is a part of many women's lives. Domestic violence against women and their lower level of education than men are issues that are shared by both merchant and weaver women and are frequent topics of discussion.

Cristina

Cristina is seventy-nine years old. She was born during the Mexican Revolution in 1910, and her childhood was marked by war and hunger. She has always had a hard life and never managed to emerge from poverty. She has been a widow for quite some time. While respected for her age, she often receives charity from her family and neighbors. She is an older woman who benefits from going to ritual celebrations because she is fed at them and receives food to bring home. Her primary source of income is weaving, a skill she recently learned and does very slowly because of arthritis pain in her legs. She also continues to card and spin wool into yarn for additional income. She produces for a nephew who is a merchant.

She is not particularly bitter about her hard life or regretful about her lack of material prosperity. She still sleeps on the ground on a mat because she prefers it and makes all of her food on the metate, not using any shortcuts such as a blender. She had few children and feels that this limited her possibilities.

Cristina only speaks Zapotec and does not know how to read or write. When she needs to do something official, she gets one of her grandchildren or children to help her. She never leaves Teotitlán and spends most of her time at home working or going to fiestas. She styles her gray hair in two braids and wears a traditional *manta* made of polyester because wool is too expensive. She is usually wrapped in a black shawl as she moves slowly down the street. The wind bothers her eyes. Because of her age, she is greeted by everyone she sees, most of whom bow in respect to her. She has witnessed many changes in the community and has her own theories about how they took place and what they mean.

I was born in 1910, I think. I don't know how old that makes me. One of the first things I can remember really well was when we went to Escipúlas, Guatemala, when I was young, maybe thirteen years old. It took over a month for us to walk to Tapachula [city close to the Guatemalan border]. Then it took another two weeks to walk to Escipúlas. We were gone for more than three months, walking. I guess it was 1923. We had a big fiesta when we came back.

[. . .] when I was a girl, on Monday and Wednesday the merchants would go to the plaza and buy blankets from people. I think there were quite a few. They would buy from people and also leave and go and sell in Oaxaca. . . . My father would buy wool in Oaxaca for weaving because not very many people here had sheep.

I was married in 1940 when I was old [she was thirty]. My husband used to go to the *monte* [communal land] with a *γolbats* [hand axe] and plant. He planted corn, beans, and squash over there on that mountain by the cave. No one plants there now, they all left.

You know when my husband went to ask for me [ask her parents for her hand] they only brought one or two candles. There was a little bit of fruit and some bread and chocolate.[1] When I was married it was simple too. We only had one meal for the *compadres*. I didn't get any presents, only one shirt. I was married in one day and that was it, there wasn't any big ceremony like *sa(^{P}a)γúil(i)* [five-day elaborate and expensive wedding ritual].

My husband didn't go to the U.S. when the others did, but about 100 men went. A lot of people thought that the men who went to the north were being signed up to go to the war. When the men were gone a lot of women made tortillas to sell and made yarn to sell to weavers. I remember that the gringos came here after the men went to the north. Before there were a lot more poor people than there are now.

They had no money so they borrowed money to live. There were a few *ricos* who made the loans. People would make blankets to pay them off. Some people were so poor they also had to borrow food. Now it's better. The money goes further. There is work.

Now women weave too. When there was a school and the girls began to go, they knew more so that they could begin to learn how to weave. Now a lot of women weave. It's the same as going to school. I learned how to weave from my grandchildren. Before only a few women knew how. Now everyone does.

. . . now there are also a lot more weavers because there are more children around. Everyone has five or six kids. Before they just died of measles and other diseases. Children don't die anymore. Before up to half of the children would die. People were afraid to go to the doctor. Now the women weave and they have more children who also weave. People aren't so poor now because their families are bigger.

Cristina's story gives us clues about many of the changes that have taken place in the class system, in weaving production, and in the celebration of rituals during this century. She begins by mentioning the pilgrimage her family made to Escipúlas, Guatemala. Until the 1960s, many families in Teotitlán as well as in other Zapotec communities undertook extensive pilgrimages to visit the sites where miraculous saints and virgins appeared. Such pilgrimages involved months of travel and were attached to some of the *mayordomías* celebrated in the community, such as that of Escipúlas. While the celebrations attached to *mayordomías* were quite elaborate, in the 1920s and 1930s life-cycle ceremonies such as weddings were very simple compared to contemporary ones. Ceremonial life for women was concentrated largely in *mayordomías*. Only later did life-cycle ceremonies become the focus of their energies.

Cristina's story also alerts us to class differences that existed in the 1920s. She refers to some of the merchants who sat in the plaza and bought blankets from people. These were the same rich people who loaned money to cover living expenses as well as to cover the costs of *mayordomía* sponsorship. Cristina grew up among the majority poor, who sometimes had to borrow money and who had to work for others in order to pay off debts.

Like Julia, she is impressed with the potential that schooling offers to women. She comments on the change in the division of labor, which now has women weaving along with men. She believes that more women are weaving now because going to school has made them more skilled and able. She notes that improved health care has allowed more children to survive, and as a result there are many more weavers in the community. For her, the option of weaving is critical—it is her only source of income. She is a poor pieceworker, but the work allows her minimally to support herself. The encouragement of her grandchildren and their belief that even as an old woman she can weave have been important to her survival. As an elderly widow weaver, her class status and the fact that she lives alone result in her being among the most economically marginalized people in the community.

Angela

Angela is forty years old, the oldest of eight children. She is a fluent Spanish speaker and also speaks a small amount of English, which she uses regularly with tourists and importers who frequent her house on the main road in town. With a commanding presence, Angela has cut her hair to shoulder length and wears simple dresses of the sort seen in many mestizo communities around Oaxaca City.

Although she went to school until the sixth grade, Angela believes that she really did not receive enough education; she considers herself to be ignorant of many things. She focuses most of her energy on her nonstop workload, overseeing a weaving workshop with up to six workers in it as well as a big family and managing a large business under her husband's orders. She is determined to move her six children out of the community and into professional jobs. Her oldest son is studying to enter medical school and her oldest daughter is finishing as a business major at a Oaxaca high school. She and her husband speak Spanish to their children; it is one of the few houses in the community where Spanish is heard more consistently than Zapotec.

Angela usually downplays how well off her household is and has a strong sense of the limitations placed on her as the wife of a merchant. Her movements are restricted and she resents the control her husband has over her as well as her ritual obligations, which make her overall workload heavier. Angela's household is one of the few merchant households with four to six workers weaving daily and also contracts pieceworkers. She has done some weaving and even produced some original pieces that brought high prices. Her favorite moments have been at the loom weaving original designs, but for the most part she has little time for this creative work.

When I was fourteen years old I went with my sisters to the cave on New Year's and asked for some things.[2] I asked that I would have money, a car, children, and a big house. There at the cave I made a big house with many rooms, a place for a car, and a place for lots of chickens and pigs. I also asked for a husband who would take care of me. See, it came true, that's why I believe in it. When I was pregnant for the first time I went there and asked to have a son. I made a little doll. I wanted to have a son because I thought that if I had a little girl my mother-in-law would kick me out. When you have a baby people ask you, *tɛŋgjuwɛ ʔénĩ(ŋ)* [is it a little man?], with a smile on their face. Women always have this expression. If it is a little girl they say, *mmmmm, težapɛ ʔɛ̃(nɛŋ)* [hmmm, it's a girl]. If it is a little boy they say, *škalbao tɛŋgjuwɛ ʔénĩ(ŋ)* [lucky you, it's a little man].

We came here to this house after we spent two years in my father-in-law's house. Felipe had money from working in the north. He went there from 1962 to 1969 to work. In 1966 we eloped and we met at his father's house [she was seventeen]. In 1969 we got married in the church. We paid for our own wedding because he worked in the United States for seven years. He used the money he earned in the United States to make the little store that used to hold our serapes. [It is now a small general store.] He also used his money from the United States to buy blankets. When we first came here there was just one little house. It was a one-room adobe house with a dirt floor. We fixed up the yard and built the store, then the porch, the kitchen, and later the other rooms.

In 1969 we had three workers. I was making *tejate* every day as well as carding wool in the afternoon. He paid the workers with money he earned in the U.S. It used to be easier to get people to come to your house to work. He had money that he saved. When he was in the U.S. he was one of the few who came back with money. He told me that when he was there he didn't drink soda pop, but drank water and that they would eat the fresh fruit and vegetables they harvested. Anyway, he came home with money. Believe it or not, we started our business with just four weavings.

We don't think about being *mayordomos*. We think of our kids. We want them all to be educated at the university—that is our *mayordomo* [. . .] I left school in sixth grade. I already knew how to card wool and spin wool and make tortillas. My grandparents told me and my parents that I should stop school and help my mother to take care of the other kids. I wanted to study more, but I couldn't. My parents wanted me to, but my grandparents have the last word in the house. So I left school. I don't want the same thing to happen to my children. Right now my grandfather still doesn't want my youngest brother to study because he and my grandmother will be left alone in the house. I don't want that to happen to my children.

Now I have to buy what my husband asks me to. He gives me a certain amount of money every day for food. He keeps the key to the money and doesn't let me handle it. He says that he knows how to take care of the money. Some women take care of all the money. In my parents' and my grandparents' house after my father or grandfather would sell a weaving they would give the money to my mother or grandmother. I don't buy anything. I don't know what to buy. Now I get up every day at about 5:30 A.M. and go to bed about 11:00. I start out by waking my son up so that he can catch the bus to Oaxaca for school. I spend most of the first half hour getting him out of bed and onto the bus. He likes to stay in bed. I have a girl named Lucía who helps me in the morning and in the afternoon my daughter Catalina comes home from school to help.

[. . .] my husband drives me to the plaza every morning so that I don't waste time and so I can't stop to talk to anyone. Today he said that I spent too much time buying meat. I didn't think it was very long, barely enough time for them to wait on me and wrap and cut up the meat. But he thought it was too long. I think that you should write that down.

We spent three days at a wedding this week. A lot of our *mozos* [weavers working on-site for a piece-rate] also went to the wedding so they are just beginning to work again. While I was at the wedding, this woman teased me for not drinking. I said that I had a sore molar and that I couldn't because I was taking medicine. Then she told me that I wouldn't drink with them [the other women], that I only drink when I am having sex with my husband. I really get angry when women talk to me like that. But she was older than I was so that I couldn't really yell at her. I had to respect her. I'm not naive about sex, but I think that talking about it at parties is really rude. Some people asked me if I was afraid of her, because she is a witch, but I said I am not. I'm not afraid of witches and I don't believe in witchcraft.

[. . .] you know men here can talk to any *muchacha* they want to and women aren't allowed to say anything. If women speak to other men they would get into trouble. Men are very jealous. . . . Once when my father was in the hospital in Oaxaca, I went to visit him with my sister. We got a ride there in someone else's truck. When I got home they slammed the door in my face [her sister-in-law and husband]. They called me all kinds of names. Imagine me, whose father is dying. I'm very sad and I come home and they shut the door in my face and call me all kinds of names for going to the city—whore, prostitute—just because I left and got a ride in someone else's truck.

You know, I don't think that money makes life easier. Just the opposite. I think that I work twice as hard as any poor person. The money makes my life harder—now we have more people working for us and I have to take care of them. Now I have a lot more things to do. For example, I promised some customers I would make them a serape. They gave me a 10,000 peso advance for my work. Felipe, my husband, put the money away and now I can't finish the work. I have no time. It's difficult.

[. . .] I'm practically not weaving at all anymore. I spend all of my time cooking for people who are working here and for my children. I did some work that sold well. I did one design that had a boat and some clouds and mountains. I made it just on the loom, I didn't use a drawing. I want to work again, but now it is impossible. I can't even leave here. When he goes somewhere I have to be here to deal with the clients who show up and might want to buy something. Today I couldn't even get to the market because he left in the morning and went to Oaxaca. I sent two of the boys to the market. When they got there they got a girl to go in because they didn't want to be seen there.

Angela's marriage to an ambitious young man who saved money while working in the United States moved her fairly rapidly into the status of a merchant wife. While she is respected by many people in the community because of the household's prominent business, her story relates her frustration at her lack of mobility. She experiences the gendered aspects of her merchant class status as more oppressive than what she believes poorer weaver women experience. She shares all women's common workload of food preparation and child care and on top of that must feed and oversee five to six weavers who work in her home on a daily basis.

Angela has a keen consciousness of her position as a woman, both at home and in the community. While she talks about her unique situation as part of a merchant household and complains about her workload because of the family business, she also emphasizes double standards that she believes all women experience, such as the preference for male children, and the inability of women to talk to other men without suffering the results of their husband's jealousy. She is able to identify with other women in the community and as a result is quite popular with both merchant and weaver women as a friend. While her personal friendships span class distinctions in the community and she feels bound by traditional norms of showing respect for all older people despite their economic status, the formal friendships of the household, which are often initiated by her husband and carried out in public, are primarily with other prominent merchant households in the community.

Alicia

Alicia is thirty-six years old and has been raising her five children alone for almost twelve years. Now a grandmother several times over, she has fought hard to support her family. Pulled out of school by her father the first day she tried to attend at age six, she never learned to read and write, but taught herself Spanish while working as a domestic in Mexico City at the age of nineteen. Like other women her age, Alicia has left Teotitlán several times in order to try to improve her lot. She has recently come to the United States for the first time with her youngest daughter in an attempt to get ahead.

Alicia began weaving as a way to support her family after her husband left her, first selling to local merchants and later to family members who opened their own businesses. For most of her life she has been living in other people's houses. As an impoverished single mother, she has had very little control over her life, moving from her parents' house to her in-laws' house and other places to work.

Alicia's appearance bridges the older and younger generations: she wears her hair in two long braids and is dressed in a modern wool skirt and an indigenous blouse. She is acutely aware of the limitations placed on her as a poor woman. Now that her children are older, she is beginning to think about how she can realize some of her own ambitions. As stated below, many of her ideas for self-improvement are tied to being able to accumulate some savings while working in the United States. She has recently spent eight months in the United States, where the interview took place.

What I remember from when I was young was that I spent a lot of time taking care of my mother's children and I made tortillas since I was really small, since I was eight years old. I remember that they sent me to wash clothes in the river and to wash dirty wool.

My father didn't want me to go to school when I was little. My grandmother went to take me to school. She bought me a notebook and a pencil and she went to bring me to school. When my father saw I wasn't at home, he went to look for me. My grandmother told him that she took me to the school. He came to the school to get me. . . . I tried to go again, but neither my father nor my mother wanted me to go to school. They told me that I didn't need to go to school because I am a woman. They said that men go to school because they are men. I took care of the babies. Every year my mother had a baby. Maybe that was why they wouldn't let me go to school. I don't know.

I was fourteen years old when I got married. I don't know how it was that I met my husband, but I loved him. When he came to get me [*robarme*] we went to his house . . . his uncle's house. I wanted to go because my father got really angry and beat my mother a lot. He beat all of us, my brothers too. I got tired of living there. When I got married I knew what I was doing, but later my husband began to drink. He began to do this in Tuxtla. . . . I went to Tuxtla five weeks after we were married and I didn't speak Spanish. I just stayed in the house. My mother-in-law used to leave with him. They would leave to buy the things we needed.

We went back to Teotitlán because his mother wanted to. When I came back I had to work again preparing wool, making tortillas, making *tejate*, making all of the meals. I had different work in Tuxtla. We made peanuts to sell. We cleaned them, peeled them, and cooked them in oil. . . . They sold them on the street. It's easier to do this than it is to work with the wool.

When I came back, I was pregnant with Luis. I gave birth to Luis in my father's house because my husband didn't want me to be with his grandparents and his mother. His mother got back together with her husband. They were separated for a while.

I also stayed there when my husband left. He went to work first in a circus that was in Oaxaca. When the circus left, he told me that he was going to go with the circus and work so that he could send me something. I told him yes. He didn't send anything. Since he left, he never sent any money, no letters, nothing. I learned to weave at my parents' house when my second son was three months old so that my children would have something to eat.

After that, when my second child was three years old, my *con-cuño* [sister-in-law's brother] came to tell me that we should go to Mexico City because I could find better work there. At the time I didn't know that my husband was with them. So I lived with my husband there for a year in Mexico City while I washed clothes.

The last time I saw him was in 1977. He never beat me, but what I didn't like was that he drank a lot. He was very irresponsible. He left . . . I felt sad, because I was left with five children who were all young. The oldest was twelve years old, the next one was nine years old, then the next one was seven years, two years, and a newborn baby. . . . It was very hard for me to think about how I was going to raise my children. My in-laws helped a little when they could. My oldest daughter began to weave when she was eleven years old and my oldest son when he was ten years old. They helped some.

Three months ago I got across the border with a coyote [person who leads people across the border for a fee] from Teotitlán, a boy from Teotitlán. I came across by the bridge on the border. There was some *migra* [immigration officers] there. We ran for a while, like half an hour. This boy I came with said that the *migra* wouldn't do anything. He said that we would go to where my brother-in-law was waiting for us. My brother-in-law and my sister paid him. When we went across the border, there were some apartment buildings there, nearly on the border. We had just gotten to where the apartment buildings were and the *migra* came. I thought they were far away, but then they were really close to us. When they shined the light on us, they told each other, "Grab them, grab them." But this coyote told me, "Let's go, let's go running through here." We went behind the building, running. . . .

When we got to San Clemente [California] there wasn't anyone there. No one was stopping people.[3] My brother-in-law told me that is where they ask for your papers in the road. . . . We passed without any problems. Some people say that they come through the mountains and that it is more difficult. A woman who lives with us went through the mountains. They got here at four in the morning. They had to walk all night before they were safe.

When I first got here I felt a little sad, a little frightened. I was afraid because I didn't know about anything. I'm still afraid to go out, to go anywhere. . . . It's like when they say the cat is guarding the mice. I am a mouse. That's how I'm living here.

It's not quite as hard here as living in my village. There I was weaving a lot but I couldn't make enough money. There are a lot

of customs in Teotitlán—weddings, engagements, other things—
you have to buy a lot of things. They are all expensive. In contrast here, I am working and I'm not spending anything. I am
working with my family. They take care of expenses, for eating.

You know when my daughter got married last year I spent a lot
of money. Some people loaned me some as well. I am going to
pay back the *guelaguetza* I owe and the loans. I spent a lot of
money—almost 3,000,000 pesos [US$1,250]. I bought a chest,
some dresses, a shawl for my daughter and also the food, the
beer, the mescal. I had to buy all of this. And also turkeys . . .
I had about forty of them.

I take care of another little girl who comes here. I get fifty
dollars per week for taking care of her and my sister also pays me
fifty dollars per week. My daughter also went to work for two
months when she first came here. She worked two months. She
got paid the same amount, fifty dollars per week. That's how she
earned a little money. After she started in school she didn't work
anymore.

In the future I am going to work to get what I don't have right
now. First, I am going to study and work more so that I can build
a house. I'm always in someone else's house. I already bought
that land, a piece of land. Now I'm going to put a house on it so
that people won't say that the land is abandoned. . . . Now that
I have my own adobe bricks I will start to build.

Alicia's story, like that of Cristina, reveals the difficulties of growing up poor and female in Teotitlán. Unlike Angela or Julia, whose
households achieved merchant status, Cristina married into a poor
family where people relied on a combination of weaving and mi-
gratory work to make a living. Many of Teotitlán's poor migrated to
Chiapas either to work in small cities or to harvest coffee and sugar-
cane. Some still go there rather than finance the longer trip to the
U.S. border. For Alicia, migration has been a long-standing survival
strategy. More recently she has tried working in the United States
as a way to pay off her *guelaguetza* debts and to accumulate some
savings.

Alicia also relates some of the difficulties of the steep ceremonial
costs of sponsoring any type of fiesta in Teotitlán. Her son's wedding
left her with many *guelaguetza* debts to pay off, which she is doing
by earning cash to purchase the turkeys, cacao, and other goods she
received as loans. Because she has no land in Teotitlán, she has few
options for growing some of the corn and beans she owes in
guelaguetza debts or for self-consumption. Selling her labor as a

weaver in Teotitlán or in the United States as a domestic or daycare worker is her best option for raising cash.

Finally, Alicia's story also relates some of the commonalities shared by all women in Teotitlán, particularly the denial of education to young girls. Her very clear memories of being told that she did not need to go to school because she was a girl have stayed with Alicia as she becomes aware of how important it is to read and write, particularly in new environments. As a result of this experience, Alicia and other women insist that their daughters receive an education equal to that of their sons. As discussed in chapter 9, increased levels of education among young women, particularly those from merchant households, may be resulting in some changes in female gender roles.

Imelda

Imelda is thirty-one years old and has two children ages five and seven. She has spent more than half of her life outside Teotitlán, an unusual situation for most Teotiteco women. She wears her hair shoulder length, cut in a shag, and sports a modern polyester dress like those worn by women in Tijuana. She has a watch and carries her money in a purse. She still uses a shawl like those worn in Teotitlán.

Her experiences living in California and in Tijuana are typical for women who have left the community for some period. Many women her age or younger have spent part of their lives working as domestics in other parts of Mexico or have come to the United States. As Imelda states below, leaving Teotitlán is one of the few ways for women to achieve some independence and begin to save some money on their own.

Since leaving home at age fourteen, Imelda spent most of her adolescence and twenties working a wide variety of physically demanding jobs. She helped her family and finally was able to open her own small business, goals for many young women and girls in Teotitlán. Imelda's story reflects the changing pool of migrants from the community beginning in the 1970s, when more young women went to Mexico City, the border areas, or the United States.

The sacrifices that Imelda made in order to help her parents and her younger siblings resulted in a lot of hardship for her, but allowed her independence later as a single woman when her family helped her to set up a small business in Tijuana. The following narrative comes from an interview in Imelda's store in Tijuana, where she now lives and works with her family. Recalling the hardships she lived through as a child and young woman, she finally feels that she has begun to accomplish some of her goals and has plans someday to return to Teotitlán.

Since we were little, we suffered a lot. I have two brothers and three sisters—six of us altogether. My grandfather had a business and my parents were living with my grandparents before I was born. Then my parents separated from them.

My parents worked a lot for my grandfather. My grandfather gave us the house. His name was Miguel Gutiérrez. He had a big business at this time and he was the only person who helped everyone in town. He bought weavings from everyone. He was a good person and he helped everyone there by buying their weavings because before the people were more ignorant. They didn't know how to sell their weavings in Mexico City. They never left town. The tourists only came to my grandfather's house, which was the Casa Gutiérrez.

My mother worked really hard and she had us help her to spin, to card, and to wash the wool. We helped her make tortillas and went to the market. In the morning we went to school. I also took care of my brothers and sisters. I had a little brother who was sick and died because of a lack of money, really. And because later my grandfather completely abandoned us.

Almost all of the girls went to the school. This was when the government demanded that all indigenous children attend school. The *presidente* fined the parents who didn't send their children to school. My father was also very demanding about school. He made us go to school.

Whether or not girls went to school had as much to do with their parents as with the government. . . . I have some friends who only went until third grade. A lot of them, about half of them, stopped going because they were older and maturing and their parents didn't want them to leave because they had to help their mothers in the kitchen. There are some who did finish and even a few who went to study in Oaxaca. I went until sixth grade. Then I didn't want to go anymore.

From what they taught me, mathematics is the thing I find most useful right now. I often tell myself that if I hadn't gone to school then I wouldn't know anything about how to keep accounts or do other things. And still, I am missing a lot. I should have studied more.

I was fourteen years old when I finished sixth grade. When I
left school I wasn't thinking about getting married. I wanted to
leave. A lot of my girlfriends got married, but I didn't think about
this. I wanted to help my parents. I saw my little brothers and
sisters who were really skinny and saw that we were really poor.
My father couldn't really get ahead with his little business of
selling what we made in Mexico City.

After I finished sixth grade, one of my cousins came who lived
in Ensenada. . . . I ran into her in the market. She said, "Don't
you want to come and work? I have a sister-in-law who needs a
girl to work in her house." Oh, I was really happy. I said, "Let's
go so that you can talk with my parents so they will let me go."
We went to talk with my parents to convince them. I asked them
to let me go. I convinced them to let me go and she brought me
to Ensenada. I was fourteen. I was in Ensenada for two months.
I worked there for this woman cleaning her house.

At that time, I had an aunt who was living in Los Angeles, one
of my father's sisters. She's still there. My father wrote to her
and told her that I was living in Ensenada. I also wrote to her
and she came to see me. I told her that I wanted to go to Los Angeles. . . . She found someone, a coyote, who took me across.
I think my aunt paid about US$200 to get me across to Los
Angeles. But I couldn't find any work because I was a minor.
I wanted to go to school, but my aunt couldn't support me.

Then my aunt got me a job working in a house taking care of
a little girl. They were people from Texas. I didn't understand
any English—nothing, nothing. They only spoke English. They
spoke to me and I answered them in Spanish. I was there for
three months. During those three months I only ate liver because I didn't know how to ask for food. The man there didn't
know how to understand what I wanted. The only thing he knew
how to say in Spanish was "Liver? liver?" So I said, "OK, liver."
So for three months it was "liver, liver" every day. When I left
there, I couldn't eat it anymore.

After that I went and learned a little English and one of my
father's brothers was working in the fields near Los Angeles in
Oxnard. He said to me, "Why don't you come with us and work
in the fields?" Then I started to work, and even though I was
younger I always said I was seventeen years old. I was working
in the harvests, picking strawberries, tomatoes, squash, string
beans. It was really hard work for me. You got paid one dollar for
a box of strawberries. You got paid by the piece, not by the hour.
Sometimes I would pick twenty-five or thirty boxes in one day.

I saved a little money, but most of it I sent to my parents, $100 per month.

There were a lot of women there from Michoacán and from Oaxaca, but from other towns. Some were from Guelatao—there were Mixtecos and a lot of people without papers. This was a big problem for me. The immigration would show up and everybody would run. Sometimes I didn't run because I would pass as my uncle's daughter. He had papers. . . . A lot of times I hid myself in cardboard boxes or in garbage cans.

There the women were paid the same as men because it was piecework. . . . A lot of people came from the unions. César Chávez came there a lot. There were strikes, the police came, and the bosses were against all of the workers. My uncles and aunts were in the strikes, but I didn't go. They left me at home— they said that it was dangerous, that there was a lot of fighting and anger. That was when they raised our wages. Our salaries went up even though we didn't have papers.

We all suffered the same because when it was hot and there wasn't any water to drink. There was water in the truck for the produce, but the water was hot, as if it had been sitting on a stove. That was where I learned how to eat tomatoes. . . . There all of the people would grab a tomato and clean it with their shirt and eat it. It was cleaner than the water, which was dirty and really hot. . . . In the winter we would get up and the plants would be white with frost and we had to go and pick them. Now when I remember, I don't want to do that work again.

Later, I began to go to night school for adults. . . . I went there for six months to learn English. During the day I worked. I was really tired when I finished working and had to go to school. . . . During this time I kept sending letters to Teotitlán. My parents wanted me to come back. But when they would write to me telling me to come back, I would send them some money and then they wouldn't tell me to come back anymore. Finally, I wrote asking them all to come and live with me in Los Angeles.

I sent them money so that they could all get here. . . . They arrived in Tijuana and I paid a coyote to get them all across. Then they came to Los Angeles. We sent my three younger siblings to school, Celerina, Ernesto, and Miguel. I had a small apartment and we all lived there. We suffered a lot because the money I earned wasn't enough for all of them. There were six of us. It was then that I began to work in a curio store. I knew a little English and I got to like the job a lot.

When I was twenty-three I had my first *novio* [sweetheart] and I got married to someone from Teotitlán. . . . I got to know him because a lot of people from Teotitlán were living in Santa Ana, California. I went to Los Angeles every week to dance or to go to the movies. He would come to my house and ask me to go dancing. I would go out with him. My parents only let me go with him because they knew him. . . . If I had been living in Teotitlán with them they wouldn't have let me go. They let me go because I had already helped them a lot. And because I was old enough, I was twenty-three.

We became boyfriend and girlfriend and then we eloped and I went to his house to live. It was a different life there. I quit working and had my son. After that I couldn't work because of the baby. Only my husband worked. On the one hand it was OK because I rested a lot, which was good, but on the other hand it was really hard. We didn't have enough money. The rent was expensive. I still didn't have any papers. The whole time I lived in the United States I never had any papers. I was going to work again when I got pregnant again. My other son was born in 1983. It was really expensive to live there with two children. When we were just living in Los Angeles, my parents moved to Tijuana.

. . . after a while it got really hard for us. So my parents said, "Why don't you come here to Tijuana, try to save some money to start a small store? It's OK here." . . . So I came here and my parents helped me with my two children. We all lived together. Me, my children, my brothers and sisters, and my parents. I started to work here again with my sister in her store. I liked it because I liked the work and I could bring my baby to work.

I worked with them for two years. My husband sent some money, but very little. He kept saying he was going to come, but he never came. . . . Now we are totally separated. With my father's help and that of all my family I was able to buy this little store [stall in the market] in 1987.

It would be very hard to be in Teotitlán alone with the two children. It's hard to have money to dress them and send them to school. My parents have a house there, but I don't. . . . I don't think I'm going to get a piece of land either. It is expensive to live there because there are a lot of fiestas with a lot of expenses. . . . And even though a woman is there alone she still has to pay a quota or provide food for the men who are doing *servicio* [required in-kind labor of town inhabitants].

I have the idea that one day if I can make some money here

in Tijuana I will go back there if I have a place to live. I will go there and set up some kind of business, something that there isn't there. Something different like a restaurant, but a restaurant that is nice, where you can get different things to eat or a general store with everything like in the city. Or a hotel or motel for the tourists. . . . But first I have to wait for my sons to get older. When they get out of primary school here, I want to take them to the United States. And because they are citizens of the United States they have the support of the government to study there, right? That's what I want to do, help them to get ahead.

Imelda's story brings together several critical issues that signal several of the transitions in gender roles being experienced by some younger women. While performing household work done by all young women in Teotitlán, such as washing wool, carding, and spinning as well as preparing tortillas and taking care of siblings, Imelda did not get married at age fourteen like some of her girlfriends. By the time she graduated from sixth grade, a larger percentage of young girls were completing their primary education, and some were leaving the community for other parts of Mexico or the United States. Most stayed for a few years. Some, like Imelda, have not yet returned to the community, but plan to eventually.

Imelda's grandfather was one of the wealthiest men in Teotitlán in the 1960s, with a large merchant business. He did not pass his wealth onto his children. This pattern has changed in the past ten years, particularly among merchant families who have moved to Tijuana. There parents help their children to set up businesses and siblings help one another. Imelda's parents did not receive the benefit of inherited wealth, but some of her younger siblings have received family assistance in setting themselves up in business. This perhaps signals a consolidation of the merchant class as well as its replication in another region of Mexico.

Like Alicia, Imelda states that it is difficult to get ahead in Teotitlán because of all the fiestas. In Tijuana, she is not accumulating *guelaguetza* debts. She also realizes that the independence she has in Tijuana would not be possible in the village. In other conversations Imelda has stated that she never would have been allowed to live and work alone as a young woman in Teotitlán as she did in the United States. She would have been treated as a dependent of her parents. Instead, because she left, she was able to support herself and win her parents' approval for her independence, ultimately by offering them support as well. She is also aware that her current status as a single mother would make it difficult for her in Teotitlán. She hopes to return when she can open her own business there, which would allow her to maintain her independence.

Conclusions

The stories of these women reflect some of the commonalities of growing up female in Teotitlán as well as important differences tied to their ages, class positions as merchants and weavers, and experiences in making the transition from weaver to merchant. Many shared a common childhood experience of extremely hard work, beginning at the age of five or six to produce yarn, prepare food, and care for their younger siblings. They have all experienced gender-linked limitations or double standards tied to lower expectations for girls, a loss of independence with marriage, and an interest in ceremonial activity. While the older women remember a common experience of poverty, the two younger women are more familiar with the current prosperity of the community and relate strongly to the kinds of material differences that exist between people. The class differences between merchants and weavers are very real in their lives and inform their perceptions of themselves and others.

All of these women mention education or lack of it as an important factor in their lives. Julia, Cristina, and Alicia all regret the fact that they were not allowed to go to school and feel that their lack of education has significantly limited what they have been able to accomplish in their lives. Imelda and Angela, who both completed the sixth grade, feel that even that was not enough to equip them for running and expanding a business. Finally, all of these women have a strong sense of themselves as filling female gender roles; regardless of their current class position, they recognize the heavy workload that they have in the gendered division of labor, whether in Teotitlán or outside of it.

In order to understand how Julia, Cristina, Angela, Alicia, and Imelda have developed their view of themselves and their world we must begin to unravel the historical, cultural, and economic context they live in and grew up in. As we explore the complex history of Teotitlán, the circumstances that frame the lives of these five women will move into sharper focus. The following chapters document how their identities as individuals and as women have been shaped not only by political, economic, and cultural changes at the local level, but also by the changing policies of the postrevolutionary Mexican state and international economics.

Chapter 4. Setting the Scene: The Zapotecs of Teotitlán del Valle, Oaxaca

This town is called Teutitlan in the Mexican language and in its own Zapotec language it is called Paguia: the ancestors gave it this name because they say that they had their idols and gods on top of a mountain that they worshiped near the town that had this name. (del Paso y Troncoso 1981 : 105)

In 1519 when we came ashore on the coast of Veracruz, we all came as Catholics. When we came ashore we gave thanks to our Lord Jesus Christ for our faith in him, which let us cross the ocean. We went through great pain and today we have ar-rived. We are here in the new land. Each one of us is a Chris-tian and is obligated to worship the mysteries, the unity of Christ in the holy trinity. Our faith states that there is only one god in the supernatural world. (Agustín, age 19, playing the part of Cortés in the Dance of the Conquest done by the danzantes *of Teotitlán)*

LOCATED IN the foothills of the Sierra Juárez, Teotitlán del Valle is an indigenous Zapotec community of approximately 5,000 located 29 kilometers from the state capital, Oaxaca, Mexico. From Teotitlán, the capital city can be reached by buses that run six to eight times per day. People from Teotitlán make frequent trips to Oaxaca to go to the bank, to visit the market, or to get on connecting buses that will take them to the other periodic markets located in the central valleys of Oaxaca.

The visitor to Teotitlán is struck by the industry of local residents and by their ability to drive a hard bargain when selling their weav-ings. A peek inside any doorway will reveal at least one weaver, male or female, slinging the shuttle across a loom as several other people work furiously winding yarn onto bobbins to keep pace. Visitors are also impressed with the conservation of the Zapotec language and the strong current of tradition found in Teotitlán. On most days, a group of Teotitecos can be seen carrying out a ritual—a wedding, funeral, or celebration for a local saint's day. The elements of ritual—candles, copal, band music, wooden saints, large feasts, and fireworks—are omnipresent.

Early in the morning and again in the afternoon, the local food market is crammed full of women, dressed in traditional plaid lengths of wool cloth or in print dresses from Oaxaca. They move briskly from stall to stall, filling their baskets with vegetables, meat, bread, and other purchases. Vendors from Teotitlán and surrounding communities come to ply their wares here because most people have some money to spend. Outside the newly built food market groups of women are selling handspun yarn, flowers, and alfalfa. Across from the market, down the hill from the church, local municipal officials are leaving city hall to go home for lunch. Young women who sell textiles in the artisan market for tourists are opening their lunches. For fear of losing a potential sale, they eat in their stalls, savoring the bundles of food brought to them by younger siblings. Everyone is busy.

Teotitlán is one of 570 *municipios* (municipalities, roughly equal to counties in the United States) found in the state of Oaxaca.[1] The high number of *municipios* is indicative of the past and present political fragmentation of the state. Teotitlán is a municipal seat that has one other community under its jurisdiction, the *agencia* of Santiago Ixtaltepec.

The state of Oaxaca holds several distinctions in relation to the other thirty-one states of Mexico. Located in the south, next to Chiapas, Oaxaca is one of the most heavily populated indigenous areas of Mexico. Approximately 35 percent of the population of Oaxaca is defined as indigenous according to languages (Instituto Nacional de Estadística, Geografía e Informática, 1984:1:1275). Currently there are fourteen different indigenous languages in Oaxaca, including Amuzgo, Chatino, Chinanteco, Chocho, Chontal, Cuicateco, Huave, Mazateco, Mixe, Mixteco, Nahuatl, Triqui, Zapoteco, and Zoque. In 1980 there were 347,006 Zapotec speakers (Instituto Nacional de Estadística, Geografía e Informática 1984: II:633).

The Economy of Oaxaca

The state of Oaxaca has the lowest per capita gross domestic product in all of Mexico. Compared with Mexico City's US$5,500, Oaxaca's

A new food market and a sixteenth-century church sit in the center of Teotitlán del Valle.

The food market in Teotitlán has been converted into a textile market for tourists. Most of the booths are staffed by young women from merchant households.

figure of US$1,136 per capita in 1980 is strikingly low. Overall, Oaxaca's economy suffers from underemployment, high out-of-state migration, and an agricultural base close to subsistence.

Approximately 60 percent of the total active labor force in Oaxaca is employed in agriculture, primarily for subsistence (Instituto Nacional de Estadística, Geografía e Informática 1984 : 1 : 750). The majority of the state's population of 2,518,157 lives in small communities of under 5,000. Most farmers in Oaxaca are working small plots of less than five hectares (about twelve acres) and struggle annually to meet their own subsistence needs.

In most communities there is a high level of underemployment during the slack months in the agricultural season. In communities where there is no local craft production, cash income is earned by wage labor, often through migration. From 1960 to 1984, 500,000 people from Oaxaca between the ages of fifteen and sixty-five went to other areas to work. More than half of them left between 1975 and 1980 (Cook 1984b). Many go to the United States. Today there are as many as 500 Teotitecos living in Southern California and other areas near the U.S. border.

Oaxaca's industrial portrait is much like that of its municipalities—numerous, but very small. According to the 1980 census, there are approximately 40,000 Oaxacans employed in manufacturing concerns, totaling about 15.5 percent of the state's gross domestic product (Instituto Nacional de Estadística, Geografía e Informática 1984 : 1 : 751). According to Oaxaca's general director of industrial, commercial, and mining promotion, there are close to 5,000 microindustries employing less than five people each (Raisz 1986 : 39). This figure, however, only includes microindustries officially registered and paying taxes.

These microindustries, many of which are craft production operations, are important sources of income for rural communities. Important rural industries include pottery, palm-weaving, embroidery, treadle and backstrap loom weaving, metate making, brickmaking, and mescal distilling (Cook 1982a). Oaxacan craft industries can be divided between those that produce for regional use and those that cater to the tourist and international market. While the weavers of Teotitlán began weaving in cotton in prehispanic times for local trade and tribute payments, Teotitecos currently weave for an international market.

Previous Ethnography of the Teotitlán Zapotecs

The Zapotecs have been one of the most heavily documented ethnic groups in the state of Oaxaca. Ethnographic work has covered the various regions in which they live as well as a range of topics.[2] The Zapotec community of Teotitlán del Valle has been researched by several ethnographers, including Jeffrey Cohen (1988), Gilberto da Silva Ruiz (1980), Jaime Segura (1979), and Robert Taylor (1960, 1966). Taylor's 1960 dissertation is highly descriptive; he concludes that Teotitlán is a "typical" Mesoamerican community based on a list of characteristics generated from the work of Redfield and Tax (1952). In a later article (1966), he emphasizes cultural conservatism in Teotitlán and ties it to two factors: the reluctance of local innovators to push others to adopt their views and the reluctance of all Teotitecos overtly to imitate nontraditional customs accepted by others. Segura's work (1979, 1980) also focuses on the cultural conservatism of the community as manifested in the civil-religious cargo system.

Other ethnographic work focuses on the economics of weaving production. The research of da Silva Ruiz (1979 : 25 – 27) documents class polarization in the community and attempts to fit a dichotomous class model of "bourgeoisie" and "exploited pieceworkers" onto the complexities of contemporary weaving production. This is discussed further in the next chapter. Cohen's (1988) work compares weaving production in Teotitlán to that of neighboring Santa Ana and evaluates both in terms of linguistic performance theory.

These previous studies of Teotitlán emphasize two striking aspects of the community central to an analysis of gender roles—its successful expansion of weaving production for export and its retention of cultural institutions and events. These two foci have led previous ethnographers to two different conclusions: that Teotitlán is culturally conservative or that the socioeconomic structure of the community has been completely altered through integration with international capitalism. As stated above, this book documents both of these tendencies and their varied effects on women in the community.

Population

The current high population level (officially 5,000, probably more) in Teotitlán is a fairly recent phenomenon. Until the 1900s, epidemics such as smallpox and typhoid kept the death rate higher than the birth rate, sometimes doubling it. During the colonial period, particularly between 1530 and 1650, the indigenous population in Teotitlán and throughout the state of Oaxaca was greatly reduced.

Estimates put the valley indigenous population at approximately 350,000 on the eve of the conquest (Chance 1978:69). The population declined steadily until the 1630s, when it reached a low of 40,000–45,000, a decline of 87 percent over 100 years (Taylor

Table 1. *Population in Teotitlán, 1890–1986*

	1890	1910	1930	1940	1950	1960	1970	1980	1986
Population	2,742	2,634	2,116	2,290	2,511	2,881	3,394	3,496	4,500

Source: 1890, Archivo General del Estado de Oaxaca; 1900–1970, Dirección General de Estadística, censuses for 1900–1970; 1980, Instituto Nacional de Estadística, Geografía e Informática 1984; 1986, household survey by Lynn Stephen.

1972:17–18). The total population of the valley had risen to nearly 70,000 by 1740 and to 110,000 by the 1790s (Taylor 1972:17). The valley had 290,000 inhabitants in 1959 (Tamayo 1960:13–31).

The chief cause of death during the colonial period was European diseases for which indigenous Oaxacans had no immunity. Smallpox epidemics, plague, measles, and other diseases swept through the valleys on many occasions during the colonial period. The high death rates caused by these epidemics are still reflected in community death records from this century, particularly for children. Until the 1950s, smallpox epidemics could kill three to four people per day in Teotitlán, resulting in an annual death toll of over one hundred (Archivo Municipal de Teotitlán del Valle, 1863–1984).

Table 1 shows population figures collected from the community archives and national censuses. They are only for the community of Teotitlán, not other communities under its jurisdiction. The population remained fairly stable from 1890 until 1960, when it began to grow. According to census figures, the first growth period came between 1960 and 1980, and a second larger period of growth between 1980 and 1986. This coincides with the expansion of weaving production. The large number for 1986 may be traced to the fact that it comes from my census of the community rather than from a national census. Discussions with informants who administered government census questionnaires suggest that official population counts of Teotitlán are often low.

Geography and Climate

Teotitlán is in the eastern Tlacolula arm of the Valley of Oaxaca, one of three arms that come together to form what are called the *valles centrales*. Other arms extend southward toward Ocotlán and northward toward the town of Etla. The Tlacolula arm of the valley is drained by the Río Salado, which flows westward to join the Atoyac River near the city of Oaxaca (Kirby 1973:7–25). The town of Teotitlán is situated between two tributaries that flow into the Río Salado, the largest of which is called *ru'óř(n)* (oven mouth river).

The *ru'óř(n)* flows from north to south from the Sierra Juárez. About one kilometer above Teotitlán, it feeds into a large lake formed by the Presa Azul, a dam built by the Mexican government in 1968 as part of a large irrigation project. The lake is currently stocked with fish. The lake bed also serves as a source of sand and gravel for community construction. The reservoir formed by the dam is the source of water for the main irrigation system of

Teotitlán, used almost exclusively during the rainy season to augment sparse rainfall.

A second dam was constructed in 1975 under the Plan Presidencial Benito Juárez. This dam, built along the tributary flowing on the eastern side of Teotitlán, has proven to be a failure. Built only of dirt and stones, it is dry throughout most of the year and has slowly eroded. The dam has been dry for much of the time it has been in operation.

The climate in the Tlacolula arm of the central valleys is semiarid. The average annual rainfall in the Tlacolula weather station between 1927 and 1975 was 542 millimeters. The heaviest months of rainfall are May through September, with little rain falling between October and April (Secretaría de Programación y Presupuesto 1981). Rainfall tends to vary greatly from year to year. From 1981 to 1984, there were three years of drought. In 1984 it rained excessively, not giving farmers enough time to plant and harvest properly. Rain falls unevenly within the geographical bounds of the community, falling more heavily at higher altitudes and east or west of the primary tract of agricultural land.

The average elevation of the valleys of Oaxaca is between 1,000 and 2,000 meters (Tamayo 1982:19). The altitude of Teotitlán is 1,590 meters, with much of the community's forest land falling at altitudes up to 2,200 meters. Until the 1950s, much greater use was made of the variety of altitudes found within the community's landholdings than currently. The land falls within areas that support both dry subtropical and coniferous vegetation (Tamayo 1982:75).

Land Distribution

Today the community of Teotitlán has a total of 8,695 hectares or 21,477 acres of land.[3] Of the total land, 2,052 hectares is *temporal* (dry land). Having no source of irrigation, *temporal* land is only worked during the rainy season. It is privately owned. There are 6,601 hectares of communal dry land, which includes forests and communal farmland. About 600 hectares of the communal land is usable as farmland (Archivo Municipal de Teotitlán del Valle 1981). An additional 50 hectares of irrigated land are held privately. The land is fed by four main channels of the large dam built on the main river; 153 households use the irrigation channels.

Unlike communities that received *ejido* land as a part of agrarian reform under Cárdenas in the 1930s,[4] all landholdings in Teotitlán are communal or private. Roughly 55 percent of the households in Teotitlán have private holdings. The remaining 45 percent are landless. People in the community who have no private holdings can apply for permission to farm and build their homes on communal lands. Most of the communal lands suitable for farming located close to the village, however, have long since been claimed. Communal land is now often treated as private land, even though individuals do not hold titles. As the population of the community grows, applying for communal land is the only option left to many young people who inherit little or no land, even for a house plot. As population pressures increase, communal land for house plots is edging farther and farther away from the central parts of the community.

Farming in Teotitlán: A Declining Occupation

As farming decreased in importance in the local economy due to the blossoming of textile production, the number of full-time male farmers dropped dramatically. While 60 percent of the households in Teotitlán listed their primary occupation as farmers in a local census in 1930, that number steadily declined as this century rolled on. While the following figures are problematic because some include

Once Teotitlán was a community of full-time subsistence farmers and part-time weavers. Now less than 10 percent of the population engages in full-time farming.

Table 2. *Percentage of Full-Time Farmers, 1930–1986*

Year	No. of Farmers/ Total Pop. Measured	% of Total Pop. Measured
1930	160/267 households recorded	60%
1950	387/901 economically active males in *municipio*	43%
1960	660/1,227 economically active males in *municipio*	54%
1970	462/1,088 economically active males in *municipio*	42%
1980	309/1,201 economically active males in *municipio* who receive farming income	26%
1986	17/154 households surveyed	11%

Source: 1930–1970, Dirección General de Estadística, censuses for 1900–1970; 1980, Instituto Nacional de Estadística, Geografía e Informática 1984; 1986, household survey by Lynn Stephen.

the population of Santiago Ixtaltepec (the *agencia* under Teotitlán's municipal jurisdiction) and others do not, they do demonstrate the trend away from farming. Most of the censuses only document male farming activity.

As seen in table 2, a 1986 random sample survey of 154 households indicated that 11 percent included full-time farmers. Up to 55 percent of the households in the survey farmed part-time. About 10 percent of those who farmed use irrigation. The nonfarming population of Teotitlán (45 percent of the households) only has access to marginal communal lands, as recorded in local land records. The majority of farming households in Teotitlán cultivate on small plots of *temporal* of less than one hectare.

Local and state figures on the number of total hectares planted in corn on an annual basis also reveal a major drop in the number of hectares planted after the early 1960s. While the number of hectares planted has increased again in the 1980s, it still has not reached the same level as during the 1960s.

Crop Yields

The triumvirate of corn, beans, and squash dominates the crops planted in Teotitlán. About fifty farmers with irrigated fields plant alfalfa year round and a few grow chickpeas during the winter

Table 3. Corn Planted and Harvested in Teotitlán, 1970–1983

	1960	1961	1962	1963	1975	1976	1977	1978	1982	1983
Total Hectares Planted	768	710	710	372	92	111	114	244	232	534

Source: Secretaría de Agricultura y Recursos Hidráulicos, Datos Definitivos de Cultivos Cíclicos, Oaxaca.

Table 4. *Irrigated versus Temporal Corn Yields for Teotitlán, 1960–1983*

	1960	1961	1962	1963	1975	1976	1977	1978	1982	1983
Total irrigated hectares planted	60	60	60	34	0	20	29	140	90	149
Total irrigated yield in tons	52	54	54	31	0	32	21	116	211	447
Average irrigated yield in tons	.87	.90	.90	.91	0	1.6	.72	.83	2.3	3.0
Total *temporal* hectares planted	708	650	650	348	92	91	85	104	142	385
Total *temporal* yield in tons	37	87	286	243	110	69	29	54	7	71
Average *temporal* yield in tons	.51	.13	.44	.70	1.2	.76	.34	.51	.05	.18

Source: Secretaría de Agricultura y Recursos Hidráulicos, Datos Definitivos de Cultivos Cíclicos, Oaxaca; Servicio Meterológico Nacional, Departamento de Archivo y Documentación Climatalógica.

months. Wheat, which was formerly rotated with corn crops and grown on communal mountain slopes, is no longer produced. The majority of agricultural production in Teotitlán is for home and local consumption. Very few families sell corn on the market outside of Teotitlán. The low yields of corn do not even supply enough to last a household through one year. Most families have to supplement their subsistence production with the purchase of corn.

While no data were available on corn yields during the period of fieldwork, data from the Secretaría de Agricultura y Recursos Hidráulicos (SARH) provide some information on corn yields in Teotitlán. Unfortunately, the data do not necessarily indicate yields for all fields planted. Farmers who reported their yields were working in some capacity with SARH. Those who were not did not report their yields. Yield data that differentiate between irrigated and *temporal* fields provide an idea of the yield for most farmers in Teotitlán.

Distinguishing between yields for irrigated versus *temporal* land makes clear the low returns that the majority of Teotitlán farmers receive on their small plots of one hectare or less. Average yields on dry land plots between the years 1960 and 1980 varied between 0.05 tons (50 kilos) and 1.2 tons (1,200 kilos) per hectare. For the years shown in the table, the yield was 540 kilos per hectare or less for seven out of ten years recorded.

The average household of six people in Teotitlán consumes at least two kilos of corn per day. The use of corn for animal feed can boost daily consumption of corn to four kilos per day in many households, particularly where there are pigs. With a minimum of two kilos per day, families with one-hectare *temporal* plots would run out of corn about eight months after the harvest in a good year. In a year such as 1982, when yields were particularly low, the average *temporal* yield from one hectare would only last about twenty-five days. Most households purchase a majority of their corn with earnings from weaving production, whether or not they are farming.

The Agricultural Cycle and the Organization of Production

Most farming activities in Teotitlán take place between March and November. Planting is timed around the arrival of the rains, which may begin in April or May. Farmers plow the fields once before the rains to open the land up to the moisture and then again after the rains begin. The land must be plowed at least once before planting and preferably twice.

Planting for flat *temporal* farming land, the majority of land under cultivation, is done in late May or early June. The planting team consists of a farmer and his two oxen plus at least two seed planters. While the plow opens the furrows, two people walk behind it broadcasting seeds and covering them with dirt using their feet. One hectare can usually be plowed and planted by a team of three in one day.

About one month after planting, the plowman goes out again to clean out between the rows and push the dirt around the young plants. This process takes a team of two men about one day per hectare. Continued time investments before the harvest depend on whether or not the land is irrigated and how much weeding is necessary. If weeding is unnecessary, then the field may be left alone until harvesting time. If weeds are prevalent, the farmer and his household make several trips to the field to pull weeds during the growing season.

Harvesting takes place in late October or November. The largest agricultural work groups are formed for harvesting. A farmer can usually harvest one hectare of corn with four helpers in about one day. Harvesting also involves hiring a pickup truck and driver or an ox cart to transport the corn. Harvesting is done by hand with men and sometimes women carrying large baskets on their backs that they fill with corn as they move down the rows.

The last step in the agricultural cycle is cutting down cornstalks, tying them together, and transporting them to the home. Cornstalks, called *zacate,* are used as animal feed and fuel. They are seen as a valuable part of the harvest, particularly by those who have oxen to feed. One hectare of *zacate* can be cut, tied, and transported in two days by a team of three men.

According to local farmers, the minimum amount of adult labor days to farm one hectare of dry land is about twenty. Many weavers who are secondary farmers spend an average of three to four weeks per year in their fields. Full-time farmers go every day to their fields or to attend animals. In the random sample survey of 154 households, the average number of days spent in agricultural activities by adult male household heads was seventy-five.

The Gendered Division of Labor in Agriculture and Labor Recruitment

While most agricultural activities associated with planting and harvesting are carried out directly by men, women also participate in agricultural production. In particular, female household workers help with weeding and harvesting. Seldom is a female seen planting or plowing. When no male labor is available, however, women also work in planting. The majority of female labor is directed toward supplying male workers with food during agricultural activities and providing supplemental labor during weeding and harvesting.

During the agricultural season, women begin their days especially early. They must prepare a meal to be served to their husbands, sons, and other laborers going to work in the field. Early morning coffee is usually served at 6 A.M. Later they bring a lunch out to the field. In many cases this involves a one-hour walk. There they prepare a hot lunch and *tejate,* a corn drink that requires several hours of grinding. They may provide another snack for workers when they return from the fields.

When weeding is done, an entire household usually goes to spend the day in a field. Food is carried by the family and prepared in the countryside. During harvesting season, women also work as supplementary harvesters, often scanning the field for ears of corn that have dropped to the ground or been missed by male harvesters. They also use the time to collect plants and herbs used in cooking and herbal remedies.

Most agricultural activities involve the recruitment of male laborers from outside the household. In rare cases where a household owns oxen and has many full-grown male sons, no extra labor is needed.

One of the chief complaints of farmers in Teotitlán is the limited number of oxen available. Oxen teams are needed for the majority of agricultural activities. Tractors can be substituted for some types of plowing. Currently there are three tractors in Teotitlán that work on a limited basis. The random sample survey of 154 households found that one in five owned at least one team of oxen. Informants estimated the ratio to be lower, with one team of oxen for every eight to ten households. Apparently a lack of rain during 1982 and 1983 caused the price of *zacate,* the primary cattle feed, to skyrocket. Many farmers could no longer afford to feed their oxen and sold them outside the community.

Securing a team of oxen and additional laborers for planting and harvesting is the responsibility of male household heads. They usually try to first rely on *guelaguetza* exchanges in order to recruit extra laborers. The demand for weaving laborers has had an effect on the availability of local labor for farming. Because weaving is the most profitable return to labor, most able-bodied men prefer to weave rather than work as hired laborers in other people's fields. This fact has doubled the cost of agricultural labor and oxen team rental in Teotitlán in comparison with neighboring communities.

Work *guelaguetza* has varying opportunity costs for different people. If members of a household are concerned about cash flow, they may try to work out a *guelaguetza* exchange in which they trade their labor for someone else's rather than shoulder the high costs of hiring labor and oxen teams from Teotitlán. If a male household head is an exceptional weaver who earns a lot of money in one day, he may try to avoid *guelaguetza* labor exchanges so that he can invest his labor in weaving. Working one day at his loom gets him a higher return for his labor than receiving one day of farming labor through *guelaguetza*.

A male household head must also be flexible in his schedule in order to participate in work *guelaguetza*. Securing *guelaguetza* laborers is dependent on the schedule of others. Most men are usually not able to schedule such labor for all of their extra labor needs. Because of the necessity to plant and harvest within strict time frames, procuring agricultural labor is often difficult. Many men have to hire laborers to augment their *guelaguetza* labor. Because of the high wages in Teotitlán, about thirty men from neighboring communities also come to work during the agricultural season. They arrive each morning on the bus to stand in the market and go with the highest bidder. There is often bitter competition for their labor as farmers become desperate to plant and harvest on time.

A second method for procuring labor for fields is to go *a medios*, which literally means going halves with another farmer in a sharecropping arrangement. Someone who owns land agrees to give half of the harvest to another person who in turn provides half of the labor. Households that have a shortage of male labor often engage in this practice as a way of cutting labor costs. But given the low yields of most dry farmland, their portion of the harvest is usually small.

Animal Production by Women

The yards of most households in Teotitlán are populated with five to ten turkeys, ten to fifteen chickens, and two or more pigs. Animal production by women provides household protein, an opportunity for savings, and a means of ritual investment for *guelaguetza*. However, animal production, like dry farming, appears to add nothing to household income. Analysis of women's animal raising suggests, in fact, that when animals are raised in the home the amount invested in them from birth is about double their worth as adults. While the economics of animal production are distinctly unfavorable to those who raise their own animals versus those who purchase them, the continued widespread occurrence of animal production in Teotitlán suggests that the motivation for production is not profit, but the possibility of accumulating a significant amount of capital through slowly investing minimal amounts. Women who raise animals describe them as a *bancomer*, a pun on a Mexican commercial bank that also means "a bank that eats." Women see animal production as one of the few ways available to them to "save money."

Women in Teotitlán use pigs as a form of savings for rituals and to accumulate small amounts of capital to invest in goods for their households. The role of women's animal production in *guelaguetza* is discussed in greater detail in chapter 8. In many households money earned through pig and turkey production is used in the purchase of initial household looms. For young households, in the early stages of the developmental cycle, animal production is often their first source of capital. In some merchant households, animal production has been a significant source of initial income to purchase wool and yarn.

Women's investments in animal production also affect their other productive activities. Animals are fed twice a day, early in the morning and again in the afternoon. In five households where animal raising activity was monitored, women spent between one and a half and three hours daily in animal care. In addition, turkeys and chickens can require constant supervision, especially if they are young. Supervision of animals goes well with the weaving activities women perform between preparing meals.

Activities that take women away from the home, however, are not compatible with animal production. When women work several days at a ritual event in another household, they all leave in midmorning and again in the afternoon to return home to check on their animals and feed them. Many women state that the reason they infrequently leave the community is concern for their animals.

Because of the importance of animal production as a means of savings, women's control over animal production gives them leverage in dealing with male household members over financial matters. Often a household emergency is met by selling a woman's pig. Because women have the capacity to sell their animals in order to take care of the household, they are able to push for more input into other types of household decisions. Through their role as supervisors of the household budget and of daily cash flow, women's roles as animal producers reinforce their control of the budget in weaving households.

Women's animal production also affects their relationship to male farming. Because animals consume fairly large amounts of corn, sometimes as much as the human members of the household, women are concerned with efficient household corn production. Some women actively encourage their husbands to cut back on farming because it becomes more expensive for them to feed their animals if farming is a low-yield enterprise. When the government subsidizes corn prices, it is always cheaper to buy corn than to produce it in the household. Recently, the government has cut back on subsidies and the price of corn has risen, making the returns on animal production even worse. Currently, women who push their husbands for more efficient corn production are encouraging them to produce for an enterprise that may have even worse returns than farming.

Current Occupational Divisions

In 1985, Teotitlán had a population of about 1,039 households. A local census stated that 125 of these households (about 12 percent of the total population) were merchant households and a majority of the remaining 914 (68 percent) were weaving households. Small farming sectors and service sectors also play an important role in the local economy. Most households and individuals have multiple occupational identities. The figures in table 5 represent the economic activity that brought in the greatest source of income (cash and in-kind) in households from a random sample survey of 154 households conducted in 1986. Weaving is regarded as a primary household occupation. The other four occupations in table 5 are more often than not considered secondary occupations. They are usually carried out in conjunction with weaving activities. The expansion of the service sector in Teotitlán has been supported not only by growth in weaving production, but by a high level of ritual consumption as well. Many of the occupations listed in table 5 receive primary support from the internal circulation of cash through purchase for rituals or through the reciprocal exchange system of *guelaguetza.*

This book concentrates on merchants and weavers as class-based

Table 5. *Economic Activity Bringing in Greatest Amount of Household Income*

Weaving	69%	
Merchant business	10%	
Farming	11%	(with weaving)
Service work	6%	(with weaving)
Musicians	4%	(with weaving)

Source: Household survey conducted by Lynn Stephen in 1986.

groups. A majority of merchants (about 95 percent) act as employers either through piecework contracts with weavers, hiring people to work in their workshops, or through commissioning complex pieces in advance. Most of the work available in Teotitlán today is available through textile merchants.

Market Links to Other Communities

Like other indigenous areas in Mesoamerica, the Valley of Oaxaca is distinguished by its market organization. Jill Appel (1982) emphasizes that in prehispanic times there is no mention of a major long-distance market in Oaxaca. She states (1982 : 146) that the valley was not used for the production and distribution of goods to traders servicing the pan-Mesoamerican system but instead specialized in the production of food as its major exchange item. While there is little ethnographic material on prehispanic markets, both Burgoa (1934) and the *Relaciones geográficas* (Acuña 1984) mention early colonial markets. What is not known is how many of the colonial marketplaces recorded in ethnohistorical sources were already in operation before the arrival of Cortés. Documented colonial markets include Ayoquezco, Chichicapan, Chilateca, Cuilapan, Etla, Mitla, Ocotlán, and Santa Ana Zegache (Appel 1982 : 147; Chance 1978).

Appel (1982 : 147) notes that, while six of the eight markets are located in local administrative centers, the majority of administrative centers are not the sites of markets. This, she suggests, indicates a lack of isomorphism between commercial and administrative functions. Within this context, Teotitlán seems to have been one of the few administrative nonmarket towns that also had a strong emphasis on commerce.

In 1670, Francisco de Burgoa singled out Teotitlán and Coyotepec as being the most commercially oriented of the nonmarket towns in the Oaxaca Valley (Chance 1978 : 110). Teotitlán had substantial numbers of traders who dealt in knives, machetes, scales, cloth, fish, and salt. These traders, known as *viajeros*, continued to operate from Teotitlán to the Isthmus and to the Sierra Juárez until the late 1950s. This is described in detail in chapter 5.

According to John Chance (1978 : 110), the largest indigenous markets in the late seventeenth century were located in San Juan Chilateca and the Villa de Etla. These markets and others mentioned above drew indigenous Oaxacans from many areas who came to trade cochineal, cotton mantles, and other products as well as creole merchants from Oaxaca who sold Castilian goods. Many of the goods indigenous peoples produced for the markets were in response to Spanish demand. Undoubtedly, Teotitecos traded in most or all of these markets. Today they continue to go on a weekly basis to sell serapes, cacao, and occasionally other trade goods in Tlacolula, Ocotlán, Mitla, and occasionally in Etla. The history and current operation of the cyclical markets of Oaxaca are best documented by Cook and Diskin (1976), who describe them as a basis for economic integration in the Oaxaca region.

Today Teotitlán serves as a primary conduit for weavings produced in two other nearby towns, Santa Ana del Valle and San Miguel del Valle. Both towns were under its jurisdiction for much of the colonial era. Merchants in Teotitlán buy weavings from these two communities on a regular basis and resell them throughout Mexico and the United States. Teotitlán also attracts laborers from other nearby communities who come to work as bricklayers and carpenters in the flourishing house construction industry.

The Religious Importance of Teotitlán in Oaxaca

The geography around Teotitlán is still associated with prehispanic gods and powers. The *Relación geográfica de Teutitlan* (Acuña 1984: 332–333) mentions a stark mountain that overshadows Teotitlán. This mountain, currently called *xiabets* (brother rock), is mentioned as a place where Teotitecos went to worship their idols and gods. The Zapotec name for Teotitlán, *šxia*, means "under the rock." According to local legend and several sources mentioned by Whitecotton (1977: 158, 312, note 118), Teotitlán is associated with a sun god in the form of a bird who descended from the heavens to his temple. The location of the temple and the spot where he is supposed to have descended is on top of *xiabets*. Interestingly enough, on the map of Macuilxóchitl that accompanies the *Relación de Macuilsúchil y su partido* (Acuña 1984: map of Macuilxóchitl), there is a picture of a large sun located by Teotitlán, perhaps a reference to this sun god associated with *xiabets*.

The *Relación de Teutitlan* states that Teotitecos worshiped stone idols to which they offered their children in sacrifice. They "killed their children in rituals performed for the Devil" (Acuña 1984: 335). They also danced and drank in front of the gods. Teotitecos still return to the site of *xiabets* today. They make an annual pilgrimage on the first day of May to the site of the sun god, but instead celebrate a Catholic holiday. Many Catholic rituals celebrated in Teotitlán contain elements that seem to be tied to prehispanic beliefs. For example, Holy Week is punctuated with small rites performed by household members to increase rainfall, provide more well water, and result in plentiful crops.

The sacred place of *xiabets* was probably visited by people not only from Teotitlán but from other communities as well. Burgoa (1934:2:119) notes that Teotitlán had a shrine that attracted people from all parts of Oaxaca. In an article on Monte Albán's hinterland, Appel (1982:144) states that the Oaxaca Valley kingdoms were interdependent religiously and economically as well as politically. She cites several instances of communities with shrines that served regional rather than local functions. Teotitlán's regional importance was reinforced religiously as well as politically, by both indigenous and colonial institutions.

During the colonial era, Teotitlán served as an administrative center for Dominican brothers. From the early 1600s until the mid-eighteenth century, it was a Dominican parish seat (Gerhard 1972: 191). During that time, the parish of Teotitlán included Tlacolula. Later, however, the parish seat was moved from Teotitlán to Tlacolula, where it was secularized after 1777. All parishes pertained to the Bishopric of Antequera during the colonial period (Gerhard 1972:191). Religious administration by parish missionaries and priests during the colonial era overlay local systems of ritual organization.

The largest rituals were *mayordomías*, organized in a hierarchy of importance. From the late nineteenth century until the 1960s, *mayordomías* were integrated with the civil cargo system of the community. This is described in detail in chapter 7. Today Teotitlán continues to be a major ritual center in the Oaxaca region, with its annual July festival of Nuestro Señor de la Preciosa Sangre (Our Lord of the Precious Blood) attracting people from many surrounding communities and bringing back hundreds of Teotitecos who have migrated to the United States. The centrality of religious ceremonies in Teotitlán is described in further detail in chapters 7 and 8.

Education and Literacy

While certain sectors of the Teotitlán population have traveled and have had extensive contact with foreigners, not everyone has been able to participate in the wider world. There have been schools in Teotitlán since before 1900, but more than 40 percent of the population is classified as illiterate, with literacy often meaning the ability to write one's name and read at a rudimentary level. About 13 percent of the population is registered as monolingual Zapotec-speaking (Brito de Martí 1982:1262). Many more understand Spanish, but cannot speak it. The majority of monolingual Zapotec speakers are women over thirty-five who never left the community or attended school.

The youngest generation in Teotitlán, those below twelve years of age, are the first to attend school in significant numbers. Most are finishing the third and fourth grades and more than 40 percent are completing their primary education. Currently, almost equal numbers of boys and girls are attending schools, although more boys are finishing the sixth grade (Secretaría de Programación y Presupuesto 1979–1985).

A few families have begun to send their children to secondary and high schools in Oaxaca. Teotitlán itself has two primary schools, a bilingual kindergarten and a secondary (junior high) school. Children from seven other surrounding communities come daily to Teotitlán to attend the secondary school.

Health Services

Because of its status as a municipal center, Teotitlán also has a government health clinic (Coordinación General del Plan Nacional de Zonas Deprimidos y Grupos Marginados, COPLAMAR), part of the Mexican Seguro Social (the national social security and health system). In addition, two doctors have established private practices there. The community has more doctors than most indigenous communities in Oaxaca. Women and children from Teotitlán also frequently travel to the district seat of Tlacolula to a larger national health clinic there, particularly for giving birth.

This abundance of medical assistance is a recent phenomenon. Before 1970, people in the community had to go to Oaxaca to receive medical treatment. Most treatment was given by local curers who used a combination of divination and herbal remedies to cure diseases. One midwife continues to practice in the community.

Political Ties

Politically, Teotitlán served as a district seat for the colonial government of Oaxaca and as a *municipio* since Mexican independence. This important position has made the community a political as well as economic center for a long time. While Teotitecos have learned to wheel and deal with state and federal officials in order to get funds for local projects such as road construction, schools, and running water, they have also achieved a significant degree of political autonomy through being able to fund a lot of their own public works projects. Due to the community's recent economic prosperity, more public works projects are funded directly by the community without going to outside sources for assistance. Recent improvements made in the primary school buildings, construction of a new market and two basketball courts, and a complete renovation of the seventeenth-century church have been paid for primarily by the community.

People in Teotitlán are proud of the facelift they are giving their community. They are also aware of the benefits of carrying out such projects independently. Receiving funds from the government for public works projects is in return for community loyalty to the Partido Revolucionario Institucional (PRI). While Teotitlán does not actively oppose the PRI, community members are reluctant to do more than cooperate with party officials when they come to monitor state and federal elections. Municipal elections do not involve the participation of political parties. In the presidential elections of 1988, the community voted overwhelmingly (80 percent) for Cuauhtémoc Cárdenas, identifying him as an alternative to the PRI and someone who understood "people like us" because he is part indigenous. The community's historical relationship to Mexican political parties is described at length in chapters 7 and 9.

When state or federal government officials want to monitor community activities, Teotitecos react with strong indignation. They feel they have the right and ability to run all of their community affairs and greatly resent outside interference. Suggestions of state taxation on looms has been met with strong local protests, a continuation of a historical trend. While Teotitecos welcome tourists and foreign importers who come to purchase their wares, they do not tolerate behavior that they deem to be inappropriate and restrictive of the freedom of people in the community. Several North Americans have been forcibly expelled from the community, and outside merchants have frequently been reminded at town meetings that they need to be on good behavior if they want to continue working in the community.

Conclusions

This overview provides background for understanding the daily world of Zapotec women in Teotitlán del Valle, who are the focus of the remainder of this book. As seen here, through their exporting and migration experience, Teotitecos have come to picture themselves in a world reaching far beyond the borders of their community. They know the daily exchange rate for the dollar and current political issues in the United States. They have a high awareness of their community's relationship to the PRI. Some Teotitecos are also informed about policies toward illegal aliens in the United States. And they are painfully aware that the Mexican national debt is making life difficult for them through runaway inflation.

At the same time, the internal life of the community expressed in weaving production, ritual, farming, and cash-based and reciprocal systems of exchange is also part of daily existence. Through their ongoing interactions, the women of Teotitlán, like other indigenous peasant women, navigate the intricate realities of the theoretical abstractions we call class, culture, ethnicity, and kinship. In order to see how the abstract categories of gender, class, and ethnicity are realized in their lives, we now turn to their stories.

Chapter 5. Contested Histories: Women, Men, and the Relations of Production in Teotitlán, 1920–1950s

In 1945 my son went away to the United States on a contract. More than 200 men went away. When the men were gone some women began to weave. They wove blankets with stripes . . . Those who didn't weave had to make tortillas and sell them or else spin wool into yarn and sell it. It was very hard on the women. We had to do all of the work, sometimes work in the fields, get firewood, haul the water in addition to doing all our other chores. (Amelia, age 85)

THE NEXT two chapters examine changes in the economic systems of Teotitlán and the three surrounding communities of Santa Ana, San Miguel, and Díaz Ordaz since the Mexican Revolution. These communities are included here because they have provided weaving labor and people in them are related through *compadrazgo* to many families in Teotitlán. They have long-standing cultural, political, and economic relations with Teotitlán.

This chapter provides information on how today's export-oriented weaving production system emerged out of an economy based on production for a regional indigenous market. Of particular interest is the role of women's labor in allowing some men to begin accumulating capital, first through earning cash as migrant workers in the United States, and later through using unpaid household labor to produce weavings that helped finance nonhousehold pieceworkers. The economic history treated here is viewed through the comparative lens of official state policy and local oral histories and archival documents. The goal of such a comparison is to understand how gender and class relations and ethnic self-identity are shaped into local history as communities respond to external markets and state-initiated economic and ideological programs of development.

Economic factors that influenced the weaving system of Teotitlán, particularly since the 1940s, include the initiation of the second United States *bracero* program in 1942; the completion of the Pan American Highway through Mexico in 1948; the loss of a regional market for handmade wool blankets to mechanized synthetic textiles made in Tlaxcala; and increasing tourism beginning in the 1950s. The first factor is examined here and the last three in the subsequent chapter. These economic changes were accompanied by political changes beginning with the Calles administration that resulted in the consolidation of the Mexican state and increased state intervention in local economies and political institutions. The Calles administration was marked by anticlericalism and the creation of national commissions such as those of agriculture, roads, and irrigation (Hamilton 1982:79–80). Continued state intervention under Cárdenas in the 1930s to support land reform, federal education programs, the establishment of *ejido* committees, detailed census and record keeping of agricultural and small industrial production, and the incorporation of labor unions and peasant groups into the government party all affected economic development in communities such as Teotitlán. In the 1940s, national policy aimed at integrating Mexico's indigenous population (at the time meaning those who spoke indigenous languages and lived under conditions of poverty in so-called Indian villages) with larger society further influenced local economic and political relations, as did government development programs promoting craft production that began in the 1950s.

The programs aimed at increasing state presence in indigenous communities and in turn integrating such communities into the national polity can also be considered in terms of their gendered content and ideology. Postrevolutionary state policy, documents, and programs promoted gender roles, including proper behavior and dress for boys and girls in school, appropriate categories of work for women (the most prominent being *quehaceres de la casa*—housework), and a bureaucratization of *municipios* that effectively put all local government positions in male hands. Women were eliminated from most formal occupational categories and were represented in few official organizations.

In general, the postrevolutionary Mexican state's programs for the development of indigenous populations provided an externally defined notion of "Indian" against which communities like Teotitlán constructed their own economic history and ethnic identity. Such histories and identities were locally based and, like that of Teotitecos, involved staking a claim to a particular economic or political resource. In the case of Teotitecos, their primary focus was laying claim to their textiles and to a secondary degree to other institutions locally associated with social reproduction, such as kin and *compadrazgo* networks, certain forms of ritual celebrations, the local language, and the notion of *respet.*

An analysis of oral histories and local correspondence suggests that Teotitecos most likely manipulated official occupational categories, including those that were gendered, in order to obscure the nature of their economy. Such efforts also worked to obscure merchant activity as the community sought to escape taxation on weaving production and marketing. Most importantly, efforts to downplay the dynamics of local textile production are indicative of a desire on the part of Teotitecos, particularly those holding political power, to retain both real and symbolic ownership over the textiles they produced. As seen in this chapter, local officials indicated an awareness of the commercial potential of their product as early as the 1930s and were quite interested in protecting it from outside interference.

The Postrevolutionary Mexican State and the Development of Indigenous Peasant Communities

Like many communities, Teotitlán had few collective or individual resources left by 1920. From 1915 until 1920, during the aftermath of the Mexican Revolution, Teotitlán was caught in the middle between the federal troops of Venustiano Carranza stationed in Tlacolula and the rebel *serrano* mountain troops of General Isaac M. Ibarra. The rebel *serranos* operated out of the Sierra Juárez directly behind Teotitlán. For five years, Teotitecos provided cattle, pigs, corn, beans, tortillas, and firewood on a regular basis to both sides. Transcripts of correspondence between Carrancista troops and the municipal president of Teotitlán show increasing pressure on the community. In an October 18, 1918, memo the municipal president apologizes to a captain in Tlacolula for not being able to send more food: "I am sending to you three head of cattle given voluntarily by the people of this town to help sustain the troops in this garrison. I hope that you can pardon us for things that have occurred in this population during the last few years that do not make it possible for us to send more things to help. The people in this town remain disposed to help you as much as we can" (Archivo Municipal de Teotitlán del Valle 1918).

The people of Teotitlán also gave food to rebel troops based in Villa Alta. Teotitlán provided a temporary market site about one mile outside of town for *serranos* who could not market their goods in Tlacolula because they would be captured by government troops.

Supplying food for both sides during the Revolution may have saved Teotitlán from armed confrontations within the community, but the price of peace was tremendous pressure on the local economy and continued poverty into the 1920s.

While it is difficult to find documentation of occupational breakdowns from 1910 until almost 1930, voting lists and the district censuses suggest that Teotiteco households engaged in both weaving and subsistence farming. Because of the economic hardship felt in the community during the Revolution and after, most elderly informants recalled that almost everyone was impoverished and trade in woven blankets diminished significantly due to the danger of continued fighting at least until 1920. Oral histories and census records do confirm, however, the existence of a small group of merchant/ traders who had more land than other households and who dominated economic relations through their indirect control on labor through obligatory *mayordomías* (Dirección General de Estadística 1906:44–45, 1936:275). These families were the primary source of employment and cash in the community, and few Teotitecos left to seek wage labor elsewhere until the 1930s. This small group of merchant/traders seems to have grown somewhat during the late 1920s as regional trade routes began to function again following the Revolution.

When Elías Plutarco Calles took office in 1926, the treadle loom weaving industry centered in Teotitlán appeared to be stabilizing. The number of merchants was on the upswing and trade was expanding into the Sierra Juárez and down to Chiapas by mule. This progress was occurring quietly in the south of Mexico without much discussion at the national level. The government had not made a detailed census count of people or production in Oaxaca since 1910. The period of the Mexican Revolution had left national information agencies in a shambles.

The decade of the 1920s in Mexico was marked by the centralization of the state and by the creation of institutional machinery set up for government intervention in the economy (Hamilton 1982:79). By the time Calles took office, institutions such as the National Commission of Roads, the National Agrarian Commission, the National Irrigation Commission, and the Agricultural Credit Bank had already been established. Calles' tenure is remembered most clearly for its rabid anticlericalism, the Cristéro Rebellion, and his interpretation of the 1917 constitution, which gave legitimacy to the concept of an interventionist, centralized state (Hamilton 1982:109).

While building its political power from a fundamentally different constituency, particularly the working class and peasants, the administration of Lázaro Cárdenas upheld the notion of an active interventionist state, controlling and directing the economy down to the local level. The agrarian reform program, in which Cárdenas redistributed more land than all of his predecessors combined, inserted the state into all areas of the local economy, including agricultural credit and *ejidal* decision-making groups. The theme of the six-year plan outlined in 1933, which was the blueprint for Cárdenas' time in office, emphasized integration. It gave the state wide leeway in directing and redirecting society, focusing on physical integration through the construction of roads and communication links as well as ideological and cultural integration through the dissemination of so-called socialist education (Hamilton 1982:136). Building on the school program begun by Calles, Cárdenas' vision of socialist education was oriented toward collective work and achievement, replacing the fanaticism and superstition generated by clerical influence (Hamilton 1982:136). Under Cárdenas the number of schools and teachers multiplied. His term also consolidated the state's indirect hold on productive land.

By the end of 1940, 47.4 percent of the total cultivated land in Mexico was held in *ejidos* linked to the state (Hamilton 1982:175). Many peasants were also tied into the official party through credit loans and membership in the National Peasant Confederation (Coordinadora Nacional de Campesinos, CNC). Communities such as Teotitlán that did not receive *ejidal* land remained at more distance from institutions such as the CNC that tied peasants directly to the state. The biggest influence on the community was probably the establishment of a more extensive education program with an emphasis on national identity. This education in national identity was to continue as the community became one of thousands targeted by promoters of indigenous integration in the 1940s. Because of the particular nature of the weavings produced in Teotitlán and surrounding communities, the integrationist policies of the National Indian Institute and later programs to promote so-called Indian crafts had a greater impact on Teotitlán than the agrarian reform policies of the Cárdenas administration.

Indigenismo and the Creation of the Official Mexican Indian

While the Interamerican Indianist Congress held in Pátzcuaro, Michoacán, in 1940 is often viewed as the initiation of indigenist policy in Latin America, Mexico had special programs aimed at educating the indigenous population of Mexico before the 1940 congress. In the early 1920s, a Department of Education and Culture for the Indian Race was set up in the Secretariat of Public Education. In 1927, the Casa del Estudiante Indígena announced its objectives: to "eliminate the evolutionary distance that separates the Indians from the present epoch, transforming their mentality, tendencies and customs . . . to incorporate them within the Mexican community" (Adams 1967:477). In 1936, the Autonomous Department of Indian Affairs was established, followed the next year by the Department of Indian Education. These programs were to provide all students with agricultural and technical techniques that would lead to success in their communities. While these educational programs operated in some areas of Mexico, it was not until the 1940s after the first Inter-American Indianist meeting that a systematic political, economic, and social policy was created for Mexico's more than fifty ethnic groups. The creation of the National Indian Institute (Instituto Nacional Indígena, INI) marked the beginning of extensive programs carried out through local centers with the general purpose of nationalizing the Indian.

As Cárdenas was winding up his six-year term, the Interamerican Indianist Congress held in Pátzcuaro in 1940 articulated the goal of "the integration of the Indian into national society, with all of his cultural trappings, giving him the instruments of civilization necessary for his articulation within modern society" (Aguirre Beltrán 1975:27). One of the primary questions preoccupying those who attended the congress was how to clearly identify Indians so that social and economic programs could be created to integrate them into national society. To aid in this identification process, material indicators were chosen to distinguish Indians from non-Indians in the Mexican population. While anthropologists who attended the Pátzcuaro congress felt that cultural characteristics needed to be considered as well, material characteristics were the initial focus of the government in identifying just who Mexico's Indians were.

In the 1940 census, indigenous people were categorized by language and material indicators. These are described in detail below. The census reflected a contradictory state policy of development that was supposed simultaneously to allow for the continuation of indigenous culture and yet to integrate indigenous communities into modern society, materially and ideologically.

Beginning with the program plan of the 1940 First Interamerican Indianist Congress, the government also took an interest in *artes populares indígenas* (indigenous folk arts). The first program plan, later adopted by the INI, called for the protection of indigenous arts, the organization of expositions, and national competitions (Marroquín 1977:39–40). Government interest in promoting indigenous arts became an important part of its contradictory program of protecting and integrating indigenous peoples into wider society. Such programs not only attempted to create new markets for crafts, but also helped the state create ethnic identities for its Indians. Since the 1950s, when the Mexican government sought to use tourism as a way of generating foreign exchange, indigenous ethnic groups have been encouraged to maintain and reproduce certain outwardly picturesque characteristics—in particular, dress, ritual, and craft production, which make them identifiable as Indians to tourists (see Cook 1984a; García Canclini 1982; Graburn 1982). Ultimately, state creation of Indian identities also influenced the construction of local ethnic identities and served as a foil against which communities such as Teotitlán created a self-determined identity not controlled by the state. An important part of creating such an identity as a subtle form of resistance involves obscuring and limiting outside access to some areas of social, economic, and political organization. In looking at this process we shall see that gender was an important element and is one of the areas in which the state had little understanding of cultural and economic relations.

The Creation of Gendered Indigenous Economic History by the State

An examination of the first six official population censuses of Mexico beginning in 1895 provides evidence of how ethnic and gendered occupational categories were constructed over a fifty-year period by the Department of General Statistics. In the discussion below, attention is focused on the names of census categories and the number of men and women reported in each. Not all categories are given, and the numbers are *not* considered in terms of statistical significance because of the difficulties in accepting census figures as accurate.

The census of 1895, which was reported at the level of the district, put all women in the district of Tlacolula (to which Teotitlán belongs) into occupational categories, reporting 1,129 female weavers and 1,179 male weavers. We can assume that most of these were located in Teotitlán del Valle and Díaz Ordaz, with a few in Santa Ana and Mitla. According to the administrative memoranda of the governor of Oaxaca in 1900, Teotitlán reported 150 weaving households that produced 10,000 pieces per year; Díaz Ordaz reported 100 weaving households producing 8,000 pieces; Mitla reported 50 households producing 4,000 pieces; and Santa Ana reported 40 households producing 2,000 pieces (Clements 1988b). Table 6 shows highest economic participation by men and women based on the 1895 oc-

Table 6. *Gendered Occupational Categories for 1895 Census, District of Tlacolula*

	Male	Female	Total
Agriculture	14,177		14,177
Merchants	52	21	73
Weavers	1,179	1,129	2,308
Seamstresses		276	276
Domestic workers	43	72	115
Washers		82	82
Lard producers	93		93
Corn grinders (female)		7,569	7,569

Source: Dirección General de Estadística 1897–1899:44.

Table 7. *Most Significant Gendered Occupational Categories for 1900 Census, Teotitlán del Valle*

	Men	Women	Total
Independent agriculturalists	9		9
Landless laborers	43		43
Muleteers/traders	18		18
Seamstresses		2	2
Corn grinders		842	842
Domestic laborers		60	60
Firewood gatherers	96		96
Weavers	565	4	569

Source: Dirección General de Estadística 1906:42–67.

cupational census for the district of Tlacolula. The majority of women were registered within specific occupational categories, with the greatest numbers as *molenderas* (corn grinders) and then as *tejedoras* (weavers). The census does not distinguish between backstrap loom weaving done almost exclusively by women and treadle loom weaving, probably dominated by men, giving women an occupational identity as weavers. Similarly, the classification of women as corn grinders under the subheading of *industria de alimentación* (food industry) also provides them with an occupational identity.

In 1900, when occupational breakdowns were given by *municipio* in the population census, women almost dropped out as weavers. For the district of Tlacolula, only 132 women were reported as weavers

compared with 1,824 men. In Teotitlán only 4 women were classified as weavers in the 1900 census.

Reporting at the level of the *municipio* in the 1900 census was
correlated with the disappearance of significant numbers of women
weavers, but most men in the community reported as weavers rather
than farmers. There is nothing in the historical record to indicate
that women stopped weaving on backstrap and treadle looms at this
time. Most likely the four women who were reported as weavers
were single heads of household who wove on treadle looms. Women
weavers who were not single heads of households do not appear to
have been reported to census officials. It is unclear why so many
men would have reported themselves as weavers. The number is un-
usually high for the period.

The 1910 census was aggregated by district only and, like the 1920
census, may indicate the general bureaucratic disarray of Mexico between 1910 and the early 1920s. In the 1910 census for Tlacolula,
the number of women reported as weavers rises to 902. Women do
not appear as agriculturalists and begin to appear in larger numbers
in the category *quehaceres domésticas* (domestic chores). However,
the majority are still registered with particular occupations.

The national census of 1920 only reports occupations for the
country as a whole, indicating that the data were probably in serious
disarray after the Mexican Revolution. What is significant about
this census, however, is that the majority of women appear in the
category of *quehaceres de la casa* (housework), subheaded as *seño-
ras y señoritas ocupadas en su casa* (married and unmarried women

Table 8. *Gendered Occupational Categories for 1910 Census,
District of Tlacolula*

	Men	Women	Total
Independent agriculturalists	9,116	27	9,143
Landless laborers	2,309	55	2,364
Weavers	1,210	902	2,112
Washerwomen		135	135
Seamstresses		530	530
Merchants	80	39	119
Door-to-door salespeople	140	18	158
Domestic workers		3,228	3,228
Maids and servants	104	165	269
Corn grinders		9,754	9,754

Source: Dirección General de Estadística 1918:925–929.

occupied in their homes). While it is not known how many women from the district of Tlacolula were included in this category, it is apparent that women dropped out of most occupations under which they were previously listed, including *molenderas* (corn grinders) and *tejedoras* (weavers).

As seen in table 9, the total number of women weavers in Mexico in 1921 is only double that reported for the single district of Tlacolula in 1895. Comparative data aggregated nationally by gender and occupation are not available for 1910 or 1930. While weaving technology was beginning to change in this period and backstrap loom weaving of cotton for commercial exchange was decreasing due to mechanization of textile production (Young 1978), local records and oral histories indicate that women continued to weave in many areas for self-consumption and for exchange. They did not simply stop weaving, but were no longer counted as weavers. The overall trend indicated by the 1921 national census and reinforced in local occupational censuses in 1930 and 1940 is that women were

Table 9. *Gendered Occupational Categories for 1921 National Census*

	Men	Women	Total
Agriculturalists	623,642	6,819	630,461
Gañanes[a] (migrant labor)	2,750,075	21,463	2,771,538
Cotton and wool weavers	10,959	2,256	13,215
Palm weavers	4,634	2,415	7,049
Clothing makers/ designers		70,563	70,563
Muleteers	20,046	43	20,089
Merchants	202,351	42,398	244,749
Door-to-door salespeople	7,050	2,862	9,912
Domestic workers		4,495,959	4,495,959
Maids, cooks, servants	35,803	153,889	189,692

Source: Departamento de la Estadística Nacional 1925–1928:82–98.

[a]*Gañanes* refers to those engaged in a wide variety of migrant labor—those who moved in order to work, not working on their own land. The census did not include the category of *peones* or *jornaleros*.

Table 10. *Gendered Occupational Categories for Teotitlán del Valle, 1930 Census and 1940 Census Compared*

	1930			1940		
	Men	Women	Total	Men	Women	Total
Agriculturalists (may employ others)	578		578	175		175
Workers, day laborers				50		50
Work alone, don't employ other laborers				119		119
Small industry (weavers)	214	2	216	567	19	586
Merchants	6		6	26	2	28
Domestic workers	1	825	826	5	870	875
Servants				5	5	10

Source: Dirección General de Estadística 1946: 567.

eliminated from many occupational categories, and their labor was lumped together in the categories of housework and nonproductive occupations.

The 1940 census for Teotitlán also indicates that large numbers of males moved from agriculture into weaving. The number seems disproportionately high, compared to earlier figures for the 1920s and later ones for 1950 and 1960. The census also records the emergence of 22 new merchant households in 1940 as well, a figure that seems more consistent with the gradually increasing number of merchant households (discussed later in this chapter). Overall, it appears that there may have been some motivation in 1940 for people to appear as weavers and merchants instead of as farmers. The gendered and ethnic dimensions of the 1940 census are discussed below.

The Indigenous Woman as Reflected in the 1920 and 1940 Census

National census documents from 1920, 1930, 1940, and after used gender and ethnicity as important categories of analysis, projecting statistical portraits of indigenous women that became the object of policies aimed at integrating the many ethnic groups of Mexico into

Table 11. *"Racial" and Gendered Literacy Rates for the State of Oaxaca in 1920*

	Women			Men		
	"Indigenous"	"Mixed Race"	"White"	"Indigenous"	"Mixed Race"	"White"
% who can read or write	7	15	42	18	32	53

Source: Departamento de la Estadística Nacional 1925–1928:46.

national society by eliminating their basis for autonomy. After the Revolution, the secretary of national statistics demonstrated a strong concern with distinguishing Indians from the rest of the population. In the 1920 census, for example, ethnic categories were used in order to discern literacy rates among the population. Table 11 shows figures for the state of Oaxaca. Indigenous women have the lowest literacy rate among the gendered ethnic groups included in the 1920 census. In 1940, in accordance with the government's endorsement of the 1940 Interamerican Indianist Congress, census officials removed overt references to ethnicity. Instead, ethnic categories were reconstituted as cultural categories. In the 1940 census being "Indian" was correlated with speaking an Indian language, bilingualism (Spanish and an indigenous language), or speaking Spanish; sleeping on the floor or using a bed, *petate* (mat), or hammock; whether or not shoes are worn and, if so, whether of "Spanish" type, *huaraches* (sandals), or other shoes of an "indigenous" type; and whether bread or tortillas are eaten.

When the data aggregated in these categories are looked at in terms of gender, a clear picture of the Indian woman emerges. For example, women from Teotitlán del Valle, Oaxaca, in the 1940 census were pictured as primarily monolingual in Zapotec (74 percent) with a low literacy rate (6.57 percent could read and write); 98 percent of those who spoke Zapotec were noted to have gone barefoot. Despite the absurdity of the cultural categories used to measure Indian identity among Mexico's indigenous population in 1940, such categories did create a national picture of indigenous women as existing on the margins of civilization—poor, barefoot, monolingual, illiterate, sleeping on the floor, and eating tortillas. While this characterization was originally the baseline from which the indigenous population was to be pushed toward modernity, in the packaging of Indian identity for sale to tourists, such marginality was converted into tradition and exoticism.

Community Reaction to the Bureaucratization of the Mexican State

In Teotitlán, detailed questionnaires began to come to the *municipio* during the Calles administration as the state moved to document agricultural and industrial production with an eye toward increasing production. They continued with the Cárdenas administration in the 1930s. An examination of Teotitlán community correspondence with different state offices during the 1930s reveals that *municipio* officials reluctantly responded to inquiries regarding the doings of local government and the specifics of economic production (Archivo Municipal de Teotitlán del Valle 1930–1939). The town is probably not atypical. After the Revolution, many indigenous communities tried to defend what little autonomy they might have gained as a result of land redistribution and broken bureaucratic links to the federal government, which fell apart during the Revolution.[1]

Instead of responding straightforwardly to official inquiries regarding their economy, Teotiteco officials avoided reporting the exact nature of weaving production. In this process they continued to report themselves as both agriculturalists and weavers and not to include specific information on the economic activities of women and children or the quantity of textiles produced in the community. By evading official inquiries about weaving production in the 1930s and 1940s and later efforts by the state to organize craft cooperatives in their community, Teotitecos successfully avoided having the state serve as an intermediary for their weaving products. This historical precedent became even more important in the late 1970s and 1980s as local merchants from Teotitlán began to negotiate directly with United States importers, cutting out both Mexican middlemen and state officials from agencies such as the Fondo Nacional de Artesanía (FONART) from their export transactions. At a time when state bureaucrats and Mexican handicraft entrepreneurs began to claim popular folk arts as the common heritage of Mexico, people in Teotitlán asserted their claim as a long-standing community of Zapotec weavers.

In their correspondence with state officials during the 1930s, municipal authorities carefully reproduced dominant ideas regarding poor, humble Indians struggling to survive, engaging in what might be called counterhegemonic activity to protect their own interests. Merchant activities were deemphasized, and uniform poverty was projected as the norm. While most of the community was poor, there were at least six to eight wealthy merchant/landowner households whose activities were not recognized—nor was the business potential of weaving production. A response from the mayor of Teotitlán to the head of national statistics in 1932 is representative of such letters (Archivo Municipal de Teotitlán del Valle 1932; my translation):[2]

1. The majority of the people in this town have looms that they use to make the beautiful blankets that have brought significant fame to our state of Oaxaca, but they do not have enough resources to work daily. They must also work as wage laborers

and during the agricultural seasons they work as subsistence agriculturalists in order to grow grain for their own consumption.

2. Commerce is very dead in our community because of a lack
of money. Many have stopped working and although names can't
be provided, I can say that there are no houses here that could be
considered factories.[3]

3. The only people who have a regular income are those *regatones* [merchants] who resell their product in Oaxaca.

4. We estimate the total income generated from production to
be about 50 pesos per month from different-sized products.

The above answer to official inquiries regarding the number of
weavers and merchants, presence of factories, and income from
farming and weaving suggests a muted version of the reality of weaving production at the time—certainly of merchant activities. While
guarding the exact nature of their production and only referring
vaguely to a few merchants operating in Oaxaca, other correspondence from the same decade indicates that the community had an
avid interest in merchant activity and in improving local infrastructure (Archivo Municipal de Teotitlán del Valle, 1930–1939).

For example, the letter below, written by Teotiteco authorities in
1931 in response to an inquiry from the subsecretary of industry,
commerce, and labor in Mexico, highlights the lack of capital resources and infrastructure in conjunction with the beauty of Zapotec
textiles. The letter ends by turning a request for production information into a petition for a post office (Archivo Municipal de Teotitlán
del Valle 1931a; my translation):

Let me inform you that the merchants, agriculturalists, and producers here all work with very scarce capital as you will see below: the merchant here who has the largest general store would
make no more than 100 pesos, the agriculturalist with the largest
piece of land plants 3 hectares. In the notable industry of wool
blankets which is undertaken here in this town, all of the inhabitants know how to weave blankets of distinct designs such as the
Aztec calendar, idols, and different animals, in fast colors. All
the people work for themselves, having in their house up to two
simple looms and up to one *arroba* [25 pounds] of wool with an
actual value of 10 pesos. Nevertheless, despite the fact that this
town is very old and large with four thousand industrious inhabitants, the government has not yet established a post office here,
something that would help this town prosper. Because we have

no post office here, our industry cannot be spread to other areas of the Mexican Republic.

If you could help us with the creation of the post office that we are soliciting, we shall remain very grateful.

On August 31, the subsecretary of industry, commerce, and labor wrote back with his recommendation for the establishment of a post office in Teotitlán (Archivo Municipal de Teotitlán del Valle 1931b). The community's effort to defend its economic interests is perhaps best reflected in a letter sent to President Cárdenas in 1938 in which the undersigned ask the president to intervene internationally to prevent the Japanese from fabricating imitations of their blankets. The very fact that Teotitecos were aware of the dynamics of international trade and marketing indicates the foresight with which they protected their interests. The adoption and use by Teotiteco municipal authorities of phrases such as "designs and idols that signify the history of Mitla and Monte Albán" suggests that the categories used to promote both Indianness and Indian crafts could be adopted and used to defend local economic interest.[4] The words *artesanía, cultura, historia, costumbre,* and others that are now a part of everyday Teotiteco Zapotec vocabulary were used in municipal documents as early as the 1930s and perhaps before, again indicating an awareness on the part of officials about what these terms mean and how to use them. The community's repeated encounters with the state in the 1930s and before are firmly entrenched in contemporary spoken Zapotec. The letter regarding the threat of the Japanese reads as follows (Archivo Municipal de Teotitlán del Valle 1938):

The native citizens of Teotitlán del Valle, Tlacolula, State of Oaxaca, state for you that we have become aware of the fact that in the country of Japan they are producing Mexican articles with the intent of passing them off as coming from Mexico. Among these articles . . . are found those from the small industry of Oaxaca blankets, adorned with designs and idols that signify the history of Mitla and Monte Albán and Zapotec and Toltec figures. We understand for certain that, among other things, Japan is producing imitations of the Oaxacan blanket, an article to which we dedicate ourselves as humble people working on simple home looms. This notice has caused us great alarm because, at the moment, we are in a precarious economic situation. It has therefore occurred to us to request that you dictate measures that will protect our small weaving industry here in Oaxaca—also international measures that will take care of this phenomenon that has come to our notice. . . .

Teotitecos clearly saw the state as necessary for protecting their interests at a national and international level, yet also resisted providing the specific information on production requested by the Office of National Statistics. While the state was busy measuring and categorizing the indigenous population of the country, indigenous people such as the Teotitlán Zapotecs were also busy building their own locally based ethnic identities and staking specific claims in terms of these identities. The voices reflected in the Teotitlán archives that make continued claims on Zapotec weavings as cultural symbols are reworking the state's strategy of adopting the Indian as part of national culture (García Canclini 1982; Marroquín 1977; Novelo 1976, 1988). Those who penned the community's official responses to government inquiries into production appear to have understood the emerging construction of Indian and the way it was being integrated with government policy. We now turn to Teotitecos' unofficial version of their history from the 1930s and 1940s as portrayed primarily in oral histories. These voices present a more complicated picture of Teotiteco identity, one that is riddled with contradictions and questions.

Unofficial Voices: Gender and Class Relations, 1930–1940

When elderly people in Teotitlán recall the past, they often begin with a description of what it used to be like to farm in the mountains surrounding the community. They point north to the Sierra Juárez stretching behind the town and recall large beans and squash carefully cultivated with hand hoes in fields where oxen could not plow. These are communal lands.

Today communal land is characterized by faint terraces that extend up into the mountains. These communal terraces remain barren, no longer used by local farmers. Most farming is done on privately held land located on the flattest parts of the landscape.

Farmers recall that all of the hillside terraces were planted until the 1940s:

> Before people started going to the United States, a lot of people would go up to the mountain and plant together. About ten to fifteen people would get together and build a big corral to protect the land from cows. Each one of them would farm a little piece

inside the corral, 1/8 or 1/4 of a hectare. We would work together planting and maintaining the corrals without pay. For example, if the fence was broken in one place, everyone would get together and fix it. The problem after the *bracería* [migration program] was that no one was around to help, so people just stopped planting in the mountains. (Antonio, age 80)

As is the case today, everyone in the community had rights to communal land. Because there were few sources of income until migration began and the export market opened up, most households devoted significant amounts of time to farming, weaving very little during the spring planting and fall harvesting seasons.

The reciprocal labor institution of *guelaguetza* also played an important part in the farming of communal land. When elderly people are questioned about the concept, both men and women recall not only ceremonially based *guelaguetza,* but also agricultural *guelaguetza* associated primarily with the working of communal land. In contrast to communal lands, small private holdings were worked by household labor pools including men, women, and children as well as *guelaguetza* labor. Larger plots owned by merchants in Teotitlán were worked by local farmers paying off loans they had taken out in order to pay their *mayordomía* expenses. This arrangement came to an end in 1930 when obligatory *mayordomías* ended. Later larger merchant-owned plots were worked by a combination of wage labor and agricultural *guelaguetza* labor.

Teotitecos identified three kinds of *guelaguetza* connected to agriculture: *xɛlgɛz dajn*—labor exchange for corral construction, planting, weeding, and harvesting on communal land in the mountains; *xɛlgɛz (h)lats(v)*—labor exchange for planting, weeding, and harvesting on flat land, mostly privately held; and *xɛlgɛz xed jaɣ*—labor exchange to gather firewood and cook communal meals for wood gatherers (usually for ceremonial purposes).

Guelaguetza labor was an institution that allowed the poor to help each other outside of the exploitative framework of debt peonage. In the minds of Teotitecos this labor was of primary importance in subsistence-level production and ceremonial events, not to mention weaving production, which later became the mainstay of the local economy. The integration of *guelaguetza* labor with wage labor under commercial capitalism became an important factor in the successful transition of production for a regional use market to an export market in the 1970s.

The division of *guelaguetza* labor for farming and wood gathering was gendered, but male and female informants differed in their descriptions of what men and women actually did. Elderly men stated that women only participated in *guelaguetza* for ceremonial purposes, where their roles were to prepare large communal meals. Women stated that in addition to preparing meals they also participated in reciprocal labor exchanges for planting, weeding, and harvesting, working in the field alongside men.[5] Today women continue to be active during weeding and harvesting seasons, pitching in alongside men as needed. In a survey of 176 women in the neighboring community of San Miguel, Helen Clements (1988a:256) notes that 29 percent of the women surveyed plant and 31 percent participate in weeding.

In the 1920s, following the Mexican Revolution, privately owned land in Teotitlán was held in greater concentration than it is now. At this time, working as a *jornalero* (day laborer) for others was the primary source of cash income for many households (Archivo Municipal de Teotitlán del Valle 1868, 1890, 1900, 1920). In addition, many people also ended up working as indentured laborers for local merchants after going completely broke from serving as *mayordomos*. Elderly informants vividly recalled the differences between the few rich and the majority poor. "The poor people who were appointed to be *mayordomos* would sell themselves to the rich people to work in their fields and in their houses. And even without being a *mayordomo*, it was the only way to earn money. I earned 50 centavos per month when I was young working in people's houses making tortillas and carding and spinning their wool. I kept doing this work even after I got married. There was no other way to pay for things" (María, age 80).

> My parents were very poor like a lot of people's. When I was a child I worked for other people taking care of their animals. I remember that I only had one set of clothing. Those of us who worked as children herding other people's cows and goats would wash our clothes by the river. We only had one pair of pants and one shirt so we would wait for them to dry by the river. The women only had one complete outfit as well. . . . You know there were a lot more poor people when things were cheap and now when things are expensive there are a lot more rich people. Before the rich people had land and oxen, and sometimes a little bit of money, but not like the money people have now. You could tell the rich by what they wore. The merchants, four or five of them, had a lot of land. The men wore leather shoes and the rich women wore *biuy* [hand-loomed fine wool cloth dyed with cochineal]. (Pedro, age 84)

Elderly informants concurred that a small group of merchant/ traders had a corner on the land market in the 1920s and, particularly with the help of forced ceremonial sponsorships, succeeded in buying up land quite cheaply as people sold it in desperation to meet the heavy financial needs of *mayordomía* sponsorship. "There were about six families who were merchants and owned oxen. They sold blankets in Oaxaca and were acquiring land for very little money. As I remember there were three sets of brothers from three families who did most of the commercial selling and were absorbing a lot of land. Everyone else worked communal lands" (Tomás, age 74).

It is unclear what percentage of the population engaged in indentured servitude in the houses and fields of the community elite. What remains strongly etched in the minds of elderly informants is the contrast between the majority poor and the few rich families. Wealth differences were clear, but class differences in the community were less obvious than they are today—the appropriation of surplus labor did not occur through the buying and selling of labor, but through merchant/landholding households controlling its product by receiving labor in return for loans made to poor *mayordomos* and their families. Because the small group of merchant/traders in Teotitlán supported the political authority of ritual elders who appointed people to be *mayordomos,* their hold on labor was effectively sanctioned by local authorities. As noted by Sider (1986:34–35), merchant capital does not exploit labor directly at the point of production, but indirectly through exchange and often through community-controlled and locally sanctioned institutions—in this case obligatory *mayordomía.* It was not until the state intervened to discourage *mayordomías* and other sources of cash became available to people in Teotitlán that the hold of local merchants over the majority of the population was loosened. Later, under conditions of commercial capitalism, labor was directly appropriated by purchasing it, but the class system also became more complex, with more middle levels between the majority poor and the few rich.

This change is somewhat consistent with the distinction Marx made between the formal versus the real subsumption of labor to capital. Under formal subsumption of labor, as under the conditions of merchant capital in Teotitlán, existing labor and production processes end up under the control of capital, but the production process itself is not changed (Bennholdt-Thomsen 1980:108). The real and more direct subsumption of labor to capital involves the production of relative surplus value through direct relations between wage-laboring producers and petty capitalists, as in the case of piece-workers working for large merchants. However, because of the ever-present mediating factors of kinship, *compadrazgo*, and the types of reciprocal exchanges attached to their relationships, labor-capital relationships in Teotitlán never become completely visible as the "real subsumption" described by Marx (1881/1967) in "Results of the Direct Processes of Production." Instead, the language of kinship and patterns of family cooperation/exploitation remain important in the formation of petty capital. And the heavy ceremonial obligations undertaken by all Teotitecos, although seemingly less by merchant households, also can act as a brake on capital formation in some instances. This is discussed further in chapter 6.

Production and Distribution for Regional Markets until 1960

To understand the international, national, and local dynamics of commercialized Zapotec weaving production, we must first trace the history of weaving production through this century to the 1960s. The weaving complex centered around Teotitlán del Valle historically included the neighboring communities of Díaz Ordaz (Santo Domingo), Santa Ana del Valle, and to a limited degree Macuilxóchitl. These communities wove cotton for local consumption as well as for tribute payments before the arrival of the Spaniards. The first documented evidence of weaving in Teotitlán is found in the *Relaciones geográficas*, which states that Teotitlán paid tribute in cotton mantles to Zaachilla (Acuña 1984:335). This cotton cloth was woven on backstrap looms. It is also probable that Teotitecos were paying tribute to the Aztecs, directly or indirectly, after Teotitlán was incorporated into the Aztec province of Coyolapan (Barlow 1949:map).

According to Oaxaca oral history, wool was introduced to Teotitlán by the first bishop of Oaxaca sometime between 1535 and 1555. In a move that changed the community's future, Bishop López de Zarate not only gave the Teotitecos sheep, but provided them with their first stand-up treadle looms as well. He taught them how to card and spin the wool and to work the large treadle looms. By the mid-seventeenth century, the woolen blanket industry inspired by López de Zarate was probably well underway. Burgoa mentions the weaving of woolen blankets and serapes as an important economic activity in Teotitlán as well as in Santo Domingo del Valle (now Díaz Ordaz), Mitla, Tlacolula, and Macuilxóchitl (Chance 1978:110).

Throughout the colonial period and independence, Teotitlán, Santa Ana, Díaz Ordaz, and Macuilxóchitl continued to weave in conjunction with subsistence farming. Censuses of Teotitlán and Santa Ana from the 1850s through the 1890s indicate the steady presence of both male and female weavers (Clements 1988b; Stephen 1987a). At the turn of this century and through the Mexican Revolution, the communities of Teotitlán, Santa Ana, and Díaz Ordaz continued to weave, each specializing in a particular type of blanket.[6]

Díaz Ordaz artisans produced a third-class blanket called a *pelusa*, which is a mixture of animal hair and cotton (Vargas-Barón 1968 : 46). This cheaper product occupied an important niche in local markets until the 1930s. Santa Ana artisans specialized in production of second-class wool blankets with little or no design, while Teotitecos wove first-class woolen blankets with complex designs.

Tracing changes in the development of the Oaxaca Valley weaving complex of Díaz Ordaz, Santa Ana, and Teotitlán, Vargas-Barón (1968) describes how the regional market for weavings expanded during the 1940s and was then replaced by a national and international market for high-quality weavings in the 1950s. As a result of this change, weaving activities have greatly declined in Díaz Ordaz while they have increased in Santa Ana and Teotitlán. As people in Díaz Ordaz abandoned weaving, they began to make technological improvements in cultivation techniques. The opposite happened in Teotitlán and Santa Ana, where increased weaving activity displaced subsistence agriculture. Vargas-Barón also points out that high-quality land in Díaz Ordaz and a superior irrigation system make farming more feasible than in Teotitlán or Santa Ana.

Until 1890, the network for sales distribution of blankets from Díaz Ordaz, Santa Ana, and Teotitlán extended only to the markets of Oaxaca and Tlacolula. From 1890 and 1920, this network expanded locally to include other valley markets in the area such as Ocotlán, Etla, and Miahuatlán. The years 1920 to 1950 mark a period of significant growth in the industry, particularly in relation to the production of first-class blankets (Vargas-Barón 1968:186). The peak in demand for *pelusa* blankets was from 1910 to 1930, according to Vargas-Barón. In the 1930s, a steady decline occurred in the number of weavers from Díaz Ordaz; *pelusa* production was extinguished in the late 1940s as factory-produced blankets from Puebla and Tlaxcala arrived in Oaxaca via the Pan American Highway.

Teotitlán and Santa Ana marketed first- and second-class woolen blankets to the Sierra Júarez and to Chiapas from 1920 until 1950. The booming market of Tlacolula was a center for salesmen and merchants who traveled by mule. About twelve to fifteen *viajeros* from Teotitlán continued to sell in Chiapas, the Isthmus, and the Sierra Júarez until the 1950s.

One way to trace the development of the weaving industry from the turn of the century is to look at the growth of the merchant sector. Census material provides sufficient evidence to show that the merchant sector grew slowly but steadily through the 1930s, and at a faster pace after 1940. Between 1930 and 1960, the number of merchants steadily increased, with the exception of *viajeros* or muleteers, who had stopped selling their wares by the early 1960s. Some of them later moved into other forms of commercial activity.

Table 12 shows the number of merchants registered in Teotitlán according to censuses and other local documents from 1868 through 1985. The table also includes the number of merchants and *viajeros* recalled by elder people from Teotitlán. Both types of data are included to provide as accurate a picture as possible. The census data may be just as problematic or more so than oral histories, given the way in which occupational categories were changed by the state and manipulated by local officials underreporting the number of weavers and merchants.[7] In addition, the great increase in the number of merchants noted from 1980 to 1985 is in part a reflection of the greater accuracy of my household occupational census than the official Mexican census. My count of merchant households was revised several times and the list of merchant households checked with over twenty informants in the community to verify its accuracy.

As seen in table 12, the number of merchants remained low until the 1940s, when the local market for the first-class blankets produced in Teotitlán opened up. With the advent of the tourist and international markets, the number of merchants more than quintupled between 1950 and 1985. Teotitecos say that since 1972 they have seen the biggest increase in demand for serapes. This growth can be linked to Teotiteco migration to the United States.

Men Migrating to the United States and Women Laboring at Home

In the 1940s, following Cárdenas' tenure in office, the initiation of the second *bracero* program had a major impact on the textile industry centered in Teotitlán. Without exception, all elderly people remember the *bracero* program as a major factor in decreasing subsistence production, pushing women into a wider range of jobs with heavier workloads, and beginning a real money economy. The labor of women maintained the local economy while men were away starting to accumulate cash in the United States.

The *bracero* program was the first opportunity most Teotitecos had to earn a substantial cash income, and significant numbers of men began to migrate to the United States in the 1940s. Estimates by elderly informants are that at least 25 percent or about 200 out of

Table 12. Numbers of Merchants in Teotitlán del Valle from 1868 to 1985

Year	Population	No. of Merchants	Census Source	No. of Merchants Cited by Informants	No. of Viajeros Cited
1868	1,899	3	Archivo Municipal de Teotitlán del Valle, 1868		
1890	2,742	3	Archivo General del Estado de Oaxaca 1890		
1900	2,540	16	Dir. General de Estadística 1906:4, 44–45		18
1910	2,634	n/a	Dir. General de Estadística 1918–1920:54		
1920	1,891	n/a	Dept. de la Estadística Nacional 1925–1928:166–167	5–6	8–10
1927				8	16
1930	2,116	6	Dir. General de Estadística 1936:275	10	
1932				9	
1940	2,290	28	Dir. General de Estadística 1946:566	6–7	
1945				15	
1948				20	
1950	2,511	19	Dir. General de Estadística 1954:445	22	
1960	2,881	27	Dir. General de Estadística 1963:1898	25	
1970	3,394	22	Dir. General de Estadística 1973:406	52	
1980	3,496	53	Instituto Nacional de Estadística, Geografía e Informática 1984:1:398	80	
1985	4,500	110	Stephen: 1986 household survey, Teotitlán		

800 male members of the municipal population over fifteen migrated to the United States in the late 1940s (Dirección General de Estadística 1954:94, 118). Many estimates are higher. Of 154 households included in a stratified random sample in 1986, 63 percent indicated that they had at least one person who had migrated to the United States. This percentage included people from two generations, those over forty as well as those under. About half of the 154 households surveyed had at least one member who temporarily migrated to another part of Mexico.

The 1940s mark the full-fledged entrance of commercial capital into the community as well as into the region as a whole (Young 1978). As male migrants returned with cash, it was used to purchase goods that had previously not been used or had been locally produced. With time, cash was also used to purchase agricultural labor to take the place of male laborers who were in the United States, changing the nature of local class relations. Labor became a commodity that was directly bought and sold on the market. In Teotitlán, paying cash for agricultural labor preceded the widespread piecework relations of production found today. Ironically, the *bracero* program placed many Teotitecos in agricultural labor jobs, but kept them from cultivating their own fields. Women were pushed into a double work shift as they pitched in to do men's jobs along with their own.

After the United States entered World War II in 1941, many growers claimed that they were suffering a severe labor shortage. Their strategy for persuading the U.S. government to establish a second *bracero* program was based on a claim that their workers had abandoned them for higher-paying jobs in the defense industry and that uninterrupted farm production was crucial to military success (Kiser and Kiser 1979:67). The second *bracero* program was carefully negotiated between Mexico and the United States. Seeking to protect workers, Mexico demanded that the U.S. government run the program. From 1942 until 1947, with the United States serving as the formal employer, laborers were guaranteed round-trip transportation to their home village, a minimum of working days, minimum or prevailing wages, and adequate housing (Kiser and Kiser 1979:68). The Mexican government seemed to maintain active control over the program during this period and kept the upper hand in protecting workers' rights, even excluding Texas from the contract process because of a history of discrimination against Mexicans.

In Mexico the program involved three state agencies,[8] the offices of state governors, and mayors of the *municipios* where migrant workers resided (García y Griego 1981:19). Notices went out through the municipal mayors that work was available. Officials from the Mexican Secretariat of Labor and Social Provisions screened *bracero* candidates and turned them over to the U.S. Department of Labor, which acted as an agent for U.S. employers (García y Griego 1981 : 20).

Teotitecos say that word of the program did not reach Teotitlán until 1944, two years after the program began. That year fifteen to twenty Teotitecos signed up for eight-week contracts for the months of May, June, and July. They were transported to the recruiting center in Mexico City, where they were inspected by Mexican officials and turned over to representatives of the U.S. Department of Labor. "The first year we went to Mexico City they took us up there, cut our hair, gave us new clothes, and got us ready. Some people in Mexico City threw rocks at us because they were angry that now the recruiters were going south for workers. There were a lot of people who needed work" (Manuel, age 70). Former *braceros* recalled that many men from Teotitlán did not go in 1944 because of rumors that they were not going to work on farms, but would be sent off to fight the North Americans' war. But in July 1944, the first Teotitecos to go to the United States returned safely with shoes, blue jeans, other items of clothing, and, most importantly, cash. In 1945, when the recruiters returned, between 150 and 300 men left the community to be *braceros*. As one man recalled, wages in the United States were extraordinarily high when compared with local wage rates in Teotitlán. "The next year a lot of people went—maybe three hundred or up to a thousand. The whole town went to the United States. In 1944 and 1945 I got paid $0.20 per box for my work picking tomatoes in the United States. I could pick thirty to thirty-five boxes per day and earn up to $8.00 per day. At that time in Mexico if I worked as a *jornalero* here I could earn about the equivalent of $0.25. You couldn't compare it" (Juan, age 68).

In recalling their time in the United States, many *braceros* commented on how easy it was to get there. They did not have to worry about obtaining official papers and transportation was taken care of. When the first groups came back safely with some money, many more were encouraged to go, seeing it as the only available opportunity to emerge from the poverty of Teotitlán.

Many Teotitecos recall 1945, 1946, and 1947 as the years when there were only women left in the community. While people varied on the numbers of men who left, they all had clear mental images of the results in the community. Most recalled that the communal lands were largely unworked. Some people left behind sons to work their land or left it *a medios* (sharecropped with another farmer), but significant amounts of land remained unplowed. The critical timing of the contracts, which fell during the planting season, also contributed to the abandonment of community lands. In addition, as contracts became longer and men began to go for longer periods, weaving production was also affected. There was a shortage of weaving labor because weaving was done primarily, although not exclusively, by men. Because weaving production had yet to be expanded for export production, however, the absence of men through migration did not result in a strong demand for female weaving labor such as occurred during the 1970s when greatly expanded production for export pushed large numbers of women and girls into the labor force. Continued male migration in the 1970s exacerbated the need for female weaving labor during that period.

Women in Teotitlán recall the *bracería* of the 1940s and the continued absence of men in the 1950s as a time of great hardship. They had no sources of income while men were gone and they were saddled with additional chores. Many women reported that their husbands sent them little or nothing, leaving them as the sole income earners for their families. While some men later returned with savings, others did not. Some women wove during this time, but also had to maintain their food processing, child care, and animal care in addition to taking care of agricultural work. Many tried to earn extra cash by selling the yarn they spun, not having time to weave it themselves or not knowing how.

Until 1947, the ease with which people got to the United States was part of the structure of the formal *bracero* contract program. After 1947, the Mexican bargaining position in the *bracero* program began to deteriorate and it became clear that Mexico could not control emigration to the United States (García y Griego 1981:22–29). After 1947, Mexico lost its ability to defend workers' rights and to prevent the deployment of *braceros* in areas that had a history of abusing them.

After 1947, the United States refused to continued in its role as formal employer and U.S. growers contracted directly with *braceros*. Unlike the U.S. government, the growers did not come all the way to Oaxaca to recruit. They recruited primarily in the northern states of Sonora and Chihuahua. Oaxaqueños had to get themselves up to the northern border in order to be contracted. This made it more difficult for poorer households to send *braceros*. They had to be able to afford round-trip transportation to the border and back. In Teotitlán, those who had already been to the United States had enough cash to continue financing trips to the border. Most of this cash was earned through previous trips to the United States as *braceros*. Continued migration was funded by previous migration. About 25 percent of the households in Teotitlán continued to send one or more workers to the United States on an annual basis throughout the duration of the *bracero* program (until 1964). Afterward, even more went as undocumented workers. Recently, some have received legal work permission under the 1986 Immigration Reform Act.

Beginning in the 1940s, a significant percentage of the women in Teotitlán had to spend long periods being the sole supporters of their families. Their continuous labor in the community since the 1940s is an important but invisible part of the process that pushed the community into conditions of commercial capitalism. It also supported many men's initial capital accumulation. Some men were able to use money earned in the United States along with unpaid family labor to move their households into merchant activities in the 1970s and 1980s.

The following narrative captures the experiences of many women who married at the ages of fourteen and fifteen, had never been alone, and then suddenly, when their husbands migrated, found themselves in charge of running a small farming and weaving enterprise as well as having to feed and clothe their children. Josefina, whose story is told below, supported her family alone from 1952 to 1964 while her husband worked for extended periods in the United States. After 1964, she had to support the family again when he returned for short trips to the United States:

I first got to be independent when my husband went to work in the United States in 1952. I had to be. He was gone most of the time from 1952 until 1964, from two to twelve months per year. The whole time he was away he only sent money twice— about $20. I didn't spend this money, I saved it until he returned. I had six children born during that period. When he left the first time, I already had two little ones.

When he was gone I carded the spun wool so that my father would make my serapes. He used to come to my house and work here. I couldn't weave because I had to take care of my children and my animals. I also used to make yarn to sell while the men were gone. This gave me money so that I could go to the market and buy things. I would also sell the blankets my father made. My children were too little to weave.

You know this whole time I worked like a mule. I would make three kilos of yarn in two days for making blankets. First I would get up and make tortillas for two other women in order to earn money. I also made *tejate* for another woman. Her husband had a lot of money so she paid me to work for her. I got paid 2 centavos [*mexicanos*] for making those tortillas. It was a hard life.

Josefina later recalled that while her husband was gone he sent money to another women he was involved with, but not to her. The fact that men were sometimes involved in multiple relationships with children in other households could further reduce the financial resources sent to their wives. In the end, most women stated that they learned how to survive. They also noted that, after their husbands returned, they no longer accepted their dominance in decision making. As one aptly stated, "If I could get along all of those years and raise eight children, why should I suddenly stop being able to decide what is best for them?"

When the men returned, their small savings were quickly spent or invested, primarily in oxen, looms, or raw wool. During the late 1950s, several men who are now the largest merchants in Teotitlán began investing savings earned in the United States in wool for yarn. Some households used their money to buy land and others to pay off ceremonial debts. Most Teotitecos recalled that the influx of cash raised local prices and the price of wage labor. Many *braceros* used their savings to begin paying other people to work for them in their fields while they went to the United States to earn more money.

Conclusions

A pattern of male outmigration while women's labor maintains households and communities is not unusual in Mexico or elsewhere. As wage labor opportunities open up for men in commercial agriculture, mining, urban construction, and assembly work, women may remain behind to engage in subsistence labor and craft production. Maria Mies (1982) has documented this pattern in relation to women lace-makers in Narsapur, India, Jette Bukh (1979) for women agriculturalists in Ghana, and Carmen Diana Deer (1979) comparatively in the Third World. In a review article on women and migration in Latin America, María de los Angeles Crummet (1987:252–254) suggests that, in cases where women remain behind, a common result is a new gender division of labor within the household where women are relegated to the subsistence sector in agriculture. She states that the work burden of women and children can increase in rural areas where male outmigration prevails. Most research shows, however, that the extent to which women are affected by migration relates to the household's economic standing within the rural community

(Crummet 1987:252; Margolis 1979; UN Secretariat 1984; Weist 1973; Young 1978). Summarizing several cases from Mexico, Crummet (1987:254) concludes: "Among landless and poor peasant households, in particular, male migration had important consequences for the household division of labor: Women increased their participation in agricultural production and wage work while retaining their traditional responsibilities for child care and family welfare. Thus the intensification of women's labor in paid and unpaid work and productive and reproductive activities sharpens not only the analysis of migration, but also of class and household relations."

The women of Teotitlán appear to have taken on an increased domestic workload during the 1950s and 1960s, years of significant male outmigration. For women from landless weaver households, the burden was probably greatest. Because only a handful of women were part of large landholding merchant households in the 1940s and 1950s, however, the burden of male migration probably fell hard on most Teotiteco women. Ironically, it was the labor of women that sustained many families in the community while significant numbers of men were off laboring in the United States, earning cash that for some would later become important in beginning a business. Male migrants in the United States suffered from exploitative labor conditions, but women who remained home seem to have derived fewer ultimate benefits for their sacrifices than migrant men. Men's experience in the United States, as described in the next chapter, gave them an advantage over women in running the increasing number of merchant businesses that began to appear in the 1970s.

The pattern of male migration in Teotitlán during the 1940s and 1950s may be different from that found in other parts of Mexico. Arizpe (1985) found in the Mazahua region of Morelos that both male and female migrants left in alternation with their parents, depending on the point in the domestic cycle. Thus only one generation of men left the household at one time. Other investigations of migration in Mexico (Nutini and Murphy 1970; Rothstein 1982) found that, in some cases when rural men migrate, there is an increase in extended family households so that women are not left alone as the sole wage earners.

Data were not gathered on migration that would permit a comparison of migration patterns from Teotitlán in the 1940s and 1950s with those of the 1960s and 1970s. The primary change in migration patterns noted was that significant numbers of young women began to migrate along with young men in the 1970s, going primarily to urban locations in Mexico. They did not begin to reach the United States until the 1980s. This marks the period when some households from Teotitlán began to establish themselves in the border area of Tijuana and Ensenada, Baja California, and through their presence formed a staging area for border crossing attempts into San Diego County. Chávez, Flores, and López Garza's (1989) research on undocumented Mexican migrants in San Diego County shows the presence of women in the population and suggests that they come for economic as well as familial reasons.

Both during the initial period of male migration and later with the expansion in weaving production, women's labor has been critical in the reproduction of the labor force as well as in maintaining household ceremonial economies. While comparative data on rates of household fiesta sponsorship and participation were not gathered for the periods of 1940–1960 and thereafter, oral histories make it clear that the ceremonial life of the community continued in the 1950s and 1960s. The labor of women was important not only in maintaining household economic production, but also in generating surpluses that could be invested in *guelaguetza, mayordomías,* and other ceremonial institutions. Women also continued to engage in reciprocal labor exchanges in relation to ceremonial activities. Male outmigration during the 1940s and 1950s was significant not only in shifting the gendered household division of labor, but in solidifying the importance of women's labor in the ceremonial activities that are as much a part of social reproduction as feeding and caring for the future labor force.

Chapter 6. Weaving in the Fast Lane: Ethnicity, Class, and Gender Relations under Commercial Capitalism

*I do a lot of the work here for my husband. I dye all of the
yarn for the people who work for us. I also cook and make
tortillas. If I need money to buy something for the house or to
pay people I have to ask him for it. The business is both of
ours, but he keeps the money. (Godelia, age 55)*

*We are weavers. Merchants don't make serapes, they have
businesses and buy them. They don't work like we do . . .
their money works for them. (Lucía, age 50)*

THE COMMERCIALIZATION of weaving production in Teotitlán that
began during the 1950s had a major impact on both class and gender
relations. It is best understood in relation to several local and national processes, which include the disappearance of local and regional markets for handwoven blankets; government promotion of
tourism; development programs to improve the quality of craft production and distribution; and Teotitecos' own efforts to gain control
over the marketing and distribution of their product. These factors
are discussed here as a backdrop to understanding changes in wom-
en's roles in weaving production and shifts in the local class structure.
    More than any other factor, the integration of weaving production
into national and international capitalist consumer markets through
commercialization has heightened some of the incipient contradictions that previously existed in the community. Class stratification
based on mercantile capitalism changed as first migration and then
the U.S. export market provided increased opportunities for more
merchant activity based on international commercial capital. Under
these changing conditions of capitalist development, a new and bigger merchant class began to emerge in Teotitlán during the 1970s.

These merchants purchased labor directly, by employing weavers in workshops and by piecework production systems. Yet, in spite of current class differentiation, the community has also maintained a strong sense of local ethnic solidarity, reflected most strongly in claims to Zapotec weaving production. It is also seen in an intensification of ritual activity specifically identified with community solidarity in Teotitlán. While authors such as James Greenberg (1989: 199–203) have identified conflicts between class- and kin-based ideologies as pitting mestizo against Indian moral orders—capitalistic institutional Catholicism against indigenous folk religion promoting reciprocity, equality, and cooperation—in Teotitlán this conflict does not correlate with ethnic differences, but is played out along gender and class lines.

The relatively egalitarian gender relations that seem to prevail in subsistence farming and weaving households today appear to erode as merchant households accumulate capital and contract laborers. Current class relations have resulted in significant differences between women based on the position of their household in the relations of production. Nevertheless, gendered class relations in the areas of production and ritual continue to be mediated by an idiom of kin-based community solidarity. The equality implied in the language of kinship, however, is experienced by few women in their relationships with other women and with their husbands. Perhaps the most egalitarian relationships remain those between weaver women and their husbands.

The Mexican Textile Industry and Markets for Indigenously Produced Wool Products, 1920–1970

The transformation of the Teotitlán-centered weaving system from production for regional use to production for tourist and export markets was tied to national and international economic factors that affected the Mexican textile industry. The textile industry has been an important part of the Mexican economy since the beginning of the colonial period. Organized first as colonial *obrajes* (textile manufactories) run largely with indigenous labor,[1] the cotton and wool textile industry in México, Puebla, and Tlaxcala remained organized around the same basic technology until the early 1900s, when the entire industry began to mechanize (Heath Constable 1982:54). While *obrajes* were built around a resident labor force that lived on the production site, later production in Tlaxcala and Puebla involved factories with a wage labor force that lived in city neighborhoods. Unlike household-based production in Teotitlán, some of these factories became large-scale enterprises. Few retained the status of household workshops and they did not evolve into piecework operations.

The first automatic looms were built at the turn of this century and imported into Mexico from the United States. In many factories, the technology imported in the first decades of this century remained in use until the early 1960s, when some factories retooled to be able to include the production of synthetic fabrics (Mercado García 1980:66). Once mechanized, many factories in Tlaxcala and elsewhere diversified their production in an effort to reach a larger consumer market. Enterprises such as La Providencia in Tlaxcala diversified and produced over 140,000 blankets, serapes, ponchos, and shawls per year sold in México, Puebla, and Veracruz (Heath Constable 1982:79). From the 1920s through the 1940s, cotton and wool factories spun thread and yarn and produced cloth for the Mexican consumer market.

During World War II, the textile industry grew significantly as pro-

Table 13. *Mexican National Production of Bland Textile Fibers, 1960–1976 (thousands of metric tons)*

Year	Cotton	Wool	Synthetic Fibers
1960	457	3.0	20.2
1961	443	3.1	19.2
1962	477	3.2	21.2
1963	490	3.2	23.7
1964	488	ND	28.6
1965	515	ND	38.6
1966	560	ND	41.1
1967	447	ND	46.0
1968	525	2.8	50.6
1969	418	2.7	60.0
1970	324	1.4	73.9
1971	352	1.3	92.4
1972	396	1.7	112.4
1973	363	1.1	144.0
1974	502	1.0	153.7
1975	228	1.0	172.3
1976	204	1.0	187.6

Source: Adapted from Mercado García 1980:138, fig. 11.

Table 14. *Evolution of the Mexican Market for Polyester,
1966–1976 (thousands of tons)*

Year	National Production	Imports	Exports	% Annual Growth of Consumption	National Con- sumption
1969	3,026	56.9	—	3,082.9	
1970	7,584	150.5	—	7,734.5	150.9
1971	17,224.8	133.2	592.3	16,788.9	117.1
1972	32,508	188.3	0.4	32,695	94.8
1973	50,000	2,967	5.0	52,692.3	62.0
1974	56,294	8,512	—	64,806	22.4
1975	70,577	1,254	—	71,831	10.8
1976	68,977	652	—	69,627	−3.2

Source: Adopted from Mercado García 1980: 149, fig. 23.

duction was interrupted elsewhere and Mexico began to export cotton and wool products in significant quantities, particularly to other parts of Latin America (Heath Constable 1982:84). In addition, the internal market grew because of a reduction in imported textiles. The growth in the industry was able to occur without any technical innovation or significant investment in new technology (Martínez del Campo 1985:73). This short-term advantage, however, quickly became a disadvantage as international production of synthetic fibers began in earnest in the late 1950s and Mexico's textile factories were not equipped to begin production of polyester (Heath Constable 1982:84; Mercado García 1980).

The growth spurt that the cotton and wool textile industry experienced during the 1940s was cut short by 1960 as the production of polyester and other synthetics began to take hold in Mexico. Between 1960 and 1976, the growth of synthetic fiber production was greater than that of all other textiles (Mercado García 1980:137–138). In 1960, synthetic fibers were 4 percent of the production of bland fibers and by 1976 they were a full 48 percent. Between 1966 and 1973, the national market for polyester grew by leaps and bounds each year, leveling off in 1974 (Mercado García 1980:35–38).

As seen in table 15, a high level of national polyester consumption continued from 1976 to 1985, with cotton and wool consumption also remaining steady, but low compared to synthetic fibers. With the development of a strong internal market for synthetic fibers by the early 1970s, producers of wool products could no longer sell goods to

Table 15. *Mexican National Consumption of Bland Fibers,*
1976–1985

	Cotton	Wool	Synthetics	Total
1976	84,870	4,885	179,858	269,613
1977	111,550	4,201	200,730	316,481
1978	129,825	5,700	212,989	348,514
1979	157,950	6,500	246,437	410,887
1980	176,400	6,900	256,610	439,910
1981	147,675	7,600	249,767	405,042
1982	82,125	5,046	213,125	300,296
1983	126,730	4,261	246,553	377,544
1984	120,750	4,615	237,664	363,029
1985	138,000	5,534	276,446	419,980

Source: Adapted from Instituto Nacional de Estadística, Geografía e Informática 1986:55, fig. 11.9.

the national population. While Mexicans continued to import wool in the 1970s, they had to find other outlets for their production.

When the Pan American Highway connected Oaxaca City and smaller towns with the larger Mexican economy, the booming textile industry of Tlaxcala and Puebla began to reach regional Oaxacan consumer markets that had previously been supplied with blankets, ponchos, and shawls produced by the Zapotecs of the central valleys and other indigenous groups. The growth of the polyester industry caused a decline in indigenous consumption of handmade blankets produced in weaving communities such as Teotitlán del Valle. The completion of a national road reaching Oaxaca also accelerated the commoditization of the Oaxacan economy, spurred on by the cash earnings that returning migrants began to spend on industrial products produced in Mexico or in the United States. By the early 1950s, local class relations were becoming firmly entrenched in commercial capital, with increased demand for commercially produced goods providing new opportunities for local and regional entrepreneurs.

If the only factor involved in the creation of markets for Zapotec weavings was internal consumption among indigenous populations, the weaving system centered in Teotitlán del Valle probably would have died on the vine by the mid-1960s. Unlike items such as metates, which continue to be locally produced and consumed, Teotiteco blankets and ponchos became quite expensive compared to machine-woven polyester-blend textiles. Because metates (Cook 1982a) and certain other indigenous implements were still cheaper and more efficiently produced by hand, they continued to have a local niche in the periodic markets of Oaxaca.[2] The current market for Teotiteco textiles had to come from elsewhere.

As the Mexican state began to promote indigenous crafts, Zapotec weavings were transformed from use objects to art objects and handicrafts. Several factors were important in the creation of a market niche for them in urban Mexico and in the United States. Always high-quality products, they are light, easily transportable, can be used as household objects abroad, and can also be art objects because of their designs. The same claims cannot be made about metates and some other indigenous crafts that have not found a market abroad. However, pottery items, especially from Coyotepec and Atzompa, have also found a market in the United States as combination use and art objects.

Kinship, Class Relations, and Gender under Commercial Capitalism

By the mid-1980s, significant capital accumulation had taken place in Teotitlán as well as in the communities of Santa Ana del Valle and San Miguel, although on a smaller scale. All three communities are characterized by growth in their merchant sectors, with Teotitlán dominating the others. The majority of merchants in Teotitlán contract weavers in local households as well as in other communities, often through kin and *compadrazgo* ties, for a certain number of pieces, designating the design, color, and shape to be produced.

Relations of production between merchants and weavers are simultaneously class relations and ties of kin and *compadrazgo*—the same relationships that form the basis of reciprocal labor networks at fiestas. Merchants tend to have more godchildren than weavers. This is due to local perceptions that it is easy for them to shoulder the heavy costs of godchild sponsorship. Many merchants have their godchildren working for them as pieceworkers in a system where *padrinos* and *madrinas* provide materials and *ahijados* and *ahijadas* produce finished weaving products in their homes.

In the relations of production, respect is so inculcated into the godparent-godchild relationship that a godchild may be in a weak position to refuse a labor request from his or her godparents. From the perspective of the godchild, having a godparent with significant financial resources also makes it possible to ask for a loan in a time of financial need, often without interest. Heads of weaving households often seek out merchants as godparents for their children in the hopes that the merchants will be able to help their children economically.

Weavers often receive interest-free loans and primary materials from merchants. When there is a shortage of weaving labor due to high market demand, weavers may have more work than they can handle. In deciding which work to do, they give priority to requests from relatives or *compadres*. If a *compadre* is unwilling to pay the wage a weaver wants, however, he or she will quietly go elsewhere to work. As long as there is a labor shortage, merchants cannot take too much advantage of their position as *compadres*. During periods of low market demand, weavers lose their negotiating power.

A census conducted in 1985 revealed that there were approximately 110 self-identified merchant households out of a total of 1,039 households in the community of Teotitlán. Teotitecos conceptually divide merchants into three types depending on the volume of their inventory. Approximately ten households are classified as "large" merchants, handling the largest share of distribution within Teotitlán and working in Santa Ana and San Miguel as well. About thirty households fall into the category of "medium" merchants, with the remainder labeled as "small." Small merchants purchase limited numbers of weavings or sell their own production in the local artisan market.

The occupational classes of merchants and weavers described in chapter 2 participate in four basic types of production units that do not necessarily coincide with households (see Cook 1988 : 5).

Independent weaver household workshops: all weavers in this production unit are household members. They are not paid for their labor. Such households own the means of production and provide their own wool, yarn, and dyes. Weavers produce textiles in their own homes that are sold to tourists, importers, or local merchants. Men, women, and children working in this type of production unit belong to the weaver class. Both men and women weave in this type of production unit.

Merchant workshops with hired laborers: labor in this type of production unit includes both unpaid merchant household members and hired weavers from weaver households. Hired weavers who work on-site at merchant workshops do not own the means of production; nor are they responsible for providing yarn or dyes. Hired weavers are paid by the piece by merchants who own the workshops. This production unit includes people from the merchant class and paid weavers from the weaver class. Paid laborers are usually male, although they may be single young women as well. Unpaid household laborers from the merchant class often include women and children. They may be weaving and/or supervising paid weavers. The paid weavers here appear in a straight labor/capital relationship with merchants.

Merchant workshops with pieceworkers: labor in this type of production unit can include both unpaid merchant household members and contracted weavers in pieceworker households who are working in their own homes. Pieceworker weavers usually own their own means of production, but often are not responsible for providing inputs. They usually are given materials and weave finished products that are paid for by the piece by contracting merchants. This production unit includes petty capitalists from the merchant class, paid laborers from the weaver class, and unpaid laborers from merchant households, usually women and children who may be weaving or doing other preparatory work to supply pieceworkers.

Pieceworker households: weavers work in their own households and utilize their own means of production. Yarn and dyes are usually supplied by a merchant. Merchant households pay weavers by the piece. This production unit only includes people from the weaver class and may involve men, women, and children who weave at home. As pieceworkers, women are much more likely to weave at home than in a merchant's household because they can combine weaving with other domestic duties, as described below.

While these are the four basic types of production units found in Teotitlán, other variations are possible. An important distinction among the four types, however, is that production units types 2 and 3 are based in households that belong to the merchant class while types 1 and 4 are based in weaver households.

While most households are related primarily to one type of production unit, laborers from a particular household may be involved in two or more types of production units simultaneously. They may, for example, work some of the time at home as part of an independent household workshop and some of the time at a merchant's house as part of a workshop with hired laborers.

One of the key issues to be explained here is how households move from weaver to merchant status under the present conditions of commercial capitalism. As we shall see, the role of gender is important in this process. Most households that have achieved merchant status within the past fifteen years used a combination of unpaid household labor and accumulation of initial capital through migration to the United States to do so, according to in-depth interviews done with twenty merchant households about how they started their businesses. In some cases this has been supplemented with cash from the sale of land or animals. Detailed information on how looms were purchased, laborers hired, and businesses financed was obtained in questionnaires given to fifty-four merchant households included in the random stratified sample described in appendix A.

The question of how weaver households become small capitalist enterprises invokes the Lenin/Chayanov debate. My work concurs with the survey research of Cook and Binford (1988 : 7 – 8), who state that "the movement of peasant-artisan household enterprises from conditions of petty commodity production to those of petty capitalism is significantly affected by household demographics through their impact on productive capacity, capital accumulation and material wealth. . . . Family labor contributes critically to the accumulation of capital and material assets in most household units which experience this movement." They emphasize that most households that experience an accumulation of capital through family labor do not cross the threshold to petty capitalist production. Those that do represent an exception to Chayanov's emphasis on simple reproduction of the household unit and "illustrate Lenin's thesis that 'family cooperation' is the 'foundation of capitalist cooperation'" (Cook and Binford 1988 : 8). The labor obligations entailed in family and household membership have allowed some households to benefit from unpaid household labor as well as to take advantage of the reciprocal obligations implied by kinship and *compadrazgo* with those outside of their immediate household, as described above.[3] In Teotitlán, the gendered dynamics of migration to the United States were critical in this process as well.

Under emerging conditions of circulation capital from the late 1940s until the early 1960s, the labor of women sustained a significant proportion of the population of Teotitlán while men were laboring in the United States. Most men did not send money home; if they did return with savings, they invested it in land, animals, or the means of production for weaving. Later the labor of women was also important in helping households to build up capital for paying nonhousehold members as pieceworkers. As tourist and export markets for Zapotec textiles steadily grew, the availability of weaving labor became a critical variable in the expansion of production. In the early 1970s, young women began to weave along with their brothers, so that the pool of family weaving labor was expanded. By the 1980s, the additional labor of women and girls was critical in helping households to begin functioning as employers. In the case of Teotitlán, the factors of migration and unpaid female and child labor seem to have been important in allowing some weavers to move ahead and begin to act as employers by paying nonhousehold workers. As demonstrated by Cook (1982a:20, 1984a) and supported by my work in Teotitlán, most current merchant households began as pieceworkers or independent producers. This situation appears to be changing as the current merchant class is consolidating and beginning to pass on capital to its offspring to be used in starting new businesses.

The Weaving Process

In order to provide a more visual idea of what textile production is like in Teotitlán, this section outlines the primary tasks involved in weaving a serape from start to finish. When handspun yarn is used, the most labor-intensive part of weaving production begins long before a weaver begins to throw the shuttle across his or her loom. Since wool is usually not available locally, Teotitecos often purchase wool in their rounds of the cyclical markets of Oaxaca, Tlacolula, and Ocotlán. Weavers may try to purchase in bulk, storing as much as they can for periods when wool is unavailable, such as during the last few months of the rainy season. Once the wool is bought, it is sorted by color and stored for future use. More and more, however, local weavers are being supplied with wool and yarn by Teotiteco merchants.

When a completely handmade textile is being produced, the proper color and grade of wool is first selected. The wool is then separated and taken down to the river for a thorough washing. Both men and women can be seen washing large lots of wool in harvest baskets. Once it has been thoroughly washed, it is spread out in the sun to dry.

Once dry, the yarn is carded. The cards used are manufactured in the neighboring community of Díaz Ordaz. Carding is usually done by women and children in spare moments or continuously if a large lot of yarn is needed. The wool is brushed back and forth between the metal toothed cards until it reaches a smooth consistency. It is then deposited in a basket for the spinner.

Spinning wheels are mounted on a low wooden bench. The wooden wheel is connected to the front spindle by a heavy woolen drive cord. The spindle is about fifteen inches long. The spinner cranks the wheel with the right hand and manipulates the wool with the left hand. A layer of carded wool is folded and split in half. The wool is attached to the spindle, and the spinner pulls the yarn outward so that a long, thin strand of yarn is created. The yarn is then wrapped around a wooden spiral holding the spindle and periodically removed.

Spinning is a respected art. Teotitecos especially value well-spun yarn. Handspun yarn from Teotitlán is higher priced than that produced in other places. Because the demand for handspun yarn is often greater than the amount available, it is purchased from other areas. One producing community, Chichicapan, has a long-standing relationship with Teotitlán as a supplier of handspun yarn. People in Chichicapan no longer weave, but continue to produce yarn. Several merchants come to Teotitlán to sell the yarn on a weekly basis. The price of Chichicapan yarn is always about 25 percent lower than the price of handspun yarn from Teotitlán.

The best spinners in Teotitlán are elderly women and men. Many widows, unable to oversee agricultural production or engage in other types of labor, work as spinners. Most work for their own families, but some are hired on a piece basis by merchants to produce the fine yarn. A good spinner can produce between one-fourth and one-half kilo of yarn per day working in conjunction with a carder. A kilo of handspun wool completed in two to three days brings about half of the wages that a weaver could earn in the same period. After wool is spun into yarn or yarn is purchased, it is wound into skeins and washed before dyeing. This is often the work of children. The four natural colors of wool used in weaving—white, black, brown, and gray—are separated to be wound onto bobbins.

Dyeing, like spinning, is a time-consuming process. Most households reserve at least one or two days per week for it. In pieceworker households and independent household workshops, the process is carried out by husband and wife teams. In merchant households, where men are often out of town or busy with clients, the dyeing process is often the responsibility of women. It is the hardest and most uncomfortable work involved in the weaving process. Large pots of water, one for each color, are set to boil over large wood fires. Dye substances, natural or chemical, are then stirred into the pots. Skeins of yarn are left in the dye for ten to thirty minutes, depending on the shade desired. When the desired hue is reached, the skeins are pulled out of the pots, washed in cold water, wrung out, and hung in the sun to dry on wooden poles. Stones are often used to weigh down the skeins so that the yarn does not shrink. Once dry, the skeins are removed from the drying poles to be spun onto bobbins using the spinning wheel. This task, which is often done by children, must be done steadily so that weavers can keep working. Often children work before and after school to create a supply of full bobbins for their parents.

The task of the weaver begins with preparation of the warp yarn for the loom. Warp yarn is usually factory made. It is a lighter grade than weft yarn and is usually 80 percent wool and 20 percent cotton. Few weavers use handspun warp yarn unless it is for a special order. The warp yarn is measured between poles inserted in the ground. When the proper number of strands have been counted, the weaver winds the yarn into a skein. If he or she is going to begin weaving immediately, the warp is attached to the fibers of the loom.

The foot-powered treadle looms used today in Teotitlán differ little from the basic model introduced by the Spanish in the sixteenth century. The only difference between current and earlier models is that looms have gotten progressively bigger. The largest loom in Teotitlán is between two and three meters long. It has eight pedals and is used for producing carpets. Most looms are mounted on four posts and sit in a tablelike construction. The batten (or beater) and the heddles are suspended from crossbars at the top of the loom. The anchor threads of the loom are on two rollers, one acting as a take-up roller as the weaving progresses and the other as a warp roller. The loom is powered by two foot pedals that are connected to the heddles by chord.

Weavers stand in the looms, often using boxes to have better access to the entire loom. The size of looms can be a problem, particularly for children. To weave, the shuttle is thrown across the loom while the warp threads are held open by the heddle attached to one foot pedal. When one trip of the shuttle across the loom is completed, the other pedal is depressed, closing the warp threads around the weft. When the weaver is weaving one color or a stripe design, the shuttle moves rapidly across the loom. Most designs, however, are more complex. In this case, the weaver must change bobbins every time there is a color change in the design. In order to do this correctly, the weaver counts the appropriate number of warp threads, lifts them up, and pulls the bobbin under. The batten suspended from overhead is then used to tighten up the weave.

Once a textile is finished, it is rolled onto the take-up wheel of the loom. Usually four to five pieces are produced at once and cut loose from the loom. They are then scraped with a metal scraper to remove loose wool and picked clean of any burrs or other material found in the wool. The final job is tying up the warp ends. When a weaver has completed several pieces, the head of the household (male or female) either delivers them to the merchant who commissioned them if they are piecework or goes from door to door trying to sell them to local merchants. After the weavings are sold, a weaver household usually invests immediately in more wool or yarn in

This man is weaving a small textile commissioned by a local merchant on a piecework basis.

Many women under thirty now spend a significant portion of each day weaving.

order to keep on working. If weavers have no cash for yarn, they may then decide to do more piecework for a local merchant. The merchant will most likely supply the materials. The production cycle thus repeats itself.

In general, older people in Teotitlán have a much wider knowledge of weaving processes than people under forty. For example, older people have greater knowledge of dyeing processes and designs. While most serapes in Teotitlán are made with "vegetable colors" (i.e., the color of vegetables, but not vegetable dyes), the majority of yarn is dyed with chemical dyes. Many young people do not know how to use natural dyes or how to find proper dyeing plants. An exception to the use of chemical dyes is found in the workshops of several high-quality weavers. In the 1970s, a local weaver studied ancient dye processes and encouraged Teotitecos to use natural dyes. The materials often used include cochineal (producing reds, pinks, and oranges), indigo (blues and greens), rock lichen (yellow), acacia beans (black), pecan shells (tan), and the dodder vine (yellow). Unfortunately, the cost of dyes such as cochineal, which is over US$100 per pound, is prohibitive to most weavers. The older generation of

Weaving itself is only one part of creating a textile. Here a weaver prepares dyed yarn for winding onto bobbins as his wife ties up the end of her completed serape.

Teotitecos still has the knowledge of how to obtain and use a wide variety of dyes, but this knowledge is exercised less and less as pressure for quick production and cost-effectiveness increases.

Ethnicity for Sale: The Mexican Indian and *Arte Popular*

While the world of Teotitlán stretched to the United States through migration, people from all over Mexico, the United States, and Europe began to arrive in Oaxaca and southern Mexico as tourists. The new Pan American Highway that passes within six kilometers of Teotitlán made the state capital of Oaxaca infinitely more accessible to Teotitecos and Teotitlán more accessible to tourists. While tourists did arrive in Oaxaca prior to the completion of the Pan American Highway and Teotitecos are recorded as selling their weavings to tourists at "elevated prices" as early as 1922 (Atl 1922: 10), the tourist market did not begin to develop in earnest until the late 1950s. Bus service from Teotitlán to Oaxaca began in 1935 and operated on Fridays and Saturdays. With the inauguration of the Pan American Highway in 1948, however, it became possible to make a trip to Oaxaca in half a day, encouraging Teotitecos to hawk their wares in Oaxaca on a more regular basis. The road also began to draw tourists to Teotitlán who wanted to see for themselves how Zapotec weavings were produced.

Tourism is now one of Mexico's biggest income generators. Since completion of the Pan American Highway, tourism has continued to grow at a steady pace in Oaxaca. Between 1976 and 1980, tourism grew by an annual average of 11 percent. Foreign tourism grew by an annual average of 18 percent (Lozano and Vargas 1982:30). To capture the interests of tourists, particular features of cultural and material production were commoditized and packaged for sale by the federal government. The ideological package that was and is sold to tourists who came to states with high indigenous populations is based on a homogenized image of "Indian culture" and the material remains of that culture that can be visited or purchased and taken home. Of primary import in this cultural package is the Mexican Indian.

The material culture or homogenized Indianness provides symbolic icons for both forging a national identity and creating commodities that, when converted from use articles to handicrafts, become a source of employment and foreign exchange. Following the revolution, *arte popular* (folk or people's art) was officially recognized in 1921 for the first time when the tenth anniversary of the Mexican Revolution was celebrated with a national artisans' exhibit inaugurated by Alvaro Obregón in Mexico City (García Canclini 1982:102). In the 1930s, intellectuals and artists declared *arte popular* to be an important part of Mexican heritage, suggesting that articles such as straw dolls, clay toys, and multicolored serapes were giving Mexicans "an elevated sense of race and a national conscience that was previously missing" (Novo 1932:56, cited in Novelo 1976).

Beyond national contests for *arte popular*, state programs to promote craft production did not reach Teotitlán until the early 1960s. Even such early efforts as national contests were not without their gendered aspects. The practice of bringing winning artisans to Mexico City and as far as London, England, for example, summarily excluded women, who usually had children to take care of and could not leave their communities. These first presentations of Mexican *artesanos* to the Mexican upper classes and to foreigners gave the impression that artisans were male. Until quite recently, no woman from Teotitlán participated in a national contest, although they began weaving long ago. Contests that recognized the weaver as the sole creator of a textile also went against community perceptions of who participates in production. Textiles are seen as belonging to all

A Teotiteco is selling his goods in the city of Oaxaca in this 1960s photograph. Note the deities in the designs along with geometrics.

who participate in producing them, including carders, spinners, and dyers—not just the weaver. While the majority of weavers probably were men during the 1940s and 1950s when such contests took place, the labor of women as spinners, dyers, and carders went unrecognized in these contests.

The Political Economy of Ethnic Handicrafts in Teotitlán

As in the case of other industrially produced items, the mechanization of textile production resulted in a desire for handmade shawls, blankets, rugs, and wall hangings. They are now consumed by the middle class and elite sectors of Mexico, the United States, and Europe, where a desire for the traditional is met with the consumption of hand-produced commodities coming from the Third World. The same mechanization that makes industrial consumers long for "genuine" crafts also eliminates peasant consumer markets for hand-produced objects as they are replaced by polyester blankets, nylon jackets, and plastic water jugs—industrial articles that are more at-

tractive because they are cheaper or are associated with modernization (García Canclini 1982:96). There is a double movement of consumption as craft production, which faced a doomed future in
regional consumer markets, can be revitalized because of a market
for the exotic and the authentic.

A key dimension in the value of crafts is their authenticity, particularly in higher-priced items such as the weavings produced in
Teotitlán and Santa Ana. An important part of authenticity has to do
with the survival of what are viewed as traditional relations of production. For U.S. consumers, Zapotec weavings are authentic handicrafts made with exotic production processes (Spooner 1986:222).
As seen in the following commercial description of Zapotec culture
and weaving production (from a California importers' brochure,
1986), the survival of seemingly exotic relations of production is the
key to the "authenticity" of the product. Most descriptions also suggest an additional dimension to the relations of production—cultural and economic dominance. Authenticity reflects the interaction of dominant consumers and dependent producers.

Their 2000 year old heritage is as deep and fertile as the Oaxacan Valley of southern Mexico where the Zapotec Indians have
woven a culture from the fibers of their own strong roots dyed
with influences from the Mayans, Aztecs, the colonial Spanish
and more recently the "modern World" as it spins towards the
21st century.

The weavers of Teotitlán del Valle, while maintaining a traditional standard of design which distinguishes them as time-
honored artisans, have evolved their wool-weaving art, adapting
and absorbing ideas from other cultures through history. The
Zapotec today, in weaving each piece, still use 100 percent
sheep's wool and natural dyes derived from the plants and insects
of this rich region. The Spanish colonial floor loom was introduced during the conquest of Mexico and has been adapted
and maintained as the machine of the predominantly male
craftsmen. . . .

Marilyn Smith, collector, personally visits the homes of the
individual weavers. In backyards throughout the village, the dyes
are prepared and piles of sheared wool, hand carded and spun, are
readied for the loom where the detailed expression of the artist
takes form. The careful individual selection and personal contact
with the weaver and his family insures the fine quality of each
collector piece.

As suggested here, more and more U.S. importers are personally selecting their merchandise on site in Teotitlán. While a majority of sales in the 1970s were to tourists in Mexico and Mexican nationals, as the spiraling devaluation of the peso began in 1982, the market for Zapotec textiles started to shift to an export market centered in the United States. After 1982, many Mexican middlemen who had been an important intermediary link among Teotiteco merchants, tourists, and U.S. importers could not afford Zapotec textiles. In addition, the purchasing power of U.S. dollars rose dramatically in Mexico in the 1980s and encouraged more North Americans to import Mexican crafts. As a result of the continued devaluation of the peso, importers saved significant amounts of money on internal airfare, hotels, automobile rental, and guides and interpreters. Many Mexican middlemen interviewed stated that their profit margins have been drastically reduced since 1982, and they cannot compete with North Americans who come to buy crafts with dollars. As Teotitecos become increasingly aggressive about marketing to foreigners and having their prices met, they are also unwilling to sell to Mexican merchants at lower prices.

Currently, most textiles produced in the four treadle loom weaving communities of the Oaxaca Valley are funneled through the dominant marketing structure of Teotitlán to an ever-expanding group of U.S. importers who distribute them through trade shows, privately owned import stores, chain import stores, interior decorators, and wholesale department stores. Today production includes highly priced original pieces, limited editions of codices and other reproductions, high-quality geometric designs, and mass-produced simple pieces produced primarily in the subordinate towns of San Miguel and Santa Ana (Stephen forthcoming).

In 1985, North American merchants interviewed reported selling Zapotec weavings in the United States at 250 percent to 600 percent of their purchase price. However, an examination of wholesale prices in Teotitlán and retail prices in U.S. stores suggests that U.S. retail prices are often as high as 1,000 percent of wholesale prices. Profits for U.S. importers are quite high, considering that most do not spend more than about 38 percent of the purchase price for taxes, shipping, broker's fees, and their traveling expenses to get the weavings to the retail market. The United States currently has an 11 percent import tax on wool goods imported from Mexico. The Mexican government has a 2 to 3 percent export tax.

Interviews also revealed that importers who purchased weavings in a number of places around the Third World are cross-fertilizing designs and materials between ethnic groups in an effort to reach new market niches in the United States. Several importers commented that, while Mexican rugs are cheaper than Navajo, Pakistani, and Afghan rugs in the U.S. market, Dhuri rugs produced in India of cotton/wool blends are cheaper and compete with Zapotec rugs at the lower end of the U.S. carpet market. These importers have contracted weavers from India to produce "Zapotec" rugs made of cotton and cotton-wool blends. Such rugs can be found in chains such as Pier 1 Imports across the United States. These same importers stated that they tried in vain to get Teotitecos to produce eastern designs so that more Zapotec rugs could compete in the high-end oriental rug market. Teotitlán weavers would not produce many of the designs, stating their preference for Zapotec geometrics.[4]

State Development Programs in Teotitlán

One of the first efforts of the federal government to promote Teotiteco weaving came through BANFOCO (Banco de Fomento de Cooperativas), a national agency with state offices in Oaxaca and elsewhere. In the early 1960s, BANFOCO attempted to run a cooperative for weavers in Teotitlán. The effort was part of a broader one to sponsor cooperatives for weaving, pottery, basketmaking, jewelry, and clothing industries throughout the Oaxaca Valley. The primary activity of the bank was to extend credit through loans to artisans for the purchase of materials.

Begun in 1963, the cooperative had a short life and ended with only eight members in 1965 (Vargas-Barón 1968 : 198). Throughout its shaky life, the cooperative had a number of problems, the most important being that the community did not decide it needed a cooperative; rather, BANFOCO officials identified Teotitlán as a good site for the program and proceeded to begin it with a few local men. Because Oaxaca BANFOCO officials did not take into account the real relations of production and distribution, the cooperative was probably doomed from the start. In particular, they did not pay attention to the structure of production in which weavers and merchants were tied together through kin and *compadrazgo* relationships. As one person explained, "Why would I sell to BANFOCO when I have been weaving for my uncle since I was fourteen years old?" Most merchants in the community opposed the cooperative because it competed with them in marketing weavings and obtaining workers. In addition, weavers in the project who received credit had no marketing skills of their own and were unsuccessful in attracting clients to purchase the weavings owned by the cooperative. There were also differences in the weavers' abilities and talents that translated into disputes about how much individuals should be paid.

Soon after the cooperative began, a number of weavers left it and began to work independently (Vargas-Barón 1968:199). They made contacts with Oaxaca merchants who paid much more than they were making by selling their work to the cooperative. They thus began to deal directly with Oaxaca merchants and circumvented the state-sponsored cooperative, a pattern that both independent producers and merchants have demonstrated since the 1960s. In general, Teotitecos claim that the cooperative was always controlled by a few men and never worked to benefit most of its members.

As far as most people recall, all of the formal members of the cooperative were men. While some women indirectly sold their weavings to the cooperative through a male household member, they were never structurally included. BANFOCO officials only approached men, probably on the assumption that all weavers were men and that as heads of households they were in charge of production decision making. This is not the case, however. At this time, women were weaving in increasing numbers and were also important in production decision making in weaving households.

Following the unsuccessful attempt of BANFOCO to create a widely supported cooperative, FONART (Fondo Nacional de Artesanía), the offspring of BANFOCO, began to work in Teotitlán. According to a Oaxaca FONART official, the mission of FONART is to "conserve, rescue, and promote popular and traditional art with commercial support, credit, and through supplying primary materials" (October 1985 interview). A major part of the FONART program revolves around a series of national stores that have huge inventories of crafts from all over Mexico. As such, FONART acts as a national intermediary for craft producers, supposedly redistributing profits to producing communities. This is done, however, only after the cost of maintaining the bureaucracy has been deducted from profits. Rather than help to support the bureaucracy of FONART and add an extra layer in the marketing process, most Teotitecos, particularly in the emerging merchant class, have avoided getting very involved with FONART.

The marketing methods of FONART have an important cultural dimension as well. FONART stores dissolve ethnic differences into nationalism, displaying crafts from Michoacán, Guerrero, Oaxaca, and Yucatán side by side as *genuino arte popular mexicano* (genuine Mexican folk art: García Canclini 1982:126–127). Ultimately, as García Canclini (1982:128) points out, the dissolution of ethnicity into nationalism also reduces particular ethnic creations to "typical crafts," *lo típico*. Since Teotitecos' claim to their textiles rests on the fact that they are Zapotec weavers producing Zapotec textiles, they lose credit for their production in state FONART stores, which homogenize hundreds of products from thirty or forty ethnic groups as "Mexican crafts." Aside from the cultural illegitimacy of FONART, the program also has had financial difficulties.

During the 1980s, FONART was consistently unable to pay artisans for their products at the time of delivery. In some cases, entire communities worked diligently to fill a FONART contract only to find that, when they finished, FONART did not have enough cash to pay them for the work they had completed. In 1985, FONART sold a large lot of merchandise to commercial stores such as Sanborn's and Sears in order to raise money owed to artisans. This cash flow problem probably further encouraged producers in Teotitlán and other communities to circumvent FONART programs and deal with commercial Mexican intermediaries. In the case of Teotitlán, some producers followed this strategy, but the enterprising merchant class of the 1970s also began to forge direct links to U.S. importers. Officially, FONART worked in Teotitlán from 1971 until 1983. The original FONART program provided credit to those weavers who were producing what were identified as traditional designs. In this project, FONART supplied loans for the purchase of primary materials such as wool and yarn. According to a Oaxaca official involved in the Teotitlán project, one of the major problems was that FONART did not have enough capital to keep the project going.

From 1972 through 1978, a group of 20 or more Teotiteco weavers were involved in a Oaxaca state FONART program at a time when there were probably more than 1,000 active weavers in the community, both men and women. In 1979, when this group was reorganized through a federal FONART program, it grew from 20 to 200. Through the federal government, they received a large sum of money to buy primary material such as wool and yarn directly from factories in Tlaxcala and Puebla. Apparently, the FONART cooperative purchased four tons of wool. The official interviewed about the program did not specify how it ended. According to those involved, however, the large wool purchase resulted in jealousy on the part of those who were not in on the deal, and the program fell apart. Significant portions of the wool remained unaccounted for as the project disintegrated.

According to many people in Teotitlán, the FONART program never reached 200 people. For many years, the Oaxaca FONART office purchased large numbers of weavings from several of the wealthiest merchants who had large piecework operations. Some independent artisans were aided with credit, but most pieceworkers continued to work in the same capacity. Now Teotitecos agree that they do not need FONART. They comment that FONART always wanted to pay below the market price for their goods, lower than what they could get from U.S. importers. As a result, FONART bought primarily from large merchants who would give them a break in price because they bought in bulk. These merchants treated FONART as they would any other client. Thus the majority of merchants and producers were not involved in the FONART project, but were busy building direct links with U.S. importers, sometimes with people they met while working in the United States.

When discussing FONART, most Teotitecos state that they prefer to make their own contacts with foreign clients or simply to produce for those in their community. The dream of every weaving household is to find a *cliente,* a foreign buyer to whom they can sell directly. If this is not possible, local merchants are preferable to officials from state craft development programs. Weavers emphasize that, unlike the government, local merchants, who are often kin or *compadres,* will give them credit and a good price for their weavings. They can also be counted on to provide help for children's education and to sponsor them at school graduations and Catholic rites of passage. They find this preferable to the government program, where they were paid less and often had to wait to obtain credit to use in purchasing yarn.

In 1985, FONART began a cooperative in neighboring Santa Ana. Apparently seventy weavers are registered with the cooperative; but, according to the FONART official in charge of the program, only twenty of them work in the program. The other fifty prefer to produce for merchants in Teotitlán. Many Santa Ana weavers still like to get their primary materials from their employers in Teotitlán and get paid for their work, rather than working in the FONART cooperative, where they can purchase wool below market price. Because social and economic ties between Teotitlán and Santa Ana are so strong, it is not surprising that weavers there prefer relations with Teotitlán merchants to relations with the government. Many of them are in *compadrazgo* relationships with people from Teotitlán and can count on them for a lot more than the government can offer.

When the peso was devalued dramatically in 1982 and 1983, many U.S. merchants who had previously bought from Mexican wholesalers as well as from FONART began to go directly to craft-producing communities. Cheaper airfares, hotel, restaurant, car rental rates, and guide fees made it attractive to do so. Textile importers no longer went through middlemen in Mexico City and Oaxaca, but directly to Teotitlán. According to the FONART official who worked there, "Since the devaluation of the peso, production has steadily increased in Teotitlán. Since that moment they no longer needed FONART. They are maintaining themselves and several other towns as well. The influx of U.S. merchants to the community was tremendous" (November 1985 interview).

The emerging merchant class in Teotitlán seems to have anticipated this change before 1982. In 1980, a local group of men who were not holding cargo positions in the *municipio*, including several prominent merchants, organized to build a paved road running directly from Teotitlán to the Pan American Highway. Previously, the community was linked to the highway with a dirt road that ran through the neighboring town of Macuilxóchitl. Apparently jealous of the success and long-standing dominance of Teotitlán, people from Macuilxóchitl frequently steered tourists and other interested parties away from Teotitlán, telling them that the town was in the opposite direction. There were also several confrontations in which buses from Teotitlán were vandalized and stopped in the road.

The move to build the road from Teotitlán was widely supported in the community, and about 75 percent of the cost of building the road was raised there. The remaining 25 percent was obtained from the Oaxaca governor's office. The road was built by community *tequio* labor in which each household provided at least one male laborer to work on the road. Several merchants who became active in the project spent almost two years overseeing the road construction. The project was supported by *municipio* authorities, but in the minds of community members it remains the project of those merchants who organized it. The road also marks an important shift in the political authority structure of the community. Merchants negotiating outside of the formal political system began subtly to challenge traditional political authority based on ritual experience and knowledge.

Another important project undertaken by the community was the conversion of what was the local food market to an artisan market for tourists in 1985. Rather than go to the state for resources, the community paid the bill for construction and local labor was used. A new food market was built with government assistance, and the new artisan market located in front of the *municipio* now houses some twenty-five stalls for local merchants and independent weavers. For the women who staff the market up to eight hours a day, their low-level involvement in its creation and their exclusion from the committee that oversees it are points of contention.

La Lanera de Oaxaca: A Controversial Development Project

One of the most controversial government-supported projects yet to have taken place in Teotitlán is La Lanera de Oaxaca (The Oaxaca Yarn Factory). The yarn factory opened its doors in 1984 on land supposedly donated by the community. In addition to the dubious community land grant, the factory was also funded jointly by federal and state agencies.[5] Its initial purpose was to provide weavers with locally produced high-quality yarn at low prices. Specifically, the project was supposed to result in lower prices than those charged by Teotiteco merchants who imported yarn from Tlaxcala.

Before 1984, the demand for machine-spun yarn was met solely by a group of local merchants who purchased industrial yarn from large factories in Tlaxcala and Toluca. They shipped it by rail and/or truck to Teotitlán as often as every two weeks. Some but not all of these merchants also had piecework weaving operations. Because of the difficulties that have plagued La Lanera de Oaxaca since it opened, yarn merchants who were supposed to be put out of business have been able to continue with no problem. The factory is, in a word, unpopular. Many Teotitecos comment that the yarn factory was never approved by the community. Some observe that even the name (which states it is Oaxacan) demonstrates that the project does not belong to the community. "The factory hasn't helped the town. . . . We don't really know who it belongs to. It seems like a private business. Didn't you see the name? The Lanera of Oaxaca? Why isn't it called the Lanera of Teotitlán?" (Lois, age 55).

Many of the problems associated with the factory can be traced to previous patterns of top-down administration that involved state officials negotiating with a few local men. When officials from the Secretariat of Oaxaca State Programs approached the mayor and his advisor in 1983 about the availability of land for a local factory, these two individuals began to negotiate on their own. A site was designated that supposedly only involved communal land, but also included some privately owned farmland. While families that owned the land were to have been compensated with other land of comparable quality, many say this never occurred. Members of these families continue to battle with the *municipio* over the loss of their land. Most people in the community complain that they were never consulted about the establishment of the factory, although it does appear to have been supported by an initial faction that backed the mayor. While most of the population was not included in the decision-making process to build the factory, many people, particularly women, have protested the actions of the factory and believe that it is the cause of escalating yarn prices in the community.

When the factory was completed, administrators for the factory offered Teotitecos jobs in the factory as apprentices. Both men and women were recruited for factory jobs. The low daily wages, about one-third of what a skilled weaver could make, discouraged most Teotitecos from applying. In addition, weavers stated that they did not want to work in a factory with set hours. They felt strongly about working in their own homes because they could control when they worked. In addition, working at home let them take time off for family affairs, ritual celebrations, farming, and domestic chores as needed. No one wanted to work in the factory. After trying to recruit local workers for a few months, the first director of the factory imported male workers from Tlaxcala. Currently no one from Teotitlán is employed at the factory except one young woman who sells yarn. The workers from Tlaxcala lead an isolated life, living in housing on the grounds of the factory. They are socially marginalized in the community.

In addition to severe political problems, the economics of factory yarn production were also dismal, offering a lesson in bureaucratic inefficiency. While the director attempted to run the factory efficiently during 1985 and 1986, he was hampered by several factors. First, because the factory was closely monitored by the government, a legitimate 15 percent sales tax was charged. In contrast, yarn wholesalers in Tlaxcala do not write receipts or keep records, so no tax is charged to Teotiteco merchants for their purchases. Essentially, the factory had to produce yarn 15 percent cheaper than Tlaxcala merchants did in order to sell it competitively in Teotitlán. A second problem centered around the logistics of production. Since the factory was built with very little capital, it had no wool-washing facility. Wool was purchased in local markets in the Valley of Oaxaca and then shipped out to Mexico City, where it was washed. It was then shipped back to Teotitlán, where it was spun. About 13 percent of the final price of the yarn sold in the factory was just for transporting the raw wool to Mexico City to be washed and returned. Finally, the factory had virtually no working capital. During local wool shortages, factory administrators had no sources of credit in order to import wool or purchase it in other areas. From November 1984 through January 1986, the director of the factory tried in vain to get government credit to import wool from Argentina. Because the wool had to be purchased with dollars, he was never granted permission since the price rose substantially every day.

The inefficiency of the factory has kept the price of local factory yarn constantly rising. In one year, 1984 to 1985, the price doubled from 900 pesos/kilo to over 1,800 pesos/kilo. Every time the price of factory yarn went up, local merchants raised their prices as well. During the rainy season when there was an annual shortage of wool, prices went up even higher, and local merchants hoarded supplies. The perception of the community is that the factory is not doing anything to provide them with cheaper yarn. Many people feel the presence of the factory actually increases the price of all yarn.

When the factory was set up, the town of Teotitlán was given a place on the board of directors. In fact, a former *presidente* (mayor) and *síndico* (mayoral advisor) were the two individuals who sat on the board representing the town. With their departure and the entrance of a new group of authorities in local government, there was initially little communication between factory administrators and the community. Strong local protests have led to increased community involvement in the workings of the factory and to the creation of a special municipal committee to oversee its operation. The latest task of this committee is to consider dismantling the factory, an outcome that seems to be desired by a majority of the community. The factory provided a community rallying point in a situation where normally weavers are often at odds with merchants. The unity around this particular issue tended to obscure the fact that it is in the merchants' interest to maintain control over yarn prices and distribution. The factory was challenging their monopoly on inputs for weaving.

Gender Relations and the Division of Labor under Commercial Production

As tourist and export markets for Zapotec textiles grew steadily during the 1970s, the availability of weaving labor became a critical variable in the expansion of production. This growing need for weaving labor was met in three primary ways. First, women and girls began to weave in greater numbers. Now almost two generations of girls and women have been socialized as weavers. In Teotitlán, approximately 35–40 percent of the weaving labor force is now female.[6] The majority of female weavers in Teotitlán are under the age of thirty-five. Most learned to weave in their natal homes or were taught by their husbands when they were married.

Second, the demand for more weaving labor was almost met by expanding the number of weavers in other communities. The population of Santa Ana began to weave on a larger scale in the 1970s when significant numbers of women entered the labor force. The most dramatic change is in the neighboring community of San Miguel, which, although it was originally populated by people from Teotitlán, never undertook weaving as a significant economic activity. Helen Clements (1988b: 22–23) reports that currently 30 percent of the community is weaving, with equal numbers of males and females participating in the textile boom. The first weavers probably began working in 1974.

Clements' study of weavers in San Miguel reveals a shift in the division of labor similar to that seen in Teotitlán, with the greatest number of female weavers concentrated at the lower end of the age pyramid. While there are more male than female weavers over the age of forty in San Miguel, women under the age of forty are weaving in equal numbers with men, even surpassing them in the fifteen- to nineteen-year-old age group. Between 1975 and 1985, the number of women who learned to weave in San Miguel tripled (Clements 1988b: 255).

The extension of weaving production into San Miguel and its growth in Santa Ana have been dominated by the community of Teotitlán, particularly by key families in the merchant sector, who now funnel a majority of the textiles produced to tourist art stores in Mexico and to an ever-expanding group of U.S. importers. While Santa Ana continues to struggle to get out of the shadow of Teotitlán and to establish an autonomous marketing structure, it seems unable to do so. In 1986, a small museum was opened in Santa Ana in order to bring tourists to the village (Cohen 1988). This effort is not sufficient, however, to overcome the dominant marketing position of Teotitlán. In some ways, the current dominance of Teotitlán is reproducing the important commercial and political position that it held as a district capital of a very large administrative territory. In its capacity as an administrative center until after independence, Teotitlán enjoyed more than 200 years of political dominance, acting as an authority and mediator among some thirty communities (Stephen 1987a: 38–39).

The third way in which the increased demand for weaving labor was met was to increase the quantity of machine-spun yarn used to produce textiles—essentially mechanizing a part of the production process. Increased use of machine-spun yarn also resulted in the freeing of significant amounts of labor, predominantly women and children, who had been dedicated to spinning and carding. Significant numbers of women and elderly men continue to card and spin, but the bulk of weaving production is now done with machine-spun yarn. Elderly women, probably the most economically marginalized sector in Teotitlán and Santa Ana, continue to hand card and hand spin. They say they are not strong enough to weave because of the stress that working the loom would put on their backs and legs. Many also believe they are too old to learn, but there are some notable exceptions to this. The high end of the textile market in the United States and Europe, which calls for handspun yarn, provides a niche for elderly laborers who earn less than weavers, further differentiating the gendered labor force by age as well.

Commercialization and the Daily Lives of Weaver Women

The commercialization of weaving production in the 1970s resulted in the long-term incorporation of Teotiteco women and girls into the weaving labor force. This process was also affected by continued male migration to the United States in the 1970s. In this process the social construction of women's work grew to include weaving as well as food processing, child care, animal production, and reciprocal exchanges. Systematic incorporation of women into the weaving labor force appears to have had mixed results for them.

While still being excluded from official census categories as weavers, female weavers in Teotitlán have not suffered a local lack of recognition for their work. Women who are spinners and dyers also receive recognition for their work. Most Teotitecos believe that women are good weavers and with enough time and practice will become equal to or perhaps better than men. Several young women have already established reputations as very talented artisans who work on intricate designs. The greatest respect is given to weavers who work on highly complex original designs.

Female weavers in Teotitlán also receive wages comparable to men's. This is unusual in comparison to lower women's wages in other types of craft production. In the embroidery, hammock, Oaxacan clothing, and shawl industries, women's piecework wages are often significantly lower than those of men, sometimes falling to less than 25 percent of the hourly rate of male workers performing different tasks within the same industry (Cook 1984b).

The schedule and rhythm of work for women weavers, however, are different from those of men. Participant observation and structured interviews in Teotitlán revealed that women weave an average of three to six hours per day, while men weave six to ten hours per day. Women weave about four hours per day no matter what season it is, while men weave considerably longer during the dry season when they are not engaged in part-time agricultural work. In general, households that engage in heavy weaving production tend to do less farming, even if they have access to land. However, women's weaving workload is not necessarily cut back in the same proportion as men's if the household is engaging in farming. Often women are expected to keep up their weaving workloads as well as to contribute to farming during the agricultural season if the household has planted crops that year. This may result in heavier workloads for women than for men. When women are left in Teotitlán by migrating husbands, they tend to give up farming and try to keep up with weaving production because it is a higher income earner than farming, which often operates at a loss. Only if their husbands or sons send home sufficient funds to hire a wage laborer to work their fields do women left alone pursue farming. If they do receive funds from husbands or sons, they are more likely to use it to purchase wool, yarn, and dyes to continue in weaving production. The time that individuals allot to weaving is also affected by their ceremonial responsibilities. In weaving households, additional cash is often raised for ritual consumption through weaving longer hours. If women are alone, they must therefore also adjust their production schedule to their ritual expenditure obligations.

On a daily basis, while men often weave in uninterrupted sessions, the weaving of women is sporadic. Most women sandwich their weaving in between meal preparations, animal care, and child care. Women often weave in the morning after preparing the morning meal and before beginning the afternoon meal. They weave again in the late afternoon when they have completed cleaning up from the midday meal. They can continue until about 7 P.M., when evening coffee must be prepared. They may weave more later at night. Many complain that since they have begun weaving they are working longer hours and no one is relieving them of their own responsibilities. "When you get married you feel the strain of weaving. With that first child a lot of women who weave feel a lot of pain because the loom mistreats your belly. It is hard to stand up for so long. Then later you have a child to take care of as well. No one helps with the children" (Josefina, age 40).

Children also affect women's ability to weave. Women with young babies rarely weave. Daughters can be important in helping to free the labor of mothers for weaving or in taking on domestic chores so that other siblings can weave. In many cases, older women continue to do domestic chores while their daughters weave. Young women often end up with quite heavy workloads, which get worse when they marry.

Those of us who started weaving in our parents' houses are usually already tired by the time we get married. Like me. I would weave in the early morning, go to the market to sell for a while, and go home and weave again. I also helped to take care of my brothers and sisters. Now that I am married it is the same except it is my children I have to take care of. I have some regrets about not staying with my parents. If I hadn't gotten married so soon, I might have been able to complete junior high school. (Ana, age 27)

The Differentiation of Women under Commercialization

An integrated approach to analyzing the changing authority roles of women in production suggests that women's positions be evaluated both within the household and in relation to the formal power structures in the community. In their recent study of women who do assembly work in their Mexico City homes, Benería and Roldán (1987: 111–114) suggest that the concept of the household/family entity be taken apart in order to uncover the underlying structures that incorporate hierarchies of class, gender, and age. While anthropologists have often resisted using the social actor as a unit of analysis, such an approach reveals the negotiation process between men and women within the household, highlighting decision-making and power struggles between household members. Allowing women to function as individual social and political actors with gendered agendas within the household as well as in extradomestic structures illuminates gender conflicts in relation to class and the construction of ethnicity. For example, as outlined in chapter 8, women's control of resources and labor for ceremonial purposes often brings them into conflict with their husbands, who may want to use the same resources for weaving production or farming. Here I am advocating an approach that allows women to function as independent-minded social actors.[7] The point is to allow them to have separate ideas and agendas from those of "the household," an analytical unit made up of social actors of differing genders and ages that is often mistakenly assumed to have a life of its own.

In Teotitlán, this approach was used to explore the dynamics of gendered household decision making in both employer/merchant households and pieceworker/employee households. The division of the population according to class position (i.e., merchants/weavers) produced significant insights into household-based gender relations. Participant observation, informal interviews, and a questionnaire suggest that, as households accumulate capital and achieve employer status, women lose authority in the sphere of production.

Women in merchant households described themselves as managers or laborers working primarily in their husbands' businesses.

Like women weavers who complained of double workloads related to weaving, merchant women had similar complaints related to the management work they had to do for their husbands combined with a heavy domestic workload. Luisa, the wife of one of the wealthiest merchants in Teotitlán, continues to make tortillas for her husband, care for six children, supervise four to six weavers who work at her house, and deal with pieceworkers.

> My husband still wants me to make tortillas every day so that
> I can save the 700 pesos I would spend buying them [about
> US$2.00]. I don't like to make tortillas. It's hot, I get burned, my
> eyes are full of smoke, and I get really tired doing this and feed-
> ing my children and the workers who come here. I do it to make
> him happy. . . . He makes the decisions about what to buy. I
> don't buy yarn or anything. I don't know how to buy it. Every
> week my husband tells me what he wants me to do. He tells me
> how to plan my time and divide my work, including overseeing
> the workers. I try to do everything he asks, but usually there just
> isn't enough time.

Cook and Binford (1986) describe similar findings in the weaving community of Xaaga, where "male-run household enterprises appropriate value from unwaged female labor-power ideologically construed as 'helping out' (*ayuda*) rather than 'work' (*trabajo*)."

In Teotitlán, a few exceptions to this are younger women married to men who have recently acquired merchant status. They have a more equal part in business decision making, partly because of their higher levels of education. They have all finished the sixth grade. Younger, more educated girls and women in merchant households are also beginning to take an active stand in community politics, and it appears that class-based authority, along with their increased confidence due to their education and commercial experience, is an important factor in their political consciousness.

In the future, young girls may grow up with expectations of participating more equally in household businesses and community politics, but they realize that their independence is limited by their roles as wives and mothers. Local custom states that women's first responsibility is to take care of their husbands and children (feed them, see to their health and comfort), then to see to the family business. Even younger merchant women who do have considerable control in family businesses are often excluded from trips to sell large lots of rugs in Mexico and the United States. Their daily responsibilities of feeding their families, shopping, and getting children off to school as well as fears of their husband's jealousy prevent them from initiating even short trips.

> Even if women do go to school more it doesn't mean that they can be merchants. They can't manage everything because they can't leave the house. If they have sons, then the sons will manage for them. Women have a lot of responsibilities at home that make it difficult for them to leave. . . . As long as women have a lot of things to do around the house they can't run businesses equally with men. . . . And men are jealous. A lot of men get jealous when their wives are gone for a long time. Even when I go to the market and have to run around looking for change I lose time. When I come home I always feel a little something. Even though my husband doesn't say anything I always explain to him. . . . The only women who can go where they want and when they want are widows. (Graciela, age 35)

When women in employer households discuss their subordinate position in production decision making, they attribute it to a lack of skills needed to conduct business. While many women do maintain control over a small pot of money for making purchases of household items, when a household accumulates capital and begins a business, this money is often kept in a separate pot controlled by men. In contrast to their husbands and sons, who have often spent several years working in the United States, most women have little experience interacting with North Americans. Many believe that their husbands learned how to deal with North Americans and accumulated capital while they labored in the United States, first as *braceros* and now as illegal immigrants. "It is very hard for women to leave the house and carry on a business because of their responsibilities. It is even more difficult for them to get together the money to start a business. They can't go to the United States to work and save some money. They usually have responsibilities" (Chavela, age 28).

In large part, the lack of female participation in production and business decisions seems to stem from unequal access to education. Until recently, women have not had the same educational opportunities as men. Discussions with older women indicated that most parents in the 1940s, 1950s, and even 1960s believed that women did not need education in their roles as wives and mothers because they seldom left the community. Because women operated primarily in the sphere of the local community or in regional markets where Zapotec is spoken, they did not need Spanish for daily use. Under

Spanish colonial custom and later under independence, women were excluded from municipal cargo roles that called for literacy. Women did not participate in outmigration to the United States, which educated many men in minimal Spanish and basic literacy, until the 1970s. By the time large numbers of former weaving households had begun merchant activity, women who had not migrated were not able to catch up with the educational skills of men who had.

Today merchants often work with large amounts of capital and their dealings with clients require at least a knowledge of spoken and written Spanish, skills in math, and minimal accounting, which is taught in the later years of primary school. They must also deal with licensing and export procedures. Knowledge of English, usually gained by migrating to the United States, is also helpful.

A questionnaire given to the male and female heads of fifty-four merchant households in Teotitlán revealed that there are important differences between men's and women's linguistic skills and level of education. While 43 percent of merchant women surveyed had been to school for one year or less and 33 percent were monolingual in Zapotec, only 2 percent of merchant men surveyed were monolingual and 21 percent had been to school for one year or less. A full 54 percent of merchant men have more than three years of education, compared to 25 percent of merchant women. Many merchant men were also able to augment their literacy and language skills in the United States. These differences are important in running a business.

While rates of monolingualism are similarly high among weaver women (45 percent of women surveyed, 3 percent of men surveyed), who, like merchant women, have little education (45 percent with one year or less compared to 18 percent of men), these skills are not

Table 16. *Male and Female Education Levels in Merchant Households*

	0–1 Year	2–3 Years	> 3 Years	Missing Data
Men (N = 54)	21%	21%	54%	4%
Women (N = 54)	43%	28%	25%	4%

Source: Random stratified household survey conducted by Lynn Stephen in 1986.

Table 17. *Languages Spoken by Male and Female Heads of Merchant Households*

	Spanish Only	Zapotec Only	Bilingual	N/A
Men (N = 54)	0%	2%	94%	4%
Women (N = 54)	1%	33%	62%	4%

Source: Random stratified household survey conducted by Lynn Stephen in 1986.

Table 18. *Management of Business Finances by Gender Reported in Merchant Households (N = 54)*

Men Alone	Men and Women	Women Alone
67%	29%	4%

Source: Random stratified household survey conducted by Lynn Stephen in 1986.

Table 19. *Management of Household Money by Gender Reported in Weaver Households (N = 100)*

Men Alone	Men and Women	Women Alone
3%	62%	35%

Source: Random stratified household survey conducted by Lynn Stephen in 1986.

as necessary for producing weavings sold within the village (N = 100 weaver women, 100 weaver men). Most transactions involved in the weaving process can be carried out verbally in Zapotec.

Data from another question included in the survey support the contention that women do not have a high level of participation in managing the financial aspects of business in merchant households. This question was asked of men and women together. They had little trouble agreeing on it. The question was phrased in terms of who controlled the key to business cash and allocated it for business

expenses. No corresponding chart is available for weaver women because in weaver households expenses for weaving, ritual, and consumption all come out of the same pot. General household money in
weaver households is managed as shown in table 19. This information was also solicited from both men and women, who had little
trouble agreeing. It was based on who controlled the key and could
give out cash. As reflected in table 18, in a majority of merchant
households surveyed (67 percent), it was stated that men manage
business finances. Participant observation supports this view. In
contrast, in a majority of weaver households, it was reported that the
household pot is managed by both men and women (62 percent). It
was also stated that a significant portion of weaver women also manage the pot alone (35 percent). "My wife María Elena has control of
the money. She guards it and keeps the key, but we both know how
much there is. When we need to buy something, like more yarn, or
pay some construction workers, we both anticipate that and know
we have to put it aside. She usually does the paying" (Eduardo, age
60). The differences between weaver and merchant women's input
into financial management are reflected in other areas of production
as well.

In contrast to merchant women, women in pieceworker and independent weaver households repeatedly characterized the production
process as a team effort with their husbands and children where they
had major control over production decisions such as the allocation
of household labor (particularly children), the timing of weaving production, the number of pieces to be produced, and the negotiation of
selling prices with local merchants. "I make a lot of decisions about
weaving. I buy the yarn, the dyes, and I sell the serapes. I also handle
all of the money we make from selling weavings and from my pigs. I
also decide about buying food, and what fiestas we will go to and
what to purchase for them. While I decide, I always tell my husband
and he agrees" (Hortensia, age 36). "We both decide what to do in our
work and in what we buy. I go and sell what we weave to merchants
and bring home the money. Then we both talk about how to spend
it, what we need" (María, age 28).

In the long run, however, women in pieceworker and independent
weaver households face contradictory results from the commercialization of weaving. On the one hand, they have retained significant control in relation to the production process. On the other
hand, their households as a whole are not reaping the material benefits from commercialization that merchant households are. The pre-
ceding analysis of women's roles in production therefore underscores

the importance of examining the gendered impact of commercialization in conjunction with class.

Conclusions

As seen in the case of Teotitlán, as use commodities were transformed into handicrafts, the relations of production, the gendered division of labor, and local ethnic identity were all affected. A new petty capitalist merchant class has emerged under conditions of commercial capitalism. This class now deals directly with U.S. importers in the distribution of textiles. Within this sector women have been marginalized because they lack experience and education and are limited by their social roles as wives and mothers. Women over thirty who grew up during a time when women were not thought to need Spanish in their daily lives and who did not receive exposure to U.S. culture and basic business skills have been further limited in their ability to participate in business by their daily obligations to shop in the market each morning, prepare meals, wash clothing, care for animals, and take care of household ceremonial needs. Even if a woman's household achieves merchant status, many of her domestic obligations continue and perhaps increase, as shown in the case study of Angela in chapter 3. Younger women who have grown up in merchant households as well as those in weaver households are receiving more education now. It has become more socially acceptable to educate girls and is even seen now as a necessity by many parents. The possibility of participating in the family business has encouraged more families to educate daughters.

In terms of the ethnic dimensions of commercialization, merchants have continued to use the idiom of kinship to reinforce the relations of production, placing weaver/merchant class relations in the same arena with *compadrazgo* and ritual reciprocal labor exchanges. At the same time, a continued claim of Zapotec ethnic identity is the basis on which Zapotec weavings now claim a handicraft status in export consumer markets. Merchants are also aware of this fact and represent themselves as the bearers of authenticity to foreign importers. Internally, the representation of local ethnic identity is in conflict with emerging class identity—merchants are increasingly acquiring political authority that stands in opposition to the authority sanctified by ritual experience and age.

Commercialization of textiles has pushed women into the weaving labor force in significant numbers not only in Teotitlán, but also in surrounding communities such as Santa Ana and San Miguel. While women weavers appear to receive equal pay to men for their work and occupational recognition—something that is still lacking for most working women in Mexico—in most cases weaving has added to the number of hours women must work in order to complete all of their daily chores.

The impact of commercialization on women and on the entire community of Teotitlán has been contradictory. The community's current economic success seems clearly tied to a history of independence, particularly with regard to defending Teotitlán's economic claim on textiles. The town first resisted government monitoring of production in the 1930s and 1940s and then avoided heavy participation in craft development projects that put the state in the position of middleman. Because they were successful on their own, Teotitecos avoided participation in government programs. This independent stance emerged again in the 1970s as local merchants began to develop their own links to U.S. importers.

Within the past fifteen years, the average level of income has gone up in Teotitlán. All Teotitecos agree that their material life has improved significantly. Because of the rapid development of a petty capitalist merchant class, however, increases in income have not been evenly distributed. People within the community as well as outside it are aware of the heightened differences between merchants and the rest of the population that have marked the past few years. Because most of today's wealthy merchants were poor farmers and weavers twenty years ago, however, many people in the community, including young women, believe it is possible to move into the merchant sector.

At the moment, a period of expansion is incorporating more laborers and communities into the system. Because expansion of textile production depends on U.S. consumers, Teotitecos do not control the expansion process. The remainder of this book examines how this expansion is operating not only between and within households, but in the arena of ritual and politics as well. There we shall see replicated, again and again, the internal contradiction of ethnicity versus class as the community's economy is integrated into the world economic system.

Chapter 7. One Man, One Vote: Changes in the Civil-Religious Hierarchy and Their Impact on Women

> *Being a* mayordoma *is important. It means everyone will re-spect you because you are supporting the town and working for the town. We call* mayordomos *the same as we call the saints and virgins. Women* mayordomas *are* nān, *like the virgins. Men* mayordomos *are* dad, *like the saints. They are the same words. They both work for the town. For example, if it isn't raining, then the* mayordomos *pray to the gods for rain. They do it for everyone. Because they do this, people listen to them and respect them. (Cristina, age 40)*

THE LOCAL political life of Teotitlán del Valle was and still is tightly bound to local ritual institutions. From the late 1800s until the 1960s, the religious cargo system of the community was the primary engine of community ceremonial life and a major arena for the de-velopment of prestige and local political authority. Both women and men actively participated in the *mayordomías* of the religious hier-archy and received authority and prestige for doing so. In this chap-ter the changing dynamics of the civil-religious hierarchy are ex-plored in relation to state attempts to wrest political control away from communities by restructuring municipal politics. Such an effort involved the appointment of local church committees in 1926 as part of local civil governments and campaigns to eliminate *may-ordomías* in the name of progress. In addition, Spanish literacy, edu-cation, and the ability to deal with political bureaucracies were em-phasized over ritual experience and community service as the primary skills necessary to hold political posts.

The eventual divorce of the civil from the religious cargo system in Teotitlán and a major decline in the celebration of *mayordomías* have had a large impact on women's political and ceremonial lives. Always excluded from formal municipal politics and then further marginalized from political relations when *mayordomía* sponsorship declined, women have increasingly turned to the notion of authority based on age and ritual experience as a way of participating politically in the community.

Breaking Traditional Images of Civil-Religious Hierarchies

Anthropological descriptions of political life in indigenous communities in the states of Oaxaca and Chiapas have focused heavily on civil-religious cargo systems and/or on *cacique* (strong-man) political machines.[1] In some cases local *caciques* have integrated themselves and their supporters into local civil-religious hierarchies (Wasserstrom 1983). Initial anthropological literature on civil-religious cargo systems described them as intertwining hierarchies of civil and religious offices that allowed individual men to advance their civil political careers as they took on religious sponsorship of cult celebrations for local saints and virgins. This original view has been amended through time by refocusing on two dimensions of civil-religious hierarchies. First, as the work of ethnohistorians has shown, the "classical" civil-religious hierarchies described by so many anthropologists are historically specific institutions that operated roughly from after Mexican independence until the 1950s. Second, while civil offices were held by men, the *mayordomía* offices of religious hierarchies were held by pairs of men and women who both received prestige and authority.

Recent ethnohistorical work (e.g., Chance 1990; Chance and Taylor 1985; Earle 1990; Wasserstrom 1983) has shown that local government during the early colonial period in indigenous communities was structured only as a civil hierarchy. Religious activities were centered in *cofradías*, religious corporations founded to pay for the cult of local saints. *Cofradías* owned land and herds, the proceeds of which paid for local cult celebrations. Only after *cofradía* property was expropriated by the church and state sanctions against religious festivals appeared did individual households begin to sponsor cult celebrations for local saints (Stephen and Dow 1990). Individual sponsorship of cult celebrations for saints probably began during the eighteenth century and eventually resulted in the marriage of religious and civil hierarchies in many communities.

John Chance's (1990) comparison of twenty-three ethnographic sources and other recent studies of cargo systems show that, in fact, the civil-religious hierarchy has undergone a structural shift in response to increasing integration of community political structures with those of the state and national governments. In his extended period of study in Zinacantán, Frank Cancian (1990) has also noted that, as entrepreneurial opportunities and social stratification increased, often in relation to state development programs, interest in sponsoring cargos declined dramatically.

Current ethnographic literature describes several contemporary forms or readaptations of the religious side of former civil-religious hierarchies. Chance (1990) focuses on what he calls "religious cargo systems," which maintain a hierarchy of public offices for the express purpose of serving local saints. He finds this to be the dominant trend in current literature on cargo systems.

Three other contemporary possibilities are also described in the literature. One is the complete disappearance of any type of cargo system. Another variety reflects back on communal support for cult celebrations offered by *cofradías* during the earlier colonial era. Stanley Brandes (1981, 1988) and others (Good 1988a) describe a system of community-wide collections, usually carried out by specially appointed committees, which support community celebrations in association with particular saints, essentially replacing household-sponsored *mayordomías*. In some communities, church committees put in place as early as the 1920s as part of the municipal government structure are also instrumental in taking up collections and organizing community rituals that were formerly planned and organized by *mayordomos* (Stephen 1990a). The final form, discussed here in chapter 8, involves a significant decrease in *mayordomía* activity and transference of the prestige and ritual forms and content associated with *mayordomías* to life-cycle rituals.

In all of these forms that reorganize civil-religious hierarchies, the formal political authority of cargo holders in relation to the state has been steadily undermined. In addition, even in those communities that preserve a prestige system built on holding offices in a religious hierarchy, such prestige may not be sufficient to qualify people to hold elected office and does not hold outside of the community. Kate Young vividly describes changes in the basis of political authority as village elders in a Oaxacan sierra community lost control of the municipal government to men who were more oriented toward national culture. She states (1976:260) that since then "the emphasis on youth, education, and wealth is in direct opposition to the former emphasis on age, service to the gods, and the fulfillment of obligations to the community."

James Greenberg (1981:191) describes a similar situation in contemporary Oaxaca, but concludes that the political authority of elders, rather than eroding, has come to coexist with the formal government of elected civil officials. A "sub-rosa structure of authority" not accessible to bureaucratic manipulation of the state is sometimes able to help communities resist pressures from mestizo-dominated political and economic institutions by causing trouble in the state's bureaucratic system (Greenberg 1990). While Greenberg's case provides an interesting and notable example, in most contemporary forms of religious ceremonial systems the political authority of cargo holders or fiesta sponsors has been undermined by the state and often by competing local systems of political authority based on class relations (Stephen 1990a).

The separation of religious from civil hierarchies in indigenous communities and the increasing secularization of formal political decision making have had important effects on the nature of women's political participation. Slowly, beginning in the 1920s and 1930s, civil office positions in Oaxaca *municipios* have been elected by village assemblies as specified by the 1917 Mexican constitution (Chance 1990). Elderly informants in Teotitlán, Santa Ana, Macuil-xóchitl, and San Miguel stated that, by tradition, such assemblies were only attended by men. Recently, women have begun to attend *municipio* assemblies only in areas where popular movements have overthrown *cacique*-run *municipios*, such as in Juchitán (Rubin 1987) and Yalálag (Equipo Pueblo 1988; Ortigoza 1986).

One of the consequences of the divorce of religious hierarchies from civil ones is that women lost their most formal remaining link to institutional community politics. As documented by Holly Mathews in Oaxaca (1985), the elimination of religious sponsorship as a requirement for political service in civil cargo systems and the emphasis on individual skills such as Spanish fluency and experience with state bureaucrats as the basis for selection to community political posts have eliminated many women from consideration. In addition, the responsibilities of many former male and female *mayordomos* are now part of male civil cargos in church committees that were mandated by Calles in the 1920s (Stephen 1990a).

In many Zapotec communities, household heads, both male and female, accrued and continue to accrue status and social position through taking on the sponsorship of *mayordomías*. While *mayordomía* titles are formally held by men in accordance with the Spanish custom of registering only male household heads in the census, *mayordomía* titles are clearly understood to be held by male/female pairs (Chance 1990; Stephen 1990c). This was documented in Chiapas (Nash 1970) and in Oaxaca (Chiñas 1973; Mathews 1985; Young 1978). Within the *mayordomía* system as well as in other formal ritual situations, both men and women have particular responsibilities and obligations that are complementary: rituals cannot be properly completed without the participation of both.

Both *mayordomas* (women) and *mayordomos* (men) were important in shaping local political opinion. According to elderly male and female informants in Teotitlán, such opinion was articulated in many areas of the community and became policy under the direction of male elders who held the highest civil cargo posts. In Teotitlán, older women emphasized the importance of women with religious authority in formulating such policy. This discussion offering two correctives about essential features of civil-religious cargo systems has important implications for our understanding of the political and ceremonial roles of indigenous women in Mexico. The historical specificity of civil-religious cargo systems can be linked to a particular type of political authority rooted in age, ritual experience, and community service. Under this system, ritual and politics were integrated entities. Respect and authority that stemmed from ritual were readily transferable to politics. For women, this was of major importance. Their participation in *mayordomías* as community ritual leaders gave them a source of authority that also allowed them to have an impact on community politics.

The ritual-political system that dominated politics in Teotitlán until the 1960s was a system that directly linked social reproduction—that is, the ritual reproduction of social actors—to politics. While this is still partially the case today, through life-cycle rituals and the ritual authority they give to women, the direct link between *mayordomías* and the civil hierarchy provided a more formal validation of women's authority. In order to understand the implications of this historical trajectory for women's contemporary political and ceremonial life in Teotitlán, we shall first look at the community's civil-religious hierarchy and the changes it went through after the Mexican Revolution.

Teotitlán's Civil-Religious Hierarchy: When *Mayordomos* Were *Mayordomos*

At the turn of the century, Teotitlán's *mayordomía* system—the basis of the religious hierarchy—was intertwined with the civil cargo system. Male and female *mayordomos* worked together to move up the religious hierarchy, while men, as representatives of their households, moved up the hierarchy of political offices, jumping from religious to political offices. Their wives remained outside of the formal civil cargo system, politicking through the extended kin and *compadrazgo* networks that operated in the arena of social reproduction, similar to the way in which many women continue to participate politically in the community today.

The prerevolutionary civil cargo system in Teotitlán had about forty cargos linked to approximately nineteen *mayordomías* celebrated in the community's ritual calendar. After the Revolution, more positions were added to the civil cargo system when the state implemented national development plans that called for new local committees such as those for schools and *ejidos*. A religious branch of the cargo system took over a lot of the work previously done by *mayordomos* and *mayordomas*.

According to elderly people in Teotitlán, the purpose of the civil cargo system was to guard local customs, keep public order, adjudicate local disputes, allocate community resources, and manage the community's relationship with the government. All male heads of households were and still are required to serve in civil cargo posts throughout their adult lives. People living together in a household were obligated to provide males for cargo positions and for communal labor. Women also contributed labor to civil cargo functions on many occasions and did so on a daily basis by making up for male household labor lost to civil cargos.

According to Teotitecos, the civil cargo system is divided into two main branches: *ayuntamiento* (governmental), and *juzgado mayor o alcaldía* (judicial). At present the *ayuntamiento* (governmental branch) is structured as indicated in figure 1.

The officials elected to the *ayuntamiento* include a president, a *síndico* (legal advisor to the president and the *ayuntamiento*), and three *regidores* (councilmen, each in charge of dealing with a specific area, such as the graveyard, water and land resources, etc.). Each of these positions has a *suplente* (alternate) who remains in the local municipal building on a rotating basis when the primary officials are absent. Other cargos stemming from the *ayuntamiento* include two employees, a secretary and treasurer, an assistant to the president and the *síndico*, ten policemen (*topiles*), two police captains (*mayores de vara*), and five section heads (*jefes de sección*). Teotitlán is divided geographically into five sections or neighborhoods. Communal labor is assigned by section.

Each section was also previously policed by officials called *gulap* in Zapotec, who are no longer part of the cargo system. No one in the community knows the Spanish name for them. They were supervised by a *comuín* and a second in command or *primer vara*.

Figure 1. Organization of the *Ayuntamiento*

Presidente
Suplente
Asistente
Síndico
Suplente
Asistente

Secretario
Tesorero

Regidor 1   *Regidor* 2   *Regidor* 3
Suplente   *Suplente*   *Suplente*
Jefes de Sección
Comuín
Primer Vara
Mayores de Vara
Topil 1   *Topil* 2   *Topil* 3   *Topil* 4   *Topil* 5
Topil 6   *Topil* 7   *Topil* 8   *Topil* 9   *Topil* 10

Figure 2. Organization of the *Juzgado Mayor*

Alcalde 1   *Alcalde* 2
Suplente 1   *Suplente* 1
Suplente 2   *Suplente* 2
Asistente   *Asistente*

They policed the community for sexual involvements between young boys and girls and had ritual responsibilities in the month of February.

The judicial branch of the cargo system, the *juzgado mayor*, includes two *alcaldes* (judges or justices of the peace), four *suplentes* (alternates, two for each *alcalde*), and two assistants, one for each judge. These local judges were the district judges while Teotitlán was a district head. They adjudicated property transfers, sales, local disputes over land and livestock, family disagreements, and other legal procedures. Today local judges in Teotitlán adjudicate similar issues.

During the colonial era, as today, local authorities were responsible for keeping order in the community and served as the links between the community and higher levels of government. All orders were passed down through the national bureaucracy to the state bureaucracies to the level of the district and *municipio*. Because Teotitlán was a district head for so long, local authorities also had to monitor the activities of other *municipios*. The community archives have clear records of legal transactions and disputes dating back to 1580. Because the district territory of Teotitlán was so extensive, the power of local officials was probably much broader during the colonial era than it is today.

In addition to these principal civil *cargo* positions, there are eleven or more committees that monitor community projects, resources, and public works. Membership is elected and is considered a part of the civil cargo system. The numerical majority of cargos are found in these committees. The structure of these eleven committees usually includes a president, sometimes a vice-president, a treasurer, a secretary, and four to five committee members.

These committees include the parents' committee for the secondary (junior high) school, parents' committee for the primary school, parents' committee for the kindergarten, committee for the (government-run) health center, committee for the Secretariat of Education (SEP), committee for running water, committee for the dam (in charge of irrigation), committee for communal lands, committee to fight fires, committee for electricity, and committee to carry out activities for patriotic holidays. In addition, the president can set up additional committees to take on public works projects or explore new issues as they arise.[2]

Today males representing particular households are elected to civil cargo positions by a large assembly (*junta*). Prior to the Revolution, they were probably appointed by a group of elders. The oldest

Figure 3. Civil-Religious Cargo Posts of Manuel Martínez,
        1952–1989

1952–1953	*šruɛz* (servant to mayor; no longer exists)
1955–1956	*topil* (paid someone to do his labor while working in the U.S.A.)
1957–1958	*mayordomo* for the Virgen de Guadalupe
1959–1960	*jefe de sección*
1961–1962	member of temporary committee to celebrate the opening of a new dam
1963–1966	member of parents' committee for schools
1970–1971	*padrino del niño Jesús,* minor religious cargo
1973–1976	president of committee for communal lands
1982	advisor to the municipal president (cargo that no longer exists)
1985–1986	president of *comité de la iglesia*
1988–1989	*mayordomía de la Preciosa Sangre*

people in Teotitlán mention a group of elders who appointed both *mayordomos* and officials for the civil cargo system. Such practices are reported for the Sierra Juárez prior to 1917 (Young 1976:159), for Juquila, Oaxaca (Greenberg 1981:66–67), for highland Guatemala (Brintnall 1979:94–99), and elsewhere in Mexico. According to some women, older women and *mayordomas* had a great deal of influence on this group of elders.

Until recently, age was a dominant factor in structuring the power relationships of local politics. Men entered the civil cargo system at a young age as helpers and slowly worked their way up to the highest positions in the system. It probably took at least twenty to twenty-five years to work through the hierarchy. Most senior officials were in their fifties or sixties and had slowly worked their way up the cargo hierarchy. Respect and prestige were closely tied to age, which in turn determined what level an individual and household were at within the cargo system. The cargo career of an elderly male who was sixty in 1985 illustrates the movement of males up the ladder of civil and religious hierarchies, moving between the two systems. This individual has continued to move between the two hierarchies, having recently taken on a large *mayordomía*. This pattern is not followed by younger men in as strict a fashion. During the twentieth century, the basis for local political power changed considerably due to structural changes imposed by the national government and changes in local cultural values related to wealth (see Stephen 1990a; Young 1976).

The religious pantheon of saints, virgins, and specific crosses in the church of Teotitlán is some twenty-one strong, with specific *mayordomías* linked to most of them in the past. Saints, virgins, and crosses in the local pantheon are shown in figure 4 with the dates of their celebration. Elderly informants remembered nineteen saints and virgins that had *mayordomos* as of 1929. These are noted with an asterisk. Under the past *mayordomía* system, each saint was cared for by at least one and often two sets of *mayordomos*. Each male-female pair of *mayordomos*, usually but not always husband and wife, organize and carry out rituals and festivities associated with the saint or virgin in their charge. The importance of the particular *mayordomía* is determined by how much money is spent on the celebration.

The *mayordomías* of Teotitlán are ranked in a hierarchy. During the 1960s, according to elderly informants, the top-ranked and still active *mayordomías* included, in order of importance, Preciosa Sangre, Escipúlas, Guadalupe, Natividad, Trinidad, San Juan, and Santísima Cruz. In the past, households began with a relatively small *mayordomía* as their initial ritual expenditure. They then would try to work up to one of the more expensive ones. In order to cut back on expenses, pairs of *mayordomos* (i.e., two male/female couples) took up sponsorship of most of the celebrations. Informants remembered the pairing system going back to before the Revolution.

The importance of both male and female contributions in the *mayordomía* system is still described today in Teotitlán by older men and women who have worked their way through two or three *mayordomías*. The system includes a fairly extensive group of offices, each of which has male and female aspects. The ritual party of the *mayordomos* includes five to six *diputados* (former high-ranking *mayordomos*) and their wives, an *escribano* (scribe) and his wife, and a couple called *biscochos*, a male-female pair who always accompany the *mayordomos*. Males and females in each pair of offices have specific functions. Those of men usually pertain to the church-related functions of the *mayordomía*, while those of women are related to planning, organizing, preparing food, and supervising activities based in the household of the *mayordomos*.

While most elderly people emphasized the equal importance of men's and women's work, some women gave greater emphasis to the

Figure 4. Pantheon of Saints, Virgins, and Crosses of Teotitlán

January 15	Escipúlas*
February 2	Candelaria*
March 19	San José*
May 3	Santísima Cruz (on Sacred *xiabets* Mountain)*
40 days after the end of Lent	Asunción
May (date changes)	Espíritu Santo
8 days after Espíritu Santo .	La Trinidad*
....	Corpus Cristi (Dadvid Jesús)*
June 24	San Juan*
June 29	San Pedro*
July 1	Preciosa Sangre*
July 16	La Santa Cruz*
July 22	Magdalena*
August 4	Santo Domingo*
August 10	San Jacinto
September 8	Natividad*
September 14	Exaltación de la Santísima Cruz*
First Sunday in October ...	Rosario*
December 2	Guadalupe*
December 18	La Soledad*
No dates remembered	San Nicolás*
	Virgen de Dolores*

female component. "Sure you need both men and women, but the work of the women is more important. The men kill chickens and hang them up, but the women always work more. They work during the fiestas of the *mayordomía* and beforehand. They make chocolate, prepare a lot of spices, and spend weeks getting ready. If there were no women there wouldn't be any *mayordomías*. Sure the men work, but not as much" (Juana, age 35). "The work of the men was important, but it was always the women who worked harder. The men would get drunk and then they couldn't do anything" (Carmen, age 62). As in other types of ceremonial occasions, both in the past and in the present, women have performed a majority of the labor necessary to carry out three to five days of communal meals and dancing. The gendered division of labor and the sequence of events in *mayordomías* is similar to those currently seen in life-cycle events described in the following chapter.

For women who have been *mayordomas*, their sponsorship involved not only work, but an important change in their status in the community. This is reflected linguistically in the terms used to address both men and women who have been *mayordomos*. Having completed a major *mayordomía*, men are called *dad*, translated as an honorific "sir," and women are called *nãn*, an honorific "ma'am." Male saints are also referred to as *dad* in Zapotec and virgins as *nãn*. Completion of *mayordomía* sponsorship gives men and women a linguistic association with the holy entities of the community, the saints and virgins in the church. "Since I have been a *mayordoma* everyone respects me. They admire me now. All of them say *ščãŋ* to me now and they call me *nãn* Lucía.[3] They never used to" (Lucía, age 55). Like the saints and virgins, *mayordomos* are also viewed as watching out for the welfare of the community. They may literally intercede for the community by praying to the gods (saints and virgins) for rain or asking for the end of disease. The only people other than *mayordomos* who are called *dad* and *nãn* are the elderly, *bɛngul*, who are deemed to have given a lifetime of service to the community. "If you see someone who is under sixty years of age and they are called *nãn* or *dad*, then it is because they were a *mayordomo*. The only way to be called this as a person who is not old is to sponsor a saint. Otherwise, you have to wait until you are old to be respected. And rich people and poor people make the expenditures to be *mayordomos*. So it is possible for rich or poor people to have these titles either by being a *mayordomo* or by waiting until they are very old" (Antonio, age 70).

The terms *dad* and *nãn* are strongly associated with respect granted to *mayordomos*, *mayordomas*, and elderly people. Accord-

Here a male *mayordomo* lights candles for Nuestro Señor de la Preciosa Sangre on the main altar of this saint in the local church.

ing to informants, the amount of *respet* depends on the size and quantity of expenses involved in the cult celebration. All but the two largest *mayordomías*, that of Nuestro Señor de la Preciosa Sangre, celebrated in July, and that of Escipúlas, celebrated in January, have been phased out. The smallest *mayordomías* were medium-sized feasts lasting three days with fifteen to twenty-five couples in attendance. The most extravagant *mayordomía* in Teotitlán, dedicated to Nuestro Señor de la Preciosa Sangre, involves three major expenditures and smaller monthly fiestas. At the largest celebrations in July, more than 200 invited guests attend and a cow, twenty-five to thirty pigs, and hundreds of chickens and turkeys are consumed, along with large quantities of liquor. This *mayordomía* was celebrated in 1989, but had no new sponsors for 1990.

In addition to sponsoring several large fiestas, *mayordomos* also pay for masses and take care of their saint's altars. This involves providing oil for lamps constantly burned, changing the flowers, and repairing the altar and the saint's clothing. Larger altars involve the purchase of twelve dozen gladiolas per week as well as considerable amounts of oil, adding to the financial burden of the *mayordomos*.

Caring for the altars usually involves four to five hours per weekend working in the church.

The sponsorship of major *mayordomías* often requires all of a household's labor for at least a year. Many years of financial sacrifice are also necessary to pay for the high level of ritual consumption maintained throughout the period of celebration. The last *mayordomía* celebrated in Teotitlán in 1988 and 1989 is estimated to have cost at least 60 million pesos or US$24,000. Costs included four large fiestas as well as smaller fiestas every month.[4]

Reciprocal labor exchanges or *xɛlgɛz šte majɪ̃dõ* are the backbone of the *mayordomía* system. Work parties to gather firewood and to prepare candles and decorations precede the extravagant celebrations. Reciprocal labor exchanges based on invited guests donating their labor make the celebrations function on their specified days. Genealogical and fictive kinship ties through the system of *compadrazgo* provide the network of people drawn together to perform the labor for *mayordomías*. In addition to reciprocal labor, year-long contracts were also made with two butchers, a family of candle makers, and at least one twenty-piece band.

In a survey done of a random stratified sample of 154 households in 1986, only about 20 percent of the households in Teotitlán had sponsored one *mayordomía*. About 7 percent had sponsored two or more. As related by some people, before the 1970s, a couple might try to sponsor two or three *mayordomías* in their lifetime. For example, in 1985, the holder of the highest ritual post in the community (*fiscal*) described his *mayordomía* career as follows: "We were *mayordomos* twice before I was made *fiscal*. The first time was in 1939. We were *mayordomos* of the Santísima Cruz. Then in 1949 we were *mayordomos* for the Santísima Trinidad. We had a lot of *guelaguetza* for each one. We had a list of things we had left with people, but someone else had to write it for us. There were about seventy people at each celebration. We had music, and danced, and burned a firework castle. We spent a lot of time and money on those *mayordomías*" (Jovenal, age 78). His wife continued the discussion of their past sponsorship: "We both thought about doing this at the same time. We really didn't have to discuss it much. We decided four years ahead of time what we would do. Jovenal went to the church to visit the Santísima Cruz and made a *promesa* for both of us that we would hold the *mayordomía*. Then we knew that we had to get ready for it" (Luisa, age 75).

While Jovenal and Luisa did not remember sponsoring their *mayordomía* out of a particular motivation, many other *mayordomos* described making a promise to hold a cult celebration in relation to a major illness or family disaster. In some cases, households combined pilgrimages with *mayordomías,* in the case of Escipúlas, where sponsors would often travel to Escipúlas, Guatemala, on foot and by burro before holding the *mayordomía* ritual in Teotitlán. Cults of local saints and virgins in Teotitlán also drew people from other communities and ethnic groups who would come to share in the miraculous power of a saint, particularly Nuestro Señor de la Preciosa Sangre.

In discussing the significance of *mayordomías,* Teotitecos continually focus on the concept of *respet,* which they identify with authority within their community. Until recently, this was the primary criterion for community leadership extended to both men and women. This slowly began to change with a government effort to eliminate *mayordomías* and to secularize local political systems beginning in the late 1920s. In Teotitlán, the government effort to eliminate *mayordomías* under Calles coincided with local dissatisfaction concerning obligatory *mayordomías.* People in the community did not want to eliminate the *mayordomías* entirely, but wanted to participate freely and not be forced to take on sponsorship. The efforts of the state, however, in conjunction with a local move to democratize participation in the *mayordomía* system, are believed by many people to have led to its eventual downfall. Both factors are important in understanding the current basis of political authority and the way in which it affects women's perceptions of themselves as political actors and their strategies for political action.

The End of Obligatory *Mayordomías* and the State's Campaign to Separate Ritual from Political Authority

Until 1931, community ritual activities in Teotitlán were organized by a group of *mayordomos* who were appointed, often against their will, by local elders. By the mid-1920s, *mayordomía a la fuerza* (obligatory *mayordomías*) had become an extremely volatile issue. Many Teotitecos believe that *mayordomía a la fuerza,* begun sometime in the late 1800s, was continued after the Revolution because of continued poor economic conditions. The economic result of obligatory *mayordomías* was a system of indentured labor and landgrabbing by a small group of wealthy merchants.

While this obligatory system was clearly undesirable to Teotitecos, the concept of ritual authority stemming from *mayordomías* was supported because it invested people who had ritually served the community with political authority. Such a system of authority also

gave the community autonomy in choosing its own leaders. Teotitecos opposed only the obligatory nature of sponsorship.

Throughout the 1800s and early 1900s, the presence of *mayordomía* offices and the political authority that stemmed from them
remained outside state control. While the civil offices of the hierarchy were tied to the state through functions such as census taking,
tax collection, and negotiations for funds and resources, the religious offices in the hierarchy remained exclusively under community control. Shortly after the Revolution, however, the autonomy of
local religious administration was challenged by state intervention.
For postrevolutionary state officials, ritual sponsorship that translated into political authority and leadership outside of official administrative structures could only be controlled by eliminating ritual sponsorship and bringing all aspects of religious leadership under
state control.

The 1917 Mexican constitution, which was actively interpreted
under the Calles regime, sought to place all local political offices
under control of state laws and strictly to regulate how local churches
were run. As part of a general campaign to loosen the ideological
control of the church over Mexican citizens, the Calles government
launched an all-out attack against the Catholic church. Strict appli-
cation of several anticlerical articles was part of this campaign. The
enforcement of these articles and additional government decrees ob-
ligating communities to organize secular *juntas vecinales* (neighborhood committees) placed community ritual activity directly under
state power in 1926 (see Stephen 1990a for a detailed description).

In 1926, Calles sent out a decree mandating that municipalities
organize *juntas vecinales* as part of the new municipal structure to
oversee church activities. This action set up an alternate administrative structure that took over many of the duties carried out by
mayordomos. Throughout the late 1920s, Teotitecos refused to
name people to the committee; the local archive contains several
exchanges in which officials from the governor's office complain
that Teotiteco authorities have yet to name the members of their
junta vecinal (Archivo Municipal de Teotitlán del Valle 1927, 1928).
By the early 1930s, the *junta vecinal* was formally constituted and
became a branch of the local civil cargo system. Now called the
comité de la iglesia, it still manages the church and also organizes
major celebrations for community saints that no longer have *mayordomos*. Its structure is shown in figure 5.

At the top of the hierarchy are the *fiscales*, positions reserved for
men who have worked their way to the top of the religious cargo sys-

Figure 5. Structure of the Comité de la Iglesia

Fiscal 1 Fiscal 2

Presidente

Vicepresidente

Secretario

Tesorero

Vocal 1 Vocal 2 Vocal 3 Vocal 4 Vocal 5

Vocal 6 Vocal 7 Vocal 8 Vocal 9

Šudao 1 Šudao 2 Šudao 3 Šudao 4 Šudao 5

Padre del pueblo 1 Padre del pueblo 2 Padre del pueblo 3 Padre del pueblo 4 Padre del pueblo 5

Sacristano 1 Sacristano 2 Sacristano 3 Sacristano 4 Sacristano 5

Acólito 1 Acólito 2 Acólito 3 Acólito 4 Acólito 5

tem. It is the last position taken before retirement and is primarily one of respect, largely ceremonial in nature. The working cargos of the church include a president, vice-president, secretary, treasurer, and nine *vocales* (committee members). There are also five sacristans, five acolytes, five bearers of religious symbols called *šudao* (who have no Spanish name), and five men who are in charge of lighting fireworks called *padres del pueblo* (town fathers). The positions of sacristan and acolyte are voluntary, often filled by people who want to avoid other cargo services or by young men who are taking the place of their fathers in the cargo system.

Attached to the religious branch of the cargo system is the *cofradía de la santa patrona*, a group headed by a treasurer that is responsible for maintaining lands that belong to the patron virgin of Teotitlán. Corn raised on the land is sold and the money used to maintain the virgin and to pay for religious festivities in her honor. The lands for maintaining the virgin were set aside in 1914. Since then the committee has served to administer the lands. The lands existed previously as communal lands located behind the church (Archivo Municipal de Teotitlán del Valle 1914).

The creation of the *juntas vecinales* was not directly designed to eliminate *mayordomías,* but it was combined with a very strong political strategy on the part of several Oaxaca governors to phase them out. Correspondence from the *Periódico Oficial,* my fieldwork in Teotitlán, and Young's (1976) research among the Sierra Zapotecs all point to a coordinated effort on the part of Oaxaca governors and their associates to discourage and undercut *mayordomos,* often in the name of moral and economic modernity (see Stephen 1990b). For example, in accordance with the party line of the Partido Socialista, precursor to the PRI, officials from San Juan Teitipac wrote to Governor Genaro Vásquez to ask his help in eliminating *mayordomías.* He responded: "I see with satisfaction the proposition that you have to rectify the customs in our towns that produce ruin or stagnancy of the moral and economic patrimony of the community" (Archivo General del Estado 1926b: 27–28; my translation).[5]

The breaking down of *mayordomía* systems and the eventual disengagement of religious hierarchies from civil ones did result in a considerable realignment of local power relations. In Teotitlán this was a slow process that began in the 1920s and was pushed further in the 1960s and 1970s with the commercialization of the weaving industry. In the late 1920s, the outcome of the anti-*mayordomía* campaign in Teotitlán was different than it was in other communities because the economy of the *mayordomía* system was heavily tied into local debt peonage.

The larger political economy of forced *mayordomías* in Teotitlán until 1931 did little to redistribute wealth, but seems to have justified or perhaps even increased economic differentiation. The redistribution of food and entertainment that took place on the part of sponsoring households during actual *mayordomías* appears to have been far outweighed by the heavy sacrifices made by poor households who had to sponsor large celebrations despite their pitiful economic circumstances. By the 1920s, economic resources were scarce in the community and people faced certain economic hardship when they were forced to make the expenditures associated with sponsorship of a local saint. Because of their unwillingness to accept sponsorships that they could not afford, many men were thrown in jail until they accepted. "I remember when we were named to a *mayordomía*. We were working and the *topiles* [police] came to get my husband. They took him to jail and then wouldn't let him out until we accepted. Then we went to the church to accept our *mayordomía*. My husband went to Tlacolula to protest this" (Rosa, age 89).[6]

The acute poverty of the community during this period made it necessary for many *mayordomos* to sell or pawn their lands and houses to local merchants in order to pay for their ritual expenses.

> People had to sell their land and their houses to the merchants. Pels Molín, Manuel Bautista, Lorenzo Martínez, *dad* Mon, all of these people got a lot of land because people borrowed money from them. People would sell their land to these merchants for very little—80 or 100 pesos. The rich merchants took advantage of people selling their land. When people were in jail to receive their *mayordomía*, their family and friends would come and visit them and offer them a little *guelaguetza* so that they could pay for their expenses. The poor people who had to be *mayordomos*. They had to sell their lands to the rich in order to fulfill their obligations. (Pedro, age 75)

If they did not have land or houses to sell, they would borrow money from merchants or other wealthy families and pay off the debt by indenturing their own and their children's labor for many years. "Before they got rid of forced *mayordomía*, people sold their houses, their land, their oxen, their children, and themselves to work for a few rich people. A lot of people had to pawn their land for money. Some people got a lot of land this way" (Luis, age 65). The *mayordomía* system guaranteed a stable and cheap source of labor for merchants as long as members of the impoverished majority in Teotitlán were forced to participate in the sponsorship system. By the late 1920s, the forced poverty stemming from obligatory *mayordomías* had become a major political issue in the community, pitting merchants and community elders who had already sacrificed and sponsored *mayordomías* against younger people who were candidates for future sponsorship.

In 1926, the Partido Socialista of Oaxaca, which in 1929 became a part of the Partido Nacional Revolucionario (PNR, precursor to the PRI), formed a local branch in Teotitlán. In 1929, the PNR urged all people in Teotitlán to free themselves from the oppression of church control and called for an end to *mayordomías*. This demand was in line with state policies (the PNR was the state party) to undercut local political autonomy and eliminate all institutions that remained outside the state's sphere of influence. While the PNR itself never gained a wide base of support in Teotitlán, the demand to end obligatory *mayordomías* did.

After 1928, many couples appointed as *mayordomos* by community elders refused to carry out their sponsorship duties. Some were held in jail for their refusals. This local *mayordomía* strike continued until 1931, when the municipal president declared the end of obligatory *mayordomía* appointments. Community elders and local merchant families protested, but they were overruled by the majority of the community (Stephen 1990a).

The end of obligatory *mayordomías* did not by any means spell the end of cult celebrations for the saints. Most *mayordomías* had sponsors until the 1960s, when they began to decline in number and frequency of celebration. Teotitlán continued to resist government efforts to eliminate *mayordomías*, maintaining voluntary celebrations. The nature of the community's reworking of Oaxaca state policy designed to limit local political autonomy following the Revolution is important for understanding contemporary community-state interaction (see Parnell 1988 for a comparative discussion). As a historical backdrop to the evolving nature of political authority in the community from the 1930s to the present, it is also critical information in understanding the participation of contemporary Teotiteco women in community political affairs.

Conclusions: The Struggle for Local Autonomy and Teotiteco Women

The eventual uncoupling of the civil and religious cargo systems in Teotitlán is a microillustration of the historical dynamics of state-local interaction and both the structural obstacles and human efforts involved in maintaining local autonomy. In Teotitlán, state efforts to undermine community control of ritual/political institutions created unintended consequences when operating in conjunction with local dissatisfaction with forced *mayordomía* sponsorship. While Teotitecos wanted to escape from the yoke of forced sponsorship, they did not want to give up control of their political institutions to the state. In spite of the efforts of state officials to wipe out *mayordomías* entirely, they continued to thrive in Teotitlán on a voluntary basis until well into the 1960s. However, structural changes in the ways in which local government was formed and the state's effort formally to separate ritual and political power probably slowly began to influence conceptions of community authority and respect in Teotitlán. As described in the following chapter, the eventual transfer of *mayordomía* content to life-cycle rituals temporarily insulated a significant part of the community's ritual life from direct outside interference by the state. While this certainly provided a measure of protection for the intimate ritual life of the community, it also distanced ritual activity from political life. For women, this was an important factor in shaping how they seek to influence community politics and to realize their own agendas.

When women participated equally with men in *mayordomía* activities that sanctified community leadership and directly linked ritual *respet* to political authority, their association with the guardian virgins of the community was widely acknowledged and validated.[7] While women still receive respect and titles for their participation in life-cycle ceremonies, the focus of such ritual events is no longer on a symbolic entity (saint or virgin) that represents the community. Women's earlier association with the holy symbolic entities of the community was a direct vehicle for authority that also translated into influence on the policy making of local elders.

At a larger level, as the Mexican state modernized and centralized under Lázaro Cárdenas in the 1930s, the role of women was paid lip service, but never taken particularly seriously. After 1917, when *municipio* authorities were supposed to be elected, women did not have the right to vote. They were unable to do so in most states until 1944. Feminist debates until the 1940s revolved around women's ability to vote and to hold elective office (Partido Feminista Revolucionario de Tabasco 1933; Primero Congreso Feminista de Yucatán 1917). However, even after women were formally given the right to vote and could legally hold public office at the *municipio* level or higher, local tradition limited attendance at community meetings to men in many parts of Mexico.

Within communities like Teotitlán, the existence of fairly complete *mayordomía* systems until the 1960s and the ritually based

BROADWAY
RENTALS LTD

① - 0 —

② - 960-5600   Sharon
                      Pasley.

③ - Jean 561-5442
         Able + Enison

④ Lary Wood 2120

         604 ~~833~~ 9979
              563-

TELEPHONE
392-2662
84 BROADWAY NORTH
WILLIAMS LAKE, B.C. V2G 1C1

authority systems that went with them were indirect mechanisms of establishing independence from the long arm of the postrevolutionary Mexican state. After the 1960s and the decline of *mayordomías*, this process continued indirectly through women who use ritual-based authority and respect as a way of claiming legitimacy as political actors in the community. With commercialization of the weaving industry in Teotitlán, however, other criteria for *respet* and political authority associated with wealth and class position have emerged. As this happened, those women who were most marginalized from the political system continued to use respect as a way of asserting their opinions. As we shall see in chapter 9, the consolidation of class relations under commercial capitalism contradicted the community solidarity expressed in ritual. A new route to respect through wealth assured that community authority was no longer equally available to all simply based on age, community service, and ritual sponsorship.

Chapter 8. Fiesta: The Contemporary Dynamics of Women's Ritual Participation

I was married in 1936. It was a very small fiesta called śa(ᴾa)-ter(t)śil [fiesta only in the morning]. It lasted only one day. About sixteen people came. We had one meal and I got a trunk, a metate, and some blouses. There was no music. Back then, only a few very rich people got married śa(ᴾa)júil(i) [with music], like when they are mayordomos. (Julia, age 70)

I was married in 1953. My husband's mother paid for the ceremony. She actually didn't have to pay much money because she had inherited her mother's guelaguetzas. She was able to call in a lot of things that people owed her mother—turkeys, corn, and cacao. She used these in the wedding. She could do this even though her mother was already dead. There were about fifty people at the wedding. We killed one pig and about twenty turkeys. I think the party went on for one or two days. There was no music and no dancing. The presents I got included a trunk, two metates, and about five or six blouses. . . . In 1968, my oldest daughter got married. It was a big party. There were about eighty couples invited and there was a band and dancing. She got two trunks, a dresser, and about eighteen different metates and some dishes. She got a lot more than I did. . . . My son was married in 1978. By then everyone had big weddings, not just the rich. There were 160 people at that wedding. There was music for two days and they killed three pigs. The bride got a trunk, a dresser, a glass case for her dishes, and lots of dishes. It was a big wedding. (María, age 52)

THESE TWO women's discussions of their own and their children's weddings document the change in Teotitlán from a ritual life focused on *mayordomías* to one centered on elaborate life-cycle rituals such as weddings, baptisms, asking a woman's hand in marriage, birthdays, and funerals. In this change, the form and content of *mayordomía* rituals that were found only occasionally in the weddings of the rich were transferred and adopted by most of the population as part of various life-cycle ceremonies. This pattern is seen in neighboring communities as well.

In Teotitlán, the reinforcement of life-cycle rituals with the form and content of the fading *mayordomía* system is part of a self-generated local Zapotec identity. The major roles that women play in ritual are valued within the community as part of this identity. When women's ritual roles and status are viewed in a larger political and economic context, however, the ritual authority of women appears to be ridden with contradictions in terms of class differences between women within the community and the limited political participation of all women within the community. Here the dynamics of class differences between merchant and weaver women are explored in the context of ritual. The interactions of women in ritual events often reflect a conflict between community solidarity and the divisions created between women by the economic inequalities of merchants and weavers. While, culturally, ritual respect status is still open to all who can achieve it, the economic realities of the labor and financial costs of fiesta sponsorship may make it easier for merchant women to achieve such status than for weaver women.

Ritual Representation of Ethnicity: Being Zapotec for Tourists and Being Zapotec for Teotitecos

As discussed in chapter 2, the construction of Teotiteco ethnicity involves different dimensions that are invoked according to particular situations. One of the strongest influences on how local ethnicity is represented is whether or not the context involves people from outside the community, particularly nonindigenous individuals who are not from surrounding Zapotec communities. The varying representations of Teotitlán local identity are also reflected in differences in local ritual activity. One level of ritual involves the maintenance of some ceremonies open to tourists and outsiders, including Zapotecs from surrounding communities. The other involves a series of life-cycle rituals and a limited number of closed religious fiestas that activate reciprocal labor and goods exchanges. The significant role of women in the ongoing construction of local Teotiteco identity is concentrated at the second tier of ritual activity, where the most intensive ceremonial life of the community is now focused. Ritually based respect, which women still pursue as a path to community authority, is also concentrated here in the face of a decline in *mayor-domías.*

The first level of ritual activity, the maintenance of saint-related ceremonies open to tourists and outsiders, has largely been taken over by men as an extension of the state-ordained *comité de la iglesia* (church committee), originally called the *junta vecinal.* The days of the community ritual calendar originally attached to *mayor-domías* are still celebrated in Teotitlán today, but, instead of being financed and organized primarily by the men and women who served as *mayordomos,* most celebrations are run on a small scale by the church committee. They are paid for collectively by tithing each household in the community for a small amount of money.

While many former *mayordomía*-sponsored rituals are still celebrated in the community, they are structured in a way that makes them available for outside nonindigenous consumption as well. Before, when saints' days were celebrated as *mayordomías,* the primary activities took place in the *mayordomos'* home, with a large final dance open to all in the community. This culminating activity took place late at night when few outsiders were likely to be present. According to elderly informants, very few tourists were ever present at these final dances because there was no place for them to stay overnight in the community. Even today, most leave at sunset. Thus most of the ritual activity for *mayordomías* took place within the space of the sponsor's compound with the exception of the final dance.

Beginning in the 1960s in Oaxaca and throughout Mexico, the state promoted indigenous ritual life as a major tourist attraction in conjunction with craft production.[1] In a sense, Teotitecos have facilitated, on their own terms, the state's promotion of Indian cultures by turning several local celebrations into performances. In Teotitlán, the celebrations for saints' days, which were formerly *mayordo-mías,* are now largely conducted in the public plaza. They take place in the same community space as celebrations of national holidays such as Mexican Independence Day, Mother's Day, and the Day of the Revolution. Both saints' day celebrations and secular ceremonies reflect a fusion of national culture and politics with local ritual tradition. While secular holidays draw a significant number of people, they are run by school officials in conjunction with local municipal officials. Regional dances, poems, and choral readings are performed by Teotitlán schoolchildren in Spanish. Local saints' day celebrations are still run by Teotitlán officials, but are now often attended by non-Zapotec outsiders as well as people from neighboring Zapotec communities, particularly during Holy Week and during the main fiesta of the community in July. The major attractions at these ritual events are performances by the local dance troupe, which acts out an unusual version of the conquest story.

By facilitating the celebration of national holidays in community space and permitting tourists and non-Zapotec outsiders to attend the celebration of saints' days, Teotitecos have given up local control over part of their ritual sphere. In doing so they have succumbed to pressure to create indigenous ritual for tourists and outside consumption and to accept the dissemination of national culture through local schools. "People come from all over to see our *danzantes*. They know that in Teotitlán we have the best dancers. During the day you can see lots of tourists here watching. For us, we can only go late in the afternoon for a little while after our chores are finished. We don't have time to go to watch. We are too busy working. We like to go to watch the end of the dance and visit the church" (Luisa, age 35). While such ritual may reflect several elements of Indianness encouraged by the state, Teotitecos have nonetheless participated in its formulation and dissemination. In this way, they have consciously added a dimension to their local Zapotec identity other than weaving production that is available for widespread consumption.

The majority of meaningful ritual content and form in Teotitlán, however, does not appear in rituals carried out in the town square. It has been transferred from *mayordomías* to life-cycle rituals carried out in household compounds, an area not readily accessible to tourists, but open to the community. As *mayordomías* were slowly abandoned, the ritual content, forms, and consumption associated with them (drinking, huge feasts, dancing, ornate decorations) were gradually transferred to rituals focused on the developmental cycle—with weddings taking on many of the characteristics and high levels of consumption formerly associated with *mayordomías*. Thus the meaningful content of *mayordomías* was transferred almost completely intact to formerly simple life-cycle celebrations, with the exception of an extravagant form of wedding ceremony, *sa(Pa)xúil(i)*, which was always celebrated by a few wealthy households. By incorporating the core ritual form and content of *mayordomías* into other rituals, the community transformed individual life-cycle rituals into semipublic celebrations that pull together large networks of kin, *compadres*, and neighbors.

Many life-cycle ceremonies have become larger and larger over the last twenty years. Teotitecos pride themselves on their high levels of ritual consumption and readily admit that occasions such as weddings have turned into contests of one-upmanship.

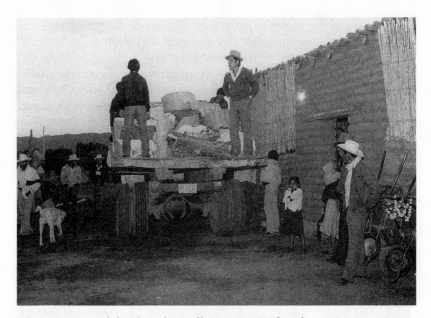

The amount of food and candles given at local engagement ceremonies is now so great that the gifts have to be transported on a flatbed truck from the house of the prospective groom to the house of his future bride.

> Even those young people who go to the United States always return. Even if a young man meets a young woman from another community they also return here to follow the custom of the wedding. If people don't follow the custom of a big wedding, others will talk about them, saying bad things—that they don't have any money. Because of what others say, people always try to carry on with the custom. People especially don't want others to think that they are poor so they will always have a big fiesta. The weddings used to be smaller, but now people spend a lot of money. They practically have a competition to see who can have the biggest one. (Octavio, age 52)

While some younger sectors of the community, particularly merchants, say they want to stop spending so much time and money on fiestas, they acknowledge that social pressure to maintain *costumbre* (custom) is very strong.

The household compound, which was also the location of most *mayordomía* rituals and is currently where life-cycle ceremonies are carried out, becomes a public space during a ritual event. While it is not public in the same sense as the market in that anyone can walk in, by bringing together a large kin-*compadrazgo* network of *invitados* (invited blood and ritual kin), the household compound becomes a focal point for a large cross-section of the community physically assembled in the same space for days on end. The group contains both weavers and merchants and brings them together in ritual relationships that reshuffle some of the inequities implied in the relations of production. Their physical presence transforms the household compound into a semipublic ritual arena while ceremonial activities are taking place. For people within the community, the household plot now provides a secure space for public ritual, temporarily protected from the presence of noncommunity members.

The Gendered Division of Labor in Life-Cycle Ceremonies

A careful look at current secular and religious events performed for community and tourist consumption in Teotitlán provides a clue to the importance of gender in the intense ritual life hidden behind the walls of individual household plots. All ritual space, whether in a home or in the town square, is divided into a male sphere and a female sphere. In the main square, married couples arrive together to view an event, but quickly split up, with the woman going to the female section and the male going to the male section.[2] Teotitecos can spot outsiders instantly, not only by how they look, but by where they stand. Many tourists and government officials inadvertently stand in the section of the opposite sex when observing ceremonial events in the main square. For Teotitecos, spatial separation by gender is a prerequisite to the creation of ritual space. This structural requirement is vividly seen in life-cycle rituals.

While many people in Teotitlán may passively observe ritual events open to outsiders, all of the community participates more actively in rituals associated with the developmental cycle of the household. Active participation of all community members in life-cycle rituals gives these rituals more importance and value than saints' day rituals, which are no longer attached to *mayordomías*. Attendance at community activities associated with saints' day rituals is optional and people are often too busy to go. An invitation to a life-cycle ritual, however, cannot be turned down. Even men and women from merchant households who try to downplay their participation in *costumbres* (i.e., fiestas) emphasize how hard it is to get out of invitations to life-cycle events. As explained by Angela, a middle-aged merchant woman:

We don't participate in many customs, but when someone asks you to go to a fiesta you can't turn them down. When someone sends a *huehuete* [ritual practitioner] to invite you, you have to go. It isn't a law written down, but you have to go. If you don't go, then people will disown you. Rumors would start to be spread about how you thought you were so important that you didn't need anyone. You know, sometimes my husband doesn't have time to go, but I have to. I am obligated to go and help. If I didn't go, I would lose a lot of friends and respect here.

Invitations imply a major time commitment. All life-cycle rituals share a similar structure, with the formal part of the celebration lasting for three days and the preparation and cleanup going on for periods up to one month.

Biological, affinal, and ritual *compadrazgo* kin perform most of the labor necessary to carry off a successful fiesta.[3] Without the labor pool available through extended family and ritual kinship networks, it would be impossible for any household to perform all of the activities necessary for sponsoring a successful fiesta.

Work groups for life-cycle rituals, like *mayordomías*, are completely segregated by gender. After men and women arrive together and offer a formal greeting to the heads of the household they are visiting, each retires to his or her separate sphere. Women make fun of men who violate the gender segregation. For example, at a wedding, two men came into the kitchen supposedly to help by carrying out a carton of beer. They were taking a long time and had overstayed their time in the women's kitchen. They were also quite drunk. The women were very open about making fun of them. "What are you two drunk chickens doing in here? You can't even walk yourselves. How can you carry that carton? You will fall over. Look at them, like babies who can't walk. They are so drunk, who could they help? Go back with the men where you belong."

Within the segregation by gender, activities are organized by age. In general, four significant age divisions are designated by Teotitecos for men and women. Outside these categories are children between the ages of seven and twelve, who also work. Categories for adults and near-adults include older teenagers (14–20) who are single and those who have recently begun to live as part of a conjugal couple (they may have small children); young people (21–35) who have young children (1–10) and whose families are growing; middle-aged people (36–60) whose children are of marriageable age; and elderly people whose children are married (60+). This includes widows and widowers.

Due to recent technological improvements such as running water and the availability of trucks, the physical labor required of men during ritual events has greatly diminished. Their primary tasks are procuring and chopping firewood, cleaning up the yard, setting up shaded work areas, hauling water, and butchering animals. The household head and his older male relatives act as bosses in these tasks, directing the other men. Those men who have already sponsored large fiestas are seen as experts and asked for advice on how to do the work. Younger men and older teenagers do the bulk of the physical labor.

Firewood is secured in a separate work party that takes place about thirty days before the main fiesta. A *guelaguetza* group is assembled by the head male of the sponsoring household. The head female organizes a parallel work party of women to feed the men. Such labor is not actually written down, but is clearly remembered by everyone involved. "We don't write it down when we go for firewood, but we remember. For example, if I already went to get firewood for someone I can ask them to help me with the harvest. They will remember that I helped them and they won't charge me for the work I ask them to do in my harvest. Usually the people who help one another the most are families or *compadres*" (Eduardo, age 30). "The same is true for women who come to make tortillas while the men gather the wood. The women who come to work during a fiesta don't get paid for their work. They are trading labor for the future" (Matilda, age 32). The men borrow or rent a truck and return with a cargo of wood sufficient to last for the entire fiesta. They do not have to work again until a few days before the fiesta.

Prefiesta male work centers around preparing the house and yard for upcoming activities. A large patio space has to be cleared and shaded areas constructed for women making tortillas and cooking. Once the activities begin, five to six men are directed by the women to haul water and firewood as it is needed. They also haul and transport anything that needs to be moved as the ritual progresses. When butchering takes place, they assist the butcher and cut the meat into large chunks. Once this work is finished, they can relax. Overall, about thirty men make active labor contributions during the course of a fiesta.

The majority of men who attend a fiesta as invited guests spend their time drinking and talking. This is not true of women. They often arrive earlier than men and spend the entire day working. They do not begin drinking until late in the afternoon or until the last day of the fiesta. While five to ten women work from five to ten days in advance preparing for a fiesta, on the actual days when ritual activities occur and meals are prepared there may be as many as two hundred women working together.

Women have mixed feelings about going to fiestas. Most of them associate it with very hard physical work and clearly state that they go to help because someday they will need other women to help them. "I only like to go to fiestas because it means the people will come here and help me. It is a lot of work to be a woman in a fiesta. If it is a close friend or *compadre* who is having the fiesta then you have to arrive really early, like at four or five in the morning. And you don't get to leave until one o'clock in the morning" (Lucía, age 28).

> Women don't really like to go to fiestas that much because it is a lot of work. *Tejate* is the worst. Tortillas are bad because of the heat. Making them makes my arms hurt and my knees sore. . . . Most people feel this way. Maybe people like my mother don't mind so much because they are older and don't have to work so hard. My mother doesn't have to do the heavy work like making *tejate* and tortillas. It is those of us who are still young who have to do all of the hard work. . . . I think that the men enjoy going to fiestas more because they only work a little bit. The men respect our work and say that we work hard. They know that the food is the most important thing about a fiesta and we do that. Therefore our work is most important, but it is hard. (Cristina, age 40)

This large female work force is organized into groups by age. Each age group has a specific task. For example, the youngest women (both married and unmarried) work grinding corn and cacao together for *tejate*. This is the hardest physical labor performed, often lasting six to eight hours. Other younger and some middle-aged women work in teams of three to four making tortillas. Older middle-aged women prepare the main ingredients—chopping meat, peeling garlic, toasting chiles, and so forth. The female head of the household and her oldest and closest relatives direct the work process.

The oldest women are in charge of cooking huge pots of food and mixing ingredients in the proper amounts and order. They are in turn advised by the hostess and her oldest relatives. Before the meat is cut up, all of the older women (*nãn*) who have achieved distinction through giving a large fiesta in their own homes are invited by the hostess to bless the meat. This invitation is a way of acknowledging an older woman's status and paying her respect.

Older women's control of the food is an important indication of

Working in teams, young women work ten to fourteen hours per day making tortillas when they are invited to local fiestas. This is *guelaguetza* labor.

their authority in ritual events. The oldest women eat last, not because they are last in the ritual order, but because they supervise the amount of food given to each person according to status. "The women who are seated in the kitchen are always the ones who are most respected. These are the women who have already been *mayordomos* or who have had a major expense like a wedding. If a woman has not given a large fiesta, like a *mayordomía* or a wedding, and she goes to sit in the kitchen, the women will look at her and later talk about her. They will say, 'Why was she in the kitchen? She hasn't even given a large fiesta yet'" (Mercedes, age 40). When all have been allocated the proper portion, they begin to eat. Men usually eat before women.

They act as waiters, carrying full plates of food to the proper person according to the instructions of the older women. When the meal is over, they return the empty plates to the women who divided the meat.

Women wash the dishes and then begin to seat themselves and to eat, with older and middle-aged women eating first, with the exception of those who are dividing the meat. Younger women follow. Once the older women who have supervised the meal finish eating, their work is over. The younger women clean up and finish up the day's work. At the end of the day people either return home or begin to drink.

Many of the older women stay until quite late, laughing, talking, gossiping, and drinking. They often comment that going to fiestas is how they find out what is going on in the community. Several commented, "Going to a fiesta is like listening to the radio. You learn all of the news." Ritual events provide women with a forum for airing opinions, discussing community politics, and demonstrating their influence in subtle ways. This is described in greater detail in the next chapter.

If the occasion calls for it, dancing takes place in the evening. If this is the case, women prepare an evening snack of bread and hot chocolate for everyone. When they have finished, both men and women move to the main patio to seat themselves—the men in one section in chairs and women in another section on palm mats. Each section of the patio is supplied with a generous supply of bottles of mescal and cartons of beer. One older relative of the sponsoring family takes on the job of liquor server, a man for the men and a woman for the women. Drinking, talking, and dancing take up the remainder of the evening, often until 4 A.M.

When dancing is called for, such as during a wedding, a *mayordomía*, or a large birthday party, the oldest male serves as *huehuete* (ritual specialist) if an actual *huehuete* is not present. He selects the people who are to dance together, with regular input from the oldest women present. Traditionally, all dancing was done with partners of the same sex. The primary dance done in Teotitlán is the *jarabe*, a three-step pass done by each dancer moving alone. Women dance backward and men move forward. More recently men and women have been assigned together as *jarabe* partners. Some older Teotitecos frown on this practice as lack of respect. Regardless of whether dancing is mixed or single sex, the oldest fiesta participants always dance first and the youngest last. The order of dancing reiterates the order found in greeting ceremonies and the seating arrangements. The most respected positions are given to the oldest people.

Men spend a significant amount of time drinking at local ceremonies—more than women because their work is usually finished
sooner.

In all ceremonial events, priority and respect are always granted to
individuals first by age, within same-sex groups. In Teotitlán, older
people are invited first, greeted first, seated in the most honorable
positions, do not do physical labor, and are called on as advisors in
work and as ritual specialists during ceremonial activities. In life-
cycle rituals, the oldest person involved in organizing events is often
a woman. If so, she has ultimate authority in terms of decision
making.

The next two sections show how women's authority in ritual activities stems from two primary institutions, *compadrazgo* and *guelaguetza*. Once we have looked at these two institutions, we shall ex-

amine how they work in conjunction with the role of gender in decision making related to life-cycle rituals and how they can be a source of conflict between women who hold different positions in the relations of production.

Compadrazgo

The *compadrazgo* system works as a hidden web pulling together the major extended families of Teotitlán into lifelong relationships through ritual commitments and continued reciprocal labor exchanges. If extended to its logical limits, *compadrazgo* could bind every member of the community together. It is a major source of material resources, labor, influence, and support for women in relation to ceremonial activities, politics, and production. But at the same time, the broader class context in which *compadrazgo* exists can cause divisions between women.

A recent study done in Oaxaca suggests that *compadrazgo* ties are inherited—that the selection of godparents is limited by lines of descent between the two households involved in the co-parenting relationship (Sault 1985b: 2–11). This is often the case in Teotitlán as well. If the heads of a household die, their children are expected to take over their responsibilities, because godparents remain important through the life cycle. Children must have godparents in order to pass through each phase of their life. "You have to have *compadres* in order to pass through different stages in the church. You need them to give testimony in the church. You need one for baptism, for first communion and confirmation. Mostly you need them to get married. You can't get married in the church without them. Before when fewer people were married in the church, not so many people were *compadres*" (Mario, age 50).

Teotitecos articulate four major categories of godparenting relationships defined by the amount of expenditures involved, the degree of long-term commitment required, and the amount of prestige attached to sponsorship. Teotitecos label co-parenting in relation to the baptism ceremony as the heaviest commitment. It entails paying for a child's baptismal clothing and accoutrements. When the child is married, the baptismal godparents must pay for the wedding clothing and offer a large gift. They also often sponsor a large party in their own house. Two lesser co-parenting categories are tied to the Catholic rituals of confirmation and first communion. Of these, the confirmation godparents are most important. They buy a child's clothing for the confirmation and must also provide a chest or cabinet for their godchild when he or she is married. First communion

Figure 6. Levels of Ritual Co-Parenthood
Relationships (*Compadrazgo*)

Baptism or marriage (highest ranking, most obligations)
Confirmation (second highest ranking)
First communion (third highest ranking)
Rosary, birthday, graduation, house crosses (lowest ranking)

godparents must give their godchildren large wedding gifts. The fourth category of godparenting is a rosary godparent. This entails buying the child a rosary, accompanying the godchild to the church, and blessing him or her in front of a particular saint or virgin. The ritual may end with a meal given by the parents for the new godparents. Often the godparents purchase clothing for the child, but further offerings are voluntary, often contingent on how well the godparents get along with the biological parents. The fourth category of godparenting also includes sponsorship of children in the one-time events like school graduations.

Asking a man, woman, or couple to be ritual co-parents to a child is a way of demonstrating respect (Sault 1985b). The majority of ritual co-parents are pairs of men and women, usually husband and wife, but not always. Mothers and sons and fathers and daughters may be co-sponsors of the same child. A male-female pair of *compadres* usually sponsor all of the children from one household, building a strong tie with the biological parents.

As first documented by Fadwa El Guindi (1986) and Nicole Sault (1985a, 1985b), women are central figures in the institution of *compadrazgo*. Sault (1987:7) argues that among the Zapotecs, "godparenthood is fundamentally a relationship between women, creating bonds which unite separate households." She found that while men must be married to begin sponsorship, girls may sponsor either alone or with a close consanguine. This is also the case in Teotitlán.

In an earlier discussion (1985b), Sault discusses the concept of "corporation"—the people that each villager can count on for support and assistance. In Teotitlán, the same idea is conveyed with the broader term *familia*. An individual with a large *familia* has many kin and *compadrazgo* ties. For women, these ties are critical in mobilizing labor for ritual events. The larger an individual woman's kin-*compadrazgo* network, the more she can mobilize for a successful fiesta. As Sault argues, by sponsoring many godchildren, a woman increases her influence and control over others. Not only does she have control over her godchildren, but also over their parents, since a child's godparents hold the superior position in the hierarchical relationship with his or her biological parents. A woman continues to expand and reinforce these hierarchical ties over generations through her children and grandchildren (Sault 1987 : 8).

An examination of data from a random sample of 154 households in Teotitlán indicates that most of the population is active in the system of *compadrazgo*. The mean number of godchildren per household in 1986 was 9—some had none, while one had 246. While there are no data on individual women and their sponsorship of godchildren in Teotitlán, Sault (1985b: 233) found in a neighboring community that the most influential women had sponsored eight to sixteen for baptism from within their own community. If sponsorship outside the village were also included, the numbers would be higher. Many influential women in Teotitlán have sponsored up to twenty children for baptism.

The number of godchildren sponsored by men and women who are household heads is likely to increase as they get older. As seen in table 20, while only half of young household heads have godchildren, almost all (97 percent) elderly household heads sponsor godchildren. While sponsorship provides a woman with access to a wide network of laborers, it can also entail considerable expense, not only in the initial sponsorship, but in the later responsibilities when a godchild marries. As discussed below, the class position of a woman's household can become an important factor in allowing her fully to carry out her ritual obligations as a *comadre*.

As women become older, particularly if they are widowed, their incomes may decline, but their ritual responsibilities multiply. In some cases, older women may be placed in contradictory positions where they hold ritual status of great honor, yet they barely have the cash available to purchase the flowers, liquor, bread, candles, and

Table 20. *Age and Sponsorship of Godchildren*

Age of Household Heads (N = 151)	Have No Godchildren	Have Godchildren
20–40 years (younger)	50%	50%
41–60 years (middle age)	28%	72%
61–80 years (elderly)	3%	97%

Source: Random stratified household survey conducted by Lynn Stephen in 1986.

presents they are required to bring to life-cycle events. As god-mothers, their contributions are always expected to be large.

Elderly women have varying strategies for fulfilling their ritual obligations. Some borrow money from their children. Others indirectly invoke lower consumption standards associated with earlier times in which ritual consumption was considerably less. For example, instead of bringing cartons of soft drinks or beer, they will bring a Coke bottle filled with local mescal. This is an acceptable substitute for a carton of commercial beer, yet costs about one-tenth of what the beer does. Twenty years ago, no one brought beer to rituals, only mescal. Elderly women also end up saving on food because many of them spend a great deal of time attending rituals, where they are fed and provided with additional food to take home. What income they do have goes toward buying ritual consumption goods rather than purchasing food. Some elderly women even attend optional rituals such as funerals for more distant kin or *compadres* (which occur quite frequently) and are fed for weeks on end. Because funerals involve heavy drinking, some elderly women also support drinking habits through attending rituals.

Extended family ties and the *compadrazgo* system organize the people of Teotitlán into social groups that may function as units for agricultural production, weaving production, and ritual participation. The existence of these units results in a high degree of cohesion between the production system and the ritual system. Often the same people work together during rituals and in weaving production. A direct consequence of this overlap is the use of *compadrazgo* relationships to recruit weaving labor, as discussed in chapter 6. In this frequent situation, the idiom of kinship, which connotes equality and ethnic unity, becomes contradictory.

When a merchant man or woman uses status as a *compadre* or *comadre* to recruit godchildren and *compadres* as laborers, relations of local ethnic solidarity conflict with the class relations of production. While Teotitecos present a unified vision of themselves to outsiders (such as tourists, state bureaucrats, and importers), internally the concept of ethnic unity is often shaken by the reality of labor relations that differentiate people into merchants and weavers. The level of unity achieved in relation to a common Teotiteco identity varies with the context and with the particular economic and political agendas of those involved.

Interviews on the meanings and criteria for choosing *compadres* also revealed contradictory ideas about the potential equality of all community members versus the notion that some are better *comadres* or *compadres* because they are wealthier. People in the poorer half of the community felt that they were recruited less for *compadres* than the well-to-do, as reflected in the statement of this poor weaver woman: "I don't have any *hijados* even though I have grandchildren. I think that a lot of people choose their *compadres* by the amount of money people have. They go for the rich, not the poor. Because I don't have a husband now I also have less money and maybe people don't like that. There is one person though who asked me to think about being a *madrina*" (Luisa, age 38). Wealthier people in the community seem to think they are selected as *compadres* based on a combination of character and wealth. "We have twelve *ahijados*. I think that most people choose their *compadres* for money and for character. They want someone with a good reputation. Because my husband has money, people like to ask him" (María, age 42). As discussed in chapter 9, as the basis for political authority and community respect has changed to include wealth as a significant criterion, the criterion for asking people to be godparents is also changing.

Compadrazgo relationships can also be used to exert pressure on invited guests as laborers in a ritual situation. Sault (1985b) documents cases where influential Zapotec women were known to overwork their godchildren and *comadres* in the kitchen because of their superior position in the *compadrazgo* relationship. Men can use their *compadrazgo* relations in a similar way to recruit laborers for agricultural work. While *compadrazgo* may appear to diminish class differences and promote ethnic solidarity, it can also be used to emphasize authority positions in the relations of production through labor recruitment and, more subtly, in the context of a ritual event. This conflict is also seen in the reciprocal exchange institution of *guelaguetza*.

Guelaguetza and Economic Change

A second institution of major importance in the structuring of ritual events is *guelaguetza*. This system of reciprocal exchange provides a basic framework for participation in ritual. The continued existence of *guelaguetza* permits many households to participate in ritual in spite of spiraling inflation in Mexico and the devaluation of the peso. In contrast to the accounting and business aspects of weaving production, which are usually controlled by men, *guelaguetza* exchange is the province of women. They are the primary investors in this system of goods and labor exchange. More often than not, men are acting as the agents of women by carrying, weighing, or writing down the details of whatever is exchanged. "*Guelaguetza* is a good custom because it helps us. You can't always save what you will need for the future in your own house. If you run out of money or someone gets sick you may have to kill your turkeys and your hens. If you made a *guelaguetza* with them, then they are safe in someone else's house and they have to bring them when you need them. As long as you have children you will need a lot of *guelaguetza* for them" (Filomena, age 54).

While the recording of *guelaguetza* debts is often done by men because until recently they were more literate than women, women are the ones who plan and prepare for making loans and for calling them in. In fact, many women interviewed could recite their entire *guelaguetza* notebooks by heart, having made mental accounts of all the transactions. Accounting and planning for loans is a complex and long-term project. Household *guelaguetza* books contain up to 200 entries for loans made to other people and items received as loans. Figure 7 shows a brief excerpt from a *guelaguetza* notebook documenting what one household owes.

The notebook goes on with over thirty more *guelaguetzas* that the household owes in relation to past *mayordomías* and another thirty-seven entries owed to them, in preparation for the weddings of their children. Following the colonial custom of recording only male

Figure 7. Sample from *Guelaguetza* Notebook

1972 What we owe from the *mayordomía*
de la Virgen de la Soledad

Tereso Rodríguez	$100 [pesos]
Mario López	Six dozen eggs
Salvador Martínez	One turkey at 6 kilos
Francisco Pérez	2 kilos of cacao
Pedro Vicente	Three turkeys that together weigh 20 kilos
Manuel Pérez	2 *almudes* of beans
Luis Martínez	6 *almudes* of corn
Enrique Bautista	3 turkeys that together weigh 21.3 kilos
Manuel del Monte	10½ *almudes* of tortillas (the amount of corn used)

names when representing households, *guelaguetza* notebooks do not reflect the fact that a majority of the transactions take place between women. Men still have the role of recorder of the transactions, but women seem to be clearly in charge of them.

> Sometimes men don't know what is needed for *guelaguetza*. I would go and leave something with someone and then tell my husband so that he would write it down. I could go and leave something and he wouldn't know about it. But he could never leave something without me knowing. Sometimes if I decided to leave something for *guelaguetza*, then I would need someone to carry it. I would get my son, a godson, or my husband. If I go, then they carry what we bring and I enter the house and talk to people about the *guelaguetza*. (Ana, age 60)

Despite the fact that women are not recorded as the transactors of *guelaguetza*, they know precisely how their accounts stand. In reality, women are often planning for several events simultaneously. In the life cycle of their families women often have to plan for twenty or more major fiestas. The greatest chore in any household-level ritual is food preparation. Women plan ahead, often years in advance, how much of each ingredient they will need (numbers of chickens and turkeys, bushels of corn, chiles, pounds of sugar and cacao, etc.) in order to have a successful feast. For example, a woman may give out over 3,000 tortillas in *guelaguetza* loans by the time she recalls them for a ritual event. If those who received the tortillas have to pay back a large debt, a second level of *guelaguetza* is invoked, with female family members donating labor to help them meet the tortilla debt. "When you have to pay back a large tortilla debt, then you have two options. You can either pay someone to make them with you, which is expensive, or get someone to work with you. When I needed to make a lot of tortillas I had a small work party and got my sisters to help me. I'll have to help them sometime as well" (Margarita, age 40).

Women's Animal Production in *Guelaguetza*

Animals are raised for investment in the reciprocal exchange system of *guelaguetza*. Most women begin keeping a brood of turkeys and pigs to prepare for their sons' weddings when the boys reach age ten. Both pigs and turkeys are raised for a period of one year or more and either sold or, in the case of *guelaguetza*, given to another household and recorded as a loan in the household notebook.

Because women plan ritual celebrations years before they actually occur, they have long-term animal production plans. For example, a woman knows that she needs to have loaned out twenty-five to fifty turkeys and one or two pigs by the time her son reaches twenty years of age and will probably be getting married. A woman who has no starting capital begins by raising chickens, which are the cheapest animals to buy and feed, although they are high-risk. If she can successfully raise and sell ten to fifteen chickens, she then has enough capital to buy several small turkeys. The turkeys can then be sold to buy piglets, which have the lowest risk in animal production.

In an article on economic exchange in Oaxaca, Ralph Beals (1970) mentions pig raising as one of the most important forms of savings engaged in by Zapotecs. While the initial investment is low, the pigs require continued care and feeding. Beals (1970:238) describes it as "forced savings," because peasants are forced to invest small sums of money on a long-term basis to feed their pigs, rather than spending a little money daily on small luxuries. When the pig is sold, the return is large enough to be used for an investment.

An analysis of pig, turkey, and chicken raising in five households in Teotitlán in 1986 supports these findings. Women in Teotitlán are aware that raising animals is a low-return venture, yet they consider it to be an effective way of "saving" a little bit of money. Table 21 summarizes the investment and risks involved in animal production. Results are averaged from ten households.

As seen in table 21, animal production does not result in a profit. On the contrary, animal production usually results in at least a 50 percent loss of investment between the total amount of income invested in the animal versus its final selling price as an adult. This does not take into account the labor invested in the animals. Nevertheless, women in Teotitlán claim that investing small amounts of money on a daily basis in their animals is the most effective means for them to save some money.

The savings notion seems to be particularly important among women from weaving households, who usually have no familiarity with conventional banks and would probably never have enough money available to make it worthwhile to open a savings account in Oaxaca. They are comfortable with animal production as a means of savings and because of their participation in *guelaguetza* are usually raising animals to pay back debts or to give out as loans.

Merchant women seem to engage in less animal production than weaver women. Merchant households often purchase animals needed for ritual consumption rather than raise them and do not rely on animal production to pay for household emergencies. Younger merchant

Table 21. *Animal Production Risks and Investments*

	Pigs	Turkeys	Chickens
Initial cost	$3,500–$5,000	$500	$350
Health care	$1,000		
Weekly maintenance	$2,570	$375	$225
# of weeks to mature	36+	24+	20+
Minimum total investment	$97,036	$9,500	$4,500
Adult selling price	$40,000	$5,000	$2,000
Difference between selling price and total investment	−$57,036	−$4,500	−$2,500
Daily time investment (minutes)	45–90	45–90	45–90 (fed with turkeys)
Risk	low	high	high

Source: Survey of ten households conducted by Lynn Stephen in 1987.
Note: Prices in 1987 pesos (440 pesos to US $1.00).

women who are taking a more active role in running the household business often leave the home periodically to supervise workers to run errands in Oaxaca. Their need for mobility is incompatible with the task of animal supervision.

Ultimately the production of animals may become an activity undertaken almost exclusively by weaver women. Their households continue to invest heavily in *guelaguetza* to finance ritual obligations and their low cash flow is often insufficient to meet unexpected emergencies. Animal production provides women from weaver households with an easy saving mechanism for ritual and household needs. Although the final returns to investment are in fact negative, the fact that low daily labor and financial inputs can yield a substantial sum when converted into cash encourages women to continue with animal production. Merchant women who have a choice of investing their money and labor in other activities choose to engage in higher-yielding activities tied to weaving or in other party businesses.

Discussion with women also suggests that animal raising has noneconomic significance for them. While men describe farming as giving them a sense of their Teotiteco identity and providing security for their families, women describe animal production as aiding them in meeting ritual obligations. Animal production is related to women's cultural identity as the organizers and workers in household ritual.

Factors in *Guelaguetza* Decision Making

When, what, and how much to loan out in *guelaguetza* is usually determined by household income. Presently, many items given as *guelaguetza* loans such as cacao, sugar, chiles, or corn are purchased outright. Animals are purchased when they are young and cared for until they are big enough to slaughter. Calculations for making *guelaguetza* loans have to be planned along with other household expenses. "Right now I am not making *guelaguetzas* because I don't have much money. People with little money don't make many *guelaguetzas* because they have to buy what they give. . . . I like *guelaguetza* because it helps out. We couldn't have had our recent fiesta without it. We bought bread and mescal, but we wouldn't have been able to buy everything. The *guelaguetza* was very necessary. Now we owe a lot" (María, age 28). *Guelaguetza* planning is particularly crucial for households that do not have a large cash flow and are not able to purchase items needed to put on a good fiesta. Instead, they must invest slowly in *guelaguetza* loans and call these in when they have the fiesta. Wealthier families who have not invested much in *guelaguetza* loans can purchase more of what they need when they sponsor a ritual event.

Labor is treated more casually in the *guelaguetza* system than goods. Labor exchanges are not recorded in notebooks, but are remembered. Ritual labor *guelaguetza* comes through invitations to attend other households' ritual events. Invitations include the unstated assumption that the couple, particularly the invited woman, will come to work for at least three days. The invited guests may be obligated to work longer, depending on how close they are to the hosts. The labor of the guests will be reciprocated by the hosts when the guests have their own fiesta.

Most women feel a strong obligation to reciprocate the help they have received from other women. When asked why they go to so many fiestas and how they feel about the hard work they do, many women reply, "It is like a *guelaguetza*. I go to help at their fiestas so that they will come and help at mine. What will I do when my children get married? If I don't help now, no one will help me when I need it."

While the ethics of *guelaguetza* exchanges imply that all labor

Table 22. Percentages and Days of Adult Labor (over Age 16) Invested in Household/Agricultural Activities, Weaving, Community Service, and Ritual (one day = 12 hours of work)

Case No./ Total Days	Household/Agr.		Weaving		Community Service[a]		Ritual	
	%	Days	%	Days	%	Days	%	Days
Merchants								
1[b] 845.5	40	334	48	402	4	33	9	76.5
2 599	44	262.5	36	213	3	18	18	105.5
3 597	38	225	38	228	13	76	11	68
4 477	46	220	33	159	5	26	15	72
5[b] 794	40	315	47	375	1	5	12	99
6 499.5	36	181	41	207	6	30	16	81.5
Weavers								
1 578.5	22	124.5	54	314	1	6	23	134
2 519	63	329	20	105	0	0	16	85
3 511	36	183	49	251	0	0	15	77
4[b] 812	55	446.5	30	243.5	1	8	14	114
5[b] 772	60	467	10	81	0	0	29	224
6[c] 346	34	119	37	128	0	0	29	99

Source: Data collected from twelve case-study households by Lynn Stephen during ten months of 1985.

Note: Totals may not equal 100% due to rounding.

[a]Community service = time spent carrying out civil cargos or engaging in *tequio*.

[b]These households had three adult laborers over age 16.

[c]This household had a laborer who became seriously ill.

will be reciprocated in future ritual events, data from a study of twelve households suggest that weavers may invest a greater percentage of their labor time in ritual events than merchants. Since the sample is quite small and the time frame limited, the data are only suggestive.

Labor allocation information in the following discussion comes from twelve study households. Amounts of adult labor allocated to ritual events, civil cargos and *tequio* (community service), and farming were tallied on a weekly basis for ten months because they can vary seasonally. Data on adult labor allocated to household reproduction (cooking, animal care, yard sweeping, loom repair, etc.) and weaving activities were collected for a six-week baseline period and then checked periodically throughout the year for accuracy. The amount of labor invested in these activities tends to be stable throughout the year. The six-week data are projected in table 22 for a period of ten months. Because of the irregularity of ritual events, individual percentages registered by households are not as important as the ranges seen for each group. The ranges are an indication of the spectrum of possible ritual labor allocations for merchant and weaver households.

As a group, merchants seem to avoid working in rituals, which can drain labor away from their businesses. While no ritual labor data are available for men and women, as a general rule, women work longer than men during ritual events. Often male merchants leave after the first day of a ritual event. Instead of coming personally on the second and third day, they send a child or a servant with an abundant supply of the necessary goods. Merchant women may work at an event for a full three days, being more likely to do so if they are a close *comadre* or relative of the sponsoring household. However, many do not seem to feel as strong an obligation as weaver

Table 23. *Percentages of Total Adult Labor Time (over Age 16) Invested in Ritual, Merchants and Weavers Compared (March 1985–December 1985)*

	Average Time Spent in Ritual	Range of Time Spent in Ritual
Merchants (N = 6)	13%	9%–15%
Weavers (N = 6)	21%	12%–29%

Source: Data collected from twelve case-study households by Lynn Stephen in 1985.

women do to fulfill their reciprocal labor obligations if they have a more distant relationship with the host woman.

These patterns suggest that weaver women are probably investing the greatest amounts of *guelaguetza* labor in life-cycle rituals. Since they cannot afford simply to send larger supplies of ritual goods with a child or servant, they usually appear personally to fulfill their labor obligations. While *guelaguetza* goods and labor exchanges are the primary means through which women build up their status in the community, such exchanges nevertheless can also underscore subtle differences of obligation within the system. Before exploring how these differences are further related to the position of households in the local relations of production, the commonalities of women's roles in rituals are explored in relation to household decision making.

Women's Control of Labor and Resources in Life-Cycle Ceremonies

Women in Teotitlán are central figures in economic decision making that pertains to household-level ritual. In both weaver and merchant households women decide together with their husbands when to attend and sponsor rituals. Once a decision has been made to attend or sponsor a ritual, women are usually the ones to decide how the ritual event will be paid for.

In merchant households, women's strong role in ritual decision making is distinct from the subordinate role they usually have in business decision making. Only in ritual decision making do merchant women seem to have an equal say with their husbands. Weaver women also seem to have a large measure of equality with their husbands in ritual decision making, as they do in decisions regarding weaving production.

In a questionnaire given to a stratified random sample of households, 82 percent of male and female informants from merchant households stated that decisions regarding the sponsorship of house-

Table 24. *Primary Decision Maker(s) by Gender for Sponsoring Fiestas*

	Male	Female	Both
Merchants (N = 51)	13%	5%	82%
Weavers (N = 100)	12%	12%	76%

Source: Random stratified household survey conducted by Lynn Stephen in 1986.

hold fiestas are carried out jointly by men and women; 76 percent of the weaver households sampled stated that sponsorship decisions were made jointly by men and women. Generalizing from the sample, it seems that women's role in ritual decision making is perceived by Teotitecos as being equal to that of men in most households. This is an interesting continuity between merchant and weaver households and provides a common experience for women. "It is women who do a lot of the things for fiestas. They have to plan months before, buy all of the food, tell people what to do to prepare. Also, on the day that a fiesta happens, women tell people what to do because they are the ones who know what has to happen" (Emiliano, age 60).

The strong role all women have in ritual economic decision making at the household level is related to the social networks and economic channels used in ritual consumption. The economics of ritual consumption are conducted by women, largely within the context of the community. Economic transactions for ritual, unlike business transactions, which often require a spoken and written knowledge of Spanish and basic math skills, are conducted entirely in Zapotec and require no writing. Because ritual economic decision making requires manipulation of economic channels located primarily within the community, women are in a strong position to take advantage of local connections and to use this fact to pressure for more control in the decision-making process with their husbands. In business decisions, women who have little or no education, cannot speak and write Spanish, and have no math skills have little ground to stand on if they want to take a stronger role in dealing with Mexican and U.S. clients. Through planning and organizing ritual events, women are able to take advantage of family and *compadrazgo* networks, where they can maximize their influence and use their organizational skills to their best advantage.

Extended kin and *compadrazgo* networks are important to economic transactions in Teotitlán. Just as many merchants tend to employ their relatives, *compadres*, and *hijados* as pieceworkers, women tend to buy from people who are a part of their extended kin and *compadrazgo* network. They much prefer to purchase turkeys or chiles for a fiesta from a *comadre* who sells in the market than from someone they are not connected to. The *comadre* will also give them a better price.

Because of their ritual labor commitments through *guelaguetza*, women are closely connected to each other in extended kin and *compadrazgo* networks. Women may work together in rituals more than twenty times per year. The close bonds that women form through working together are also used in procuring the necessary items for a ritual event. Women can often get a better price than men because of their personal links in the community with women who sell ritual goods. They are thus more successful than men in making purchases for ritual purposes. In addition, the strong role that women have in planning and organizing ritual events and the connections they have in the community through extended family and *compadrazgo* networks reinforce the local *guelaguetza* system and the use of primarily local vendors for the purchase of ritual goods.

Conclusions: The Impact of Merchant and Weaver Status on Women's Ritual Authority

Through their roles in the institutions of *compadrazgo* and *guelaguetza,* women are the primary sustainers of ritual activity focused on life-cycle ceremonies. Through their decisive roles in the household ritual economy, all women effectively channel significant amounts of resources and labor into life-cycle rituals. While this gives them an important status within the community, this status does not hold up outside of Teotitlán and may result in conflicts between women who hold different positions in the relations of production.

Does economic wealth give women an advantage in ritual? Does household wealth make a difference in the ways in which women from weaver and merchant households participate in ritual and the status they derive from that participation? Many, but not all, of the women in Teotitlán who sponsor large numbers of godchildren also come from merchant households. They are desired as *madrinas* because they not only have the resources to fulfill the expensive obligations of godparenthood, but may also be able to offer more, most notably employment, to their godchildren. Thus when a merchant woman who has many godchildren invites their mothers to a ritual event signaling that they have been recruited as laborers, the consequences of noncompliance for the invited women may not only be that their *comadre* does not return the favor. She may also be able to withhold other resources or opportunities from them and their families. While such power differences are never overtly stated between women, a woman almost always complies more quickly with the request of a *madrina* or *comadre* than with that of another woman, particularly if the godmother stands in an employer relationship to her or to a family member.

It is important to emphasize that a significant number of women who are godmothers and have sponsored many godchildren are not merchants. They were chosen because of their high status in the community as *mayordomas* and as well-liked people. Nevertheless, as wealth becomes more important in determining political power and access to resources both within and outside the community, merchant women become more desirable as godmothers. This may result in a concentration of *comadres* among merchants in the future.

Wealth differences also have a very real effect on what the cost of obtaining ritual status is for different women in the community. While all households have minimal social obligations for both sponsoring and attending ritual events, there are important differences between households in terms of the percentage of total cash outflow invested in ritual and the strategies used to provide this cash and in-kind goods for ritual consumption. Data from six merchant and six weaver households were collected to investigate this trend.

Ritual and farming expenses were tallied on a weekly basis for ten months for the twelve case-study households. Household reproduction (food, clothing, building materials, medical costs, school costs) and weaving expenses (for production and/or business) were collected for a six-week baseline period and then checked periodically throughout the year for accuracy. Weaving and household costs were found to be stable, while ritual and farming costs can vary throughout the year.

The information in the sample suggests that, while the average amounts that weaver and merchant households spend on ritual are similar (approximately US$292 for merchants and US$245 for weavers), weavers spend a significantly higher percentage of their total cash outflow on ritual consumption than merchants do—an average of 19 percent and a range of 8 to 45 percent for weavers and an average of 4 percent and a range of 3 to 7 percent for merchants. While the data are limited, they do suggest possible trends. The full cash outflow data for the case-study households are found in appendix B. Table 25 is a summary of ritual versus total cash outflow. These differences have important implications for the ways in which women in merchant and weaver households carry out budgeting and labor allocations as they try to meet their ritual responsibilities and build up their status in the community.

Any household that is sponsoring a major fiesta or is invited to attend a series of ritual events must have cash for ritual consumption as well as for taking care of household expenses. In merchant households, where there is a relatively large cash flow, it does not cause a major disruption to the household budget if women divert a relatively small amount of cash for immediate ritual consumption or for *guelaguetza* goods. The choices are usually different for

Table 25. Cash Outflow Data from Case-Study Households (March 1985–December 1985, in US$)

	Average Cash Outflow	Range of Total Cash Flow	Average Amount Allocated to Ritual	Average % of Total Used for Ritual Expenses	Range of Amount Allocated to Ritual	Range of % of Total Used for Ritual Expenses
Merchants (N = 6)	$7,298	$3,544–$18,269	$292	4	$219–$510	3–7
Weavers (N = 6)	$1,332	$528–$2,227	$253	19	$106–$798	8–45

Source: Data collected from twelve case-study households by Lynn Stephen in 1985.

women in weaving households, who have a much smaller cash flow and less disposable income.

If a woman from a weaving household is going to sponsor a ritual event, she plans well ahead of time and invests as much as she can in the *guelaguetza* system. However, she is usually not able to plant enough loans to cover all of her ritual consumption needs. If cash is needed for ritual consumption either immediately or in the future, women in weaving households push household members to speed up production, resulting in a greater number of blankets and rugs to be sold. Labor is funneled into weaving activities to build up a cash surplus for ritual consumption.

Often women in weaver households have to push their children and husbands hard in order to accumulate sufficient cash reserves to invest in ritual consumption, particularly for the sponsorship of events such as weddings. Because ritual consumption can eat up such a large percentage of household cash flow in some years, weaver women may find themselves in an ongoing set of confrontations with their husbands as they plan to procure all of the necessary items for a large ritual event and must also take care of daily expenses. The ritual status and authority that weaver women achieve through sponsorship of life-cycle rituals is the same as that obtained by merchant women, but they have often made greater family and personal sacrifices to get it. Because ritual spending is a much smaller overall percentage of merchant household budgets, merchant women do not engage in domestic struggles to fund their participation in and sponsorship of rituals.

Personal and household struggles to achieve ritual authority can be a source of tension between women as they act in their ritual statuses. While a large ritual event allows the woman who planned and sponsored it to increase her status if it is carried out correctly, such events also underscore the differing resources to which individual women have access as a result of their position in the relations of production. The contradictions of ethnicity and class that are often softened in the ritual sphere can subtly reappear in the close relations women develop as they work together in ceremonial events.

Chapter 9. Hidden Voices: Women's Political Participation in Teotitlán

A little while ago I went to a meeting in the kindergarten. I don't think the men were used to hearing the women talk. One woman got up to nominate a man for a committee. Some men who were present objected and made fun of her for naming someone. A lot of people still don't think women know how to talk. Sure, women want to go to more meetings, but they can't. And when they do, they aren't listened to like men.
(Josefina, age 24)

FEMINIST SCHOLARSHIP and grassroots development projects in Latin America have increasingly concentrated on the circumstances that promote or inhibit women's ability, both individually and collectively, to confront and participate in dominant political structures. Recent studies of the dynamics of women's conflicts and coalitions in local political life emphasize women's roles in overtly political institutions such as local committees in *municipios* and school committees, as well as in other institutions not usually associated directly with politics, such as mothers' clubs, ritual institutions, and health organizations.[1] These studies demonstrate that an emphasis on the gendered roles associated with local culture often illuminates instances where women's initial political participation is not through formal institutions, but through networks, channels, and events stemming from cultural institutions associated with social reproduction.[2]

Until recently in Teotitlán, the symbolic reproduction of the community through the celebration of *mayordomías* linked political and ritual authority together through the civil-religious hierarchy. In the 1960s, as the *mayordomía* system declined and the population became more formally differentiated between merchants and weavers, the links between ritual and political authority have become more tenuous. As a result, women's roles in the social reproduction of the community are less visible and focus primarily on life-cycle rituals, which now reflect much of the symbolic content of *mayordomías*. Despite their distancing from formal politics since the decline of *mayordomías*, many Teotiteco women continue to place great importance on the ceremonial life of the community and the ritual authority that stems from active participation in it. Many continue to use *respet* as a basis for achieving influence and gaining a right to hold influential political opinions. The differentiation process that has separated the population into more permanent groups of weavers and merchants, however, has also affected women and their perceptions of themselves as political actors and the types of strategies they use to achieve their goals within the community.

Here the changing criteria for the ritually based notion of *respet* are examined in relation to women. As wealth becomes a source for the legitimization of authority and a basis for earning *respet* and in some cases political power, merchant and weaver women are showing different patterns of political participation and opinions about their ability to participate. Often these differences translate into varying linguistic abilities and experiences in negotiating with outsiders. While the community currently has a high degree of interaction with U.S. importers and tourists, only people from merchant households, particularly women staffing market stalls and stores, are involved in this interaction. The commercial experience of merchant women has given them an edge over weaver women in feeling comfortable in voicing their opinions, particularly in relation to local and outside authorities.

The Changing Basis of Community Authority and Respect: Wealth or Ritual Experience?

The political scenario in Teotitlán is informed by class stratification. Here I focus on the influence of weaver and merchant class positions on women's participation in local politics. The ideological split in Teotitlán between merchants and weavers is also readily acknowledged to exist on a material level as well.

In order to measure potential material differences between merchants and weavers, I collected indices of material wealth and consumer goods from 74 weaver households and 54 merchant households included in a random stratified sample. House type and land ownership were chosen as primary wealth indicators and recorded in terms of size and quality of house construction and size of land holding. House type is measured by construction material (adobe versus brick) and the number of rooms. The divisions were suggested by Teotitecos in discussions of how houses are upgraded. Other wealth

This is an example of the poorest housing type in Teotitlán, which reflects the conditions of most houses before the commercialization of weaving. It is made of adobe, cane, and tile roofing with a dirt floor.

indicators including ownership of trucks, refrigerators, stoves, beds, sewing machines, televisions, and looms were recorded in terms of the numbers owned. The comparative results are shown in table 28.

A summary of the data in table 26 through table 29 is provided in table 30 in relative comparative terms of merchant and weaver wealth. Merchants do not have an absolute monopoly on consumer goods, land, and good-quality housing, but they definitely possess a greater amount of material wealth. Significantly, this does not include their rug inventory, also considered to be an indication of wealth. Merchants were unwilling to provide any information on the amount of merchandise they had stockpiled and other invest-

Table 26. *Merchant and Weaver Households Compared by House Type*

	Merchant		Weaver	
	#	%	#	%
1 rm. adobe without floor	0	0	13	17.6
1 rm. adobe with floor	3	5.6	11	14.9
1–2 rm. brick	14	25.9	30	40.5
3 rm. brick	16	29.6	15	20.3
4–5 rm. brick	15	27.8	4	5.4
6 rm. or more	6	11.1	1	1.3
Total	54	100.0	74	100.0

Source: Random stratified household survey conducted by Lynn Stephen in 1986.

Table 27. *Merchant and Weaver Households Compared by Land Ownership*

	Merchant		Weaver	
	#	%	#	%
No land	13	24.1	45	60.8
0.01–1.0 hectare	35	64.8	26	35.1
1.01–2.0 hectares	4	7.4	2	2.7
More than 2.0 hectares	2	3.7	1	1.4
Total	54	100.0	74	100.0

Source: Random stratified household survey conducted by Lynn Stephen in 1986.

Table 28. *Merchant and Weaver Households Compared by Ownership of Consumer Goods*

	Merchant (N = 54)		Weaver (N = 74)	
	#	%	#	%
Own television(s)	49	90.7	46	62.2
Own a truck or car	26	48.1	2	2.7
Own refrigerator(s)	35	64.8	15	20.3
Own sewing machine(s)	35	64.8	29	39.2
Own at least 1 bed	53	98.1	48	64.9
Own a stove	49	90.7	50	67.6

Source: Random stratified household survey conducted by Lynn Stephen in 1986.

Table 29. *Merchant and Weaver Households Compared by Ownership of Looms*

No. of Looms	Merchant		Weaver	
	#	%	#	%
0–1	7	13.0	10	13.5
2–3	24	44.4	49	66.2
4–5	15	27.8	12	16.2
More than 5	8	14.8	3	4.1
Total	54	100.0	74	100.0

Source: Random stratified household survey conducted by Lynn Stephen in 1986.

Table 30. *Merchant and Weaver Wealth Compared*

House Type
   27% more weavers than merchants live in the poorest-quality housing, adobe structures of one room
   32% more merchants than weavers live in the best-quality housing, brick with four or more rooms

Land
   37% more weavers than merchants are landless

Consumer Goods
   45% more merchants than weavers own cars or trucks
   45% more merchants than weavers have refrigerators
   23% more merchants than weavers have stoves
   33% more merchants than weavers have beds
   26% more merchants than weavers have sewing machines
   29% more merchants than weavers have televisions

Looms
   22% more merchants than weavers have more than three looms

ments. Several have begun to buy up local land and have real estate in Oaxaca and in the cities of Tijuana and Rosarito in Baja California.

Once I had collected information on material wealth indicators from 54 merchant and 74 weaver households according to my criteria, I also wanted to see how people from Teotitlán would rank the same households by their own criteria of wealth. Three men and three women, including both weavers and merchants of varying ages, were asked to rank the merchant and weaver households (along with another 26 farmer and service households) into groups by wealth. The names of all of the household heads included in a random sample survey of 154 households were put on slips of paper with their Zapotec nicknames on them as well. The six informants then ranked these households in relation to each other. They began by comparing two households and built their wealth groups up from their initial comparison.

Initially two informants ranked the households into five groups, one informant ranked them into four groups, two informants ranked them into seven groups, and one informant ranked them into three groups. When asked what was the minimum number of groups, all collapsed them into three groups. The six informants' wealth rankings (of high, mid, and low) for each of the 54 merchant and 74 weaver households in the sample were averaged and frequencies were run (see appendix A for further discussion). According to the six informants, the merchant and weaver households in the sample have the average wealth rankings shown in table 31.

The averages of six informant rankings of merchant versus weaver wealth suggest that, conceptually, Teotitecos believe there are significant wealth differences between merchants and weavers. While a sample of six people is certainly not enough to generalize to the whole population, it does support the idea that Teotitecos identify differences in wealth with merchant and weaver class positions. The fact that the six informants themselves represent different sectors of the class system also helps to ensure a more complete picture.

Informant averages ranked 59 percent of the merchants in the sample in the highest wealth rank and only 12 percent of the weavers;

Table 31. *Average Wealth Rankings of Merchant and Weaver Households by Six Informants*

	Low (little money, few things)		Middle (neither rich nor poor)		High (have money and things)	
	#	%	#	%	#	%
Weaver (N = 74)	46	62	19	26	9	12
Merchant (N = 54)	6	11	16	30	32	59

Source: Ranking exercises carried out with six informants by Lynn Stephen in 1986.

62 percent of the weavers in the sample were placed in the lowest wealth ranking in comparison with 11 percent of the merchants. Almost equal percentages of weavers and merchants were ranked into the middle wealth category.

When sorting households into groups, informants always defined high wealth levels in positive terms. The wealthiest in the community were described as having "large, well-built houses," "cars or trucks," "a business," "a large stockpile of weavings to sell," and "good-quality land." The lowest-ranking households were defined completely by negatives such as "they don't have a good house," "they don't have any land," "they have no business," and "they don't have anything [weavings] to sell." The possessions of the wealthiest set the terms for evaluating everyone else.

Apart from wealth, Teotitecos emphasized *respet* as another way to rank households. When I originally asked people to rank households, they told me that ranking by wealth—*rap(a)daŋ med(ʒ)*, they have money; *rap(a)daŋ kos*, they have things—was not the only way that people were evaluated. People repeatedly emphasized that wealth and *respet* were different, and that one did not necessarily imply the other. "*Respet* and being rich are not the same thing. Even poor people can become important here. They can become *presidente* [mayor] or *síndico* [legal advisor]. The people who have the most respect are the elderly. Both they and people with money can have *respet* here" (Gregorio, age 65). "We are Teotitecos. We are all united here. We don't have disagreements and fights. Everyone can be respected" (Marcos, age 30).

In a second exercise, the same six informants who ranked 54 merchant households and 74 weaver households by wealth were asked to rank the same set of households into groups by respect. The respect rankings of the six informants were then averaged for each household. When the averaged informant wealth rankings for each household were correlated with the averaged respect rankings for each household, the resulting Spearman correlation coefficient of 0.44 (with a significance level of .005) suggests that respect is no longer simply associated with age, ritual experience, and service to the community in the minds of the six informants who participated in the exercise. In addition, extended interviews, linguistic behavior, and the political strategies of several large merchants suggest that wealth has also become a road to *respet*, community authority, and political influence.

The conceptual overlap between wealth and *respet* expressed in the correlation is indicative of a wider contradictory dynamic in the community that underlies the projected unifying ethnic identity tied to social reproduction and the ability of all community members to receive *respet*. This unifying identity is now constantly challenged by the fact that having more wealth in combination with being an employer can give an individual quite a bit of leverage in production relations, ritual relations, and local politics. The conceptual overlap between wealth and *respet* is indicative of the shifting economic and political relations that women navigate on a daily basis.

The importance of wealth in relation to respect is also expressed in extending the use of the honorific titles of *dad* and *nān* to a few wealthy merchants in the community who have not sponsored major fiestas or engaged in extensive cargo service. The wealthiest man in town is now referred to by some people as *dad*, the honorific title given to *mayordomos* and old men. "Now people who have a lot of money also get respect, like old people. For example, Miguel. They say *dad* Miguel to him. I am the same age as him and I have been a *mayordomo* and he has not, but they still call him *dad* Miguel. He has a lot of money and a lot of godchildren. He is very well known. That is why he is called *dad* Miguel" (Clemente, age 58). "Well, I respect the rich people in this town, like Miguel and Luisa. People say *dad* to him for his money. Because he has a lot of money he has a lot of godchildren too. That's why people respect him" (Margarita, age 32).

In a few cases, respect terms are extended to women as well. Merchant men and women who are addressed as *dad* and *nān* are placed in the same category as elderly couples who have sponsored at least one *mayordomía* and worked their way through the ranks of the civil cargo system. The linguistic association of *dad* and *nān* also extends to the religious metaphors for saints and virgins who are the guardians of the community.

Picking up on the linguistic symbolism used to legitimate their high-respect position, some male merchants are trying to manipulate ritual symbolism to reinforce their authority and political positions in the community. While some male merchants are adamantly against ritual expenditures, several of them have given large parties for themselves on their birthdays. These parties contain traditional ritual elements, such as complicated foods, single-sex *jarabe* dancing, and band music. The merchants sponsoring these rituals put themselves in the position of ritual leaders without having gone through the proper training and sacrifice. By sponsoring fiestas on secular occasions, merchants demonstrate their material wealth and also attempt to validate their rank by acting in a ritual capacity. "They throw these big parties so that they will be respected and to show how much money they have. Giving these big birthday parties can be more important than having a big wedding for the purposes of showing off your money. People say, 'How impressive. He had a big party.' You know women don't do that kind of thing. Only men do that for themselves" (Irene, age 50).

In some cases, merchants try to convert their purchased ritual *respet* into political authority. The wealthiest merchant in town, who is also accorded high levels of respect, has made several efforts to become mayor. He has never come close but continues to work subtly to build a position of power in the community. As indicated by other Teotitecos, one of the ways in which he wields great influence is through the record number of *ahijados* he and his wife have sponsored—246 as of 1986. While not holding a formal political office in the *municipio*, he is always a major political figure to be reckoned with in the community, indicating that the base of political power may be shifting outside of the *municipio* into class-based authority.

The purchasing of ritual respect indicates a realignment of the basis of political authority in the face of a persistent ideology that still gives credence to ritually based *respet* as a basis for influence. For women who have been shut out of the formal political institutions of the community, the traditional arena of age and ritually based respect can still be an important focus for their efforts to influence community politics. The degree to which they use this as a strategy, however, is influenced by their class position and the degree of wealth accumulated by their households. The strong association between high material wealth, high levels of respect, and merchant/employer status in the community is likely to cause merchant and weaver women to have differing political strategies.

Women's Exclusion from *Municipio* Meetings and Cargo Positions

As discussed in chapter 7, almost all of the formal cargo positions in the *ayuntamiento, juzgado mayor,* and *comité de la iglesia* are held by males. However, a few women have held committee positions on the kindergarten committee, the health committee, and the committee for the Secretariat of Education (SEP). In contrast to their exclusion from community *municipio* meetings, women do attend committee meetings held in relation to school business and health. All of the committees where women have held low-level offices and/or regularly attended meetings are state-initiated—women's participation was actively encouraged and often required.

Women's visible attendance at school committees has been important to demonstrating that it is possible for them to participate in official municipal politics. "I know a lot of women who could go to assemblies. They don't go because they only see men going. But now when there are meetings at the school women go. This is good because they can see that there are women there with good ideas. But in the *municipio*, since from the beginning only men went, it is difficult for women to go" (Cristina, age 37). Some women who had attended the meetings, however, found that there was still a great deal of resistance to women's participation. "Of course women have a right to go to public meetings. They go to school meetings. Sometimes, however, when a woman speaks up there, the men say that she doesn't know what she is talking about. But she has the right to speak" (Rosa, age 34).

The greatest factor preventing women's participation in general *municipio* assemblies is not a formal law that forbids them from coming, but *costumbre*. When asked whether or not assemblies would be better if women attended, both men and women repeatedly stated *sí, pueden participar, pero no es la costumbre* (yes, they can participate, but it isn't the custom). Many also pointed out, however, that women's participation in the various school committees had been valuable and signaled their ability to take part in public meetings.

Overall, men and women felt that it would be better for women to participate in all public meetings, but the facts that they are often held at night, that women might attend alone, and that meetings violate the norms of spatial separation by gender were named as obstacles.

Of course, it would be better if women went to *municipio* assemblies. Once they had a meeting in the afternoon and women went. In this meeting women had more courage than the men. They are better at working things out than men. Women are more honest when they say things. The problem is that they always have the meetings at night so that women can't go. The problem is that the men are in charge and they have the meetings in the evening. If they had meetings during the day and invited the women they would be much better. (Leonora, age 40)

Both in the past and currently, much of women's political discussion takes place in space that is strongly segmented by gender. In Teotitlán, as well as in other indigenous communities, any time men and women come together outside their immediate household for an event, they congregate in physically separate spaces. Many political discussions take place during ritual celebrations, in markets, and during reciprocal labor exchanges in which men and women occupy physically distinct places. Women acknowledge the importance of these discussions and feel that their experience there is a valid basis for participating in community assemblies.

> There are some women in this town who are really articulate. I know that they can express themselves very well and would be really good at *juntas* [assemblies]. We always talk about politics at fiestas and that way you can see who the really influential and articulate women are. Often we talk about what the men do and say. It's too bad that the *costumbre* keeps us from going to *juntas* because we know how to do things. Fiestas are very important to us because that is where we talk about things, things that men discuss in their *juntas*. A lot of women know how to talk really well, but they are afraid to talk in front of men. (Isabela, age 50)

Even in formal civic functions or community religious festivities that take place in the public square, men and women self-segregate their seating. People in Teotitlán defined this as an indication of mutual respect on the part of men and women. In some cases, this discourages women from wanting to attend meetings with men. "I'm not sure that women are ready to go to meetings with men. You can't have men and women together in the same place. It isn't respectful" (Soledad, age 25).

In Teotitlán, both men and women are socialized to discuss politics in gendered spheres and in a manner that resembles small discussion groups rather than formal meetings in which a designated leader calls on participants and opinions must be expressed in front of large numbers of people. As individual men and women accumulate capital, engage in businesses, and attend school, they may learn alternate ways of discussing politics and asserting their opinions. This in turn can affect their self-perceptions as political actors and the strategies they choose.

Merchant and Weaver Men's Attitudes toward Women's Political Participation

Male attitudes toward women's political participation vary somewhat, depending on whether they are merchants or weavers. The limitations that merchant men place on their wives' participation in business are also indicated in their attitudes toward women's political participation. In the questionnaire given to 54 merchant house-

Table 32. *Men's Attitudes toward Women's Attendance at Municipio Meetings*

	Believe Meetings Would Be Better If Women Attended	Do Not Believe Meetings Would Be Better If Women Attended	Total
Merchant men (N = 25)	56%	44%	100%
Weaver men (N = 40)	78%	22%	100%

Source: Random stratified household survey of male and female household heads conducted by Lynn Stephen in 1986.

holds and 74 weaver households, a subset of questions was asked concerning women's political participation. Respondents included 67 men and 84 women. In 3 households, both men and women insisted on responding simultaneously, making it impossible to differentiate their responses. In some cases not all of the questions were answered.

In the random sample of merchant and weaver men, only 56 percent of merchant men interviewed compared with 78 percent of weaver men thought that local assemblies would be better if women participated in them. Extreme comments focused on the fact that community assembly space was traditionally all male and should stay that way, with women meeting in their own forums such as in fiestas and at the market. "I think it should just be men. I don't think that both men and women should be in meetings together. The men would get jealous if their women came. The custom says that it is only men. That is how it should be. Women have their own places to go" (Mario, merchant, age 54). "I do tell my wife what goes on in the municipal meetings, but women can't go to them. They are not for women. They don't have any reason to get involved with affairs that belong to men—the affairs of the community" (Francisco, merchant, age 60).

More weaver men (85 percent) than merchant men (68 percent) thought that women were capable of holding civil cargo posts. Merchant men emphasized increased numbers of better-educated young women as those who might be qualified for such posts. In contrast, weaver men often focused on knowledge that women already had as

Table 33. *Men's Opinions on Women's Ability to Hold Cargo Posts*

	Believe Women Are Qualified to Hold Cargo Posts	Do Not Believe Women Are Qualified to Hold Cargo Posts	Total
Merchant men ($N = 25$)	68%	32%	100%
Weaver men ($N = 40$)	85%	15%	100%

Source: Random stratified household survey of male and female household heads conducted by Lynn Stephen in 1986.

a basis for their participation in community political discussions. "I think that there are a lot of women who are capable of holding office, but their husbands won't let them. It would be better with them there because sometimes we can't work things out alone. They know different things than we do" (Raúl, weaver, age 36). In a few cases, weaver men thought women might be even better for cargo posts than men. "Women are capable of carrying out cargos. . . . Women know better than men what goes on here. They have more ideas about what to do. Women don't forget things. If they say they are going to do something, they do it. Men only remember for a little while" (Pedro, weaver, age 48).

Despite the fact that a majority of both merchant and weaver men surveyed thought that women were capable of holding cargo positions and that community meetings would be improved by their presence, many men do not seem to share political information from municipal meetings with their wives and daughters. While only 21 percent of the males surveyed said that they did not share information with the women in their households, 42 percent of women surveyed stated that men in their households did not share information with them. This may indicate different perceptions on the part of men and women about what political information is and what constitutes sharing. In several interviews, men and women began to argue with one another about whether or not information was shared. Women maintained that information was not shared with them or that what was shared was superficial.

Table 34. *Women's Perceptions of Men's Sharing of Political Information*

	Believe Men in Their Household Share Political Information	Do Not Believe Men in Their Household Share Political Information	Total
Merchant women (N = 25)	46%	54%	100%
Weaver women (N = 59)	65%	35%	100%

Source: Random stratified household survey of male and female household heads conducted by Lynn Stephen in 1986.

The stronger feeling among merchant men that community assemblies would not be improved by the presence of women was also reflected in the number of merchant women who responded negatively when asked if their husbands discussed the content of community assemblies with them. While 35 percent of the weaver women interviewed stated that their husbands did not discuss the business of community assemblies with them, 54 percent of merchant women responded negatively to the question. Many of the merchant women who indicated that their husbands did not discuss assembly business with them stated that they felt distant from the political process that took place in the *municipio*. They said that they found out what went on by discussion with other women in the market the following morning.

The Self-Perceptions and Political Strategies of Merchant and Weaver Women

Given differing male opinions regarding the desirability of women in community meetings and women's perceptions of how much men in their households discuss assembly business with them, we might now ask: what is the impact of male attitudes and the structure of *municipio* assemblies on women's own attitudes and strategies for political participation?

While a majority of merchant (60 percent) and weaver (56 percent) women surveyed agreed that community assembly meetings would

Table 35. *Women's Opinions about Their Own Ability to Attend* Municipio *Meetings and Hold Cargo Posts*

	Believe Meetings Would Be Better If Women Attended	Do Not Believe Meetings Would Be Better If Women Attended	Believe Women Are Qualified to Hold Cargo Posts	Do Not Believe Women Are Qualified to Hold Cargo Posts
Merchant women (N = 25)	60%	40%	80%	20%
Weaver women (N = 59)	56%	44%	64%	36%

Source: Random stratified household survey of male and female household heads conducted by Lynn Stephen in 1986.

be better if both men and women attended, they felt differently about the capacity of women to hold cargo offices such as president, secretary, or treasurer. While 80 percent of merchant women interviewed stated that they felt women were capable of holding such offices, 64 percent of weaver women agreed. The difference is not huge, but significant, particularly when related to differences between merchant and weaver women in linguistic skills and experience in dealing with outsiders. "There are women who could hold these jobs because now there are women who can read and write. It would be good if these women had cargos. They would say things more correctly and get things done" (Godelia, age 58).

As discussed previously, education and Spanish literacy have become increasingly important in determining who is qualified to function in the elected positions of the *municipio.* The individuals holding such offices become the primary political brokers for the community in formal relations with the state bureaucracy, particularly concerning the use of state funds for public works such as construction of roads, schools, bridges, running water, and irrigation schemes. As such they are also crucial in prioritizing the needs of the community.[3]

Merchant women believe women are more qualified to fill official positions in the *municipio* than weaver women do. Many of them have expressed their desire to do so. Several merchant women and one woman from an independent producing weaving household have already served as secretaries on parents' committees for kindergarten and primary school. Others have served on the government-mandated health committee. That committee followed the principle of gender separation and had a male and a female component. For several young women who served on it, it was a positive experience. "I was named with six other young women on the *comité de salud* [health committee]. There was a women's committee and a men's committee. In the process we were able to talk freely about our own ideas and participated equally with men in the project. I learned how to give injections and traveled to some other towns as part of my experience. It was good and I was listened to. . . . But in the kindergarten where men and women are together, they made fun of a woman because she spoke up" (Claudia, merchant, age 24).

The influence of women's linguistic abilities on their perceptions of themselves as political actors may be reflected in the relatively small but significant difference in this area between merchant and weaver women. Weaver women have a higher level of Zapotec monolingualism. Those who do speak Spanish do not practice it as often as merchant women, who may interact in Spanish on a daily basis because they sit in the local artisan market selling to tourists. Weaver women remain in their homes and only use Spanish when they go to the state capital of Oaxaca to shop. While there are not significant differences in the educational level of merchant and weaver women, merchant women are more inclined to exercise their minimal literacy skills in their interactions with tourists and importers.

These differences can have important consequences for when and how merchant and weaver women feel they will be politically effective. The strongest indication of differences in women's perceptions

Table 36. *Linguistic Skills of Merchant and Weaver Women Compared*

	Mono-lingual Zapotec	Bilingual Zapotec/ Spanish	Spanish Only	No Data
Weaver women (N = 59)	45%	51%	1%	3%
Merchant women (N = 25)	33%	62%	1%	4%

Source: Random stratified household survey of male and female household heads conducted by Lynn Stephen in 1986.

Table 37. *Minimum Literacy Skills of Merchant and Weaver Women Compared*

	One Year or Less	Two Years or More	No Data
Weaver women (N = 59)	45%	53%	2%
Merchant women (N = 25)	43%	53%	4%

Source: Random stratified household survey of male and female household heads conducted by Lynn Stephen in 1986.

of themselves as political actors can be seen in the strategies taken by merchant and weaver women, particularly in relation to their age. Several young merchant women and girls (approximately ages 14–24), most of them daughters of prominent merchants, have indicated a willingness to confront the structure of the *municipio* and demand equal participation with men on one of the committees. Many of these young women run stalls for their families' businesses in the local artisan market. They are bilingual, sometimes trilingual with rudimentary English. Most have completed at least the sixth grade and are interested in questions of accounting and investments. Through their socialization in the public school system of Mexico, they have received an education in Spanish that defines political participation in terms of voting in local and state elections, albeit for the PRI, the ruling party in Mexico. They have been taught that it is important for women to vote.

Decisions regarding local price controls and market policy are made by an all-male market committee attached to the local municipal government. Members of the committee are elected in the same all-male meetings in which local officials are elected. Several of the young women who run market stalls have fathers who sit on the committee. These men are seldom present in the market on a daily basis.

This group of approximately twenty-five young women has emerged with a vocal critique of the committee that excludes them. Some have also criticized the municipal structure for excluding women. "There is a committee that meets to regulate the serape market where I work with my daughters and a lot of other girls and women. We all want to go to the meetings. The problem is that the *presidente* [chairman] of the committee is a man and he only calls the men from the families who sell in the market to the meeting. They call the husbands and fathers who don't know what is going on. We know what is going on in the market because we are there all day. The problem is that men run the meetings" (Concepción, age 35). Many of them have voiced their dissatisfaction to their fathers who are on the committee, but expressed frustration at having to silence their critique due to their fathers' position of authority within the household. Younger men in the community have brought up the possibility of including women on more local committees, such as the market committee, at the behest of their young wives.

These young women from merchant households are in a contradictory position. On the one hand, they have decreasing influence over production and business decision making as their households accumulate capital. On the other hand, they have gained significant business expertise through going to school and through their daily interactions with tourists and importers. Because they have the skills that are identified with being able to hold municipal office and participate in wider national politics, they seem more willing to question the authority structure that excludes them.

This is also seen in the willingness of literate merchant women to confront outside authorities, such as the director of the yarn factory in Teotitlán. One of the most volatile political issues since 1984 has been a lack of community involvement in the building and administration of the yarn factory. On almost a daily basis, locals would question both the quality of production and the price of wool yarn (Stephen 1987a:159–163). Merchant women were in the forefront of many of these confrontations, talking directly to the manager and the director, threatening them with personal boycotts and action from local authorities. At one point, these confrontations frightened factory workers so badly that production was halted for several days for fear of violence.

Many of the merchant women who confronted factory management purchased significant amounts of yarn (100 to 200 kilos) for their husbands. Their role as important customers of the factory as well as the value of their opinions because of their position in the community made factory officials take them seriously. Like the market committee, however, when a formal municipal price control committee was set up to negotiate with the factory, its members were all male.

Weaver women and older monolingual Zapotec merchant women had different strategies in dealing with the factory price increases. They would talk with one another in fiestas, at the market, and at the community wells, advocating boycotts of the factory and urging people to purchase from local yarn merchants. The channels they used to hold political discussions, influence public opinions, and coordinate unified activity were more subtle and did not involve a direct confrontation of officials or threats to disrupt the *municipio*. Instead they worked through what do not appear to be overtly political channels, but channels and events connected with social reproduction. Older merchant women and many weaver women emphasize the influence they have over public opinion by virtue of their status as *mayordomas* or other measures of ritual status such as the number of godchildren they have. When they conceptualize their sphere of community influence, it is in reference to the number of people they are connected to through kin and *compadrazgo* networks. They work to influence their own kin-based networks of people in a particular direction instead of opting to work through the formal structure of the *municipio*.

Weaver women, who cannot rely on wealth or education as a source of authority, turn to the concept of respect and the institutional links of social reproduction as a source of power. By using this strategy, they are militating against the use of wealth as the sole basis of political authority. Like the young merchant women who are pushing for acceptance within the formal political system, they are broadening the boundaries of the political process in the community.

Conclusions

The situation in Teotitlán suggests that women will push to be formally included in the municipal structure of government, yet also continue to use the institutions of social reproduction as a basis for political influence. The case study also highlights the influence that the competing factors of ethnic solidarity and class formation can have on women as a group. Not all women are likely to have the same perceptions of themselves as political actors or be attracted by the same institutional possibilities or strategies. In addition, their strategies for change tend to reflect the different positions they hold in the relations of production and corresponding levels of literacy and language skills, which have become vital in determining formal political authority at the level of the *municipio*. In Teotitlán, poorer, older, illiterate, and monolingual women will continue to use ritually based *respet* as a way to gain influence. Younger, literate, bilingual, and wealthier women will construct a political position in relation to a claim of superior knowledge and wealth.

The case of Teotitlán underlines the importance for women of class/ethnic conflicts that are reflected in changing notions of respect. In Teotitlán local criteria of respect and the ranking of community participants in terms of these criteria help to determine political authority and influence. In situations where broader popular movements are not reordering traditional, male-run political structures, disenfranchised women who do not have language and literacy skills or wealth generated through entrepreneurial activities continue to use the networks, events, and institutions of social reproduction to influence community political agendas and to mobilize people to take specific action. In this process, they are indirectly militating against the use of wealth and occupation as the sole criteria for determining political participation.

Chapter 10. Creating New Political Spaces: Mexican Peasant Women in Local Politics

For the first time in the history of our community, women are participating in a fully conscious way and organizing to fight for self-determination. (Juana, age 55, activist from Unión de Mujeres Yalatecas)

THE VARIETY of means that Teotiteco women use to influence local political life are also reflected in the participation of Mexican women in organizations that form the basis of popular movements in Mexico,[1] such as the CONAMUP (Coordinadora Nacional del Movimiento Urbano Popular, National Coordinating Body of the Popular Urban Movement) in Mexico City, where women are a majority of the members. While women's participation in urban popular movements has been reasonably well documented, little analysis has been done of peasant women's popular participation in groups such as *ejido* unions, independent peasant organizations, and efforts to democratize *cacique-* or PRI-dominated *municipios*. The limited literature that does exist often describes women as the surplus labor of rural movements and characterizes them as largely marginalized from the center of power relations (Camarena 1988; Carbajal Ríos 1988; Comisión Organizadora del Encuentro de Mujeres de los Sectores Populares de México, Centroamérica y el Caribe et al. 1987; Documentos del Movimiento Campesino 1984; Magallón Cervantes 1988; Las Mujeres Tenemos la Palabra 1988). While descriptions of women's participation in Mexican rural movements are rare yet exist, no comparative work has been done to suggest why women are excluded from leadership and decision making in the Mexican peasant sector or to suggest what changes might be made in organizational structures and procedures to include them.

As a beginning step toward that end, this chapter compares women's political participation in Teotitlán, where there are no independent peasant organizations, with three cases where women's presence has been established in popular political organizations. The gendered political dynamics of indigenous peasant communities such as Teotitlán,[2] which exhibit more contradictory forms of resistance to cooptation, can help us to understand the different ways in which women do and do not participate in more formal movements. The three cases discussed include the creation of a women's union through an effort to democratize the *municipio* of Yalálag in Oaxaca, women's efforts to achieve support for their productive projects and their presence within an *unión de ejidos* in Nayarit, and efforts to create an official women's presence within a national independent peasant organization, the CNPA (Coordinadora Nacional "Plan de Ayala").

Key questions to be raised in conjunction with the three cases and Teotitlán are:

1. What type of leadership and political style and skills do women develop organically in communities where they are structurally excluded from *municipio* politics and peasant organizations?

2. How are such skills encouraged or discouraged by the ways in which peasant organizations and actions are structured?

3. What are the factors that trigger women's presence in municipal politics or peasant organizations? Ethnicity? Unintended consequences of state recognition of women through providing them with resources and programs? External organizers such as the church, feminist organizers, and bureaucrats from state agencies?

Political organizations are constantly undergoing changes. Two of the organizations described in this chapter have changed since the data were collected. The Unión de Mujeres Yalatecas in Oaxaca still exists but has decreased significantly in size. The women's union in the Unión de Ejidos Lázaro Cárdenas in Nayarit became significantly strengthened in 1990 through the development of government-funded projects in many of the Agro-Industrial Units for Women (UAIMs). The women's union is also getting along better with the male leadership of the Unión de Ejidos Lázaro Cárdenas. As always, what happens within these two organizations as well as the other group discussed in this chapter, Coordinadora Nacional "Plan de Ayala" (CNPA), is always subject to change.

The Political Toolbox of Indigenous Peasant Women: Lessons from Teotitlán

The description of Teotiteco women's political participation in the previous chapter offers some general insights that can help to explain the current nature of indigenous women's marginalization within formal political organizations—what has been described as women's support roles versus their active presence as leaders and key decision makers. First, women have been largely excluded from formal political institutions, both in municipal offices and in peasant organizations. Even after 1971, when the agrarian reform law was formally amended to grant legal equality between men and women and provided for the creation of Agro-Industrial Units for Women (UAIMs), women were not participating formally as *ejidatarios* with men (Arizpe and Botey 1987; Camarena 1988). In some cases where government offices such as the Agrarian Reform Ministry and Rural Bank gave women legal legitimacy within *ejido* structures as part of UAIMs, the autonomy of such groups was threatened not only by nonacceptance by the male directorates of *ejidos,* but by attempts to coopt and take over the UAIMs by the CNC, the state-controlled peasant union (Camarena 1988).

Often women achieve legitimate political status at the level of the *municipio* only when the state formally intervenes and requires that women be put on specific municipal committees or sets up programs aimed at integrating women into production (Dalton 1990). This is the case in Teotitlán, where the only civil cargo posts held by women are on committees for health and education, areas where government officials urged and sometimes required women's participation. Many government programs that tried to integrate women into the labor force have only turned unpaid domestic work into paid labor as women work in sewing cooperatives and food processing, thus never altering the traditional gendered division of labor (for example, the UAIMs, the PINMUDE [Programa de Desarrollo Comunitario con la Participación de la Mujer: Program for Community Development with Women's Participation] in Oaxaca; see Dalton 1990).

Second, the structure of women's political discussions and the ways in which they formulate opinions are distinct from the way in which many formal meetings are constituted in *municipios* as well as in independent peasant organizations. In Teotitlán, such discussions take place informally in gendered spheres such as the market, at wells, at the river during bathing and washing clothes, and to a large extent in ritual fiestas. Such discussions are characterized by fluidity and a lack of formal procedures and leadership. The limited literature on Mexican women's participation in peasant politics points to formal meeting structures, with an emphasis on public speaking ability and the ability to negotiate with bureaucratic officials in Spanish as factors limiting many women's participation (Camarena 1988; Magallón Cervantes 1988:420; Martin 1990). Those few women who are comfortable confronting bureaucratic officials or putting forth their opinions in Spanish may be those who have commercial experience and a higher degree of education or have served on municipal committees, as reflected in Teotitlán. The majority of women will most likely participate in those aspects of a political struggle that coincide with their normal range of activities, for which they receive status and recognition outside of formal political organizations, such as the ritual respect gained by women in Teotitlán for their labor, planning, and direction of complex ritual fiestas. In many cases these are the activities described by observers as support work.

A third factor of critical importance brought home by women's political and social participation in Teotitlán is the importance of segregation by gender. Ritual and community space (which cannot necessarily be divided up into public and domestic space) is often strongly segregated by gender. As the concept of mutual respect between men and women from Teotitlán suggests, the immediate integration of women into previously male spaces may not only undermine women's ability to participate, but can also clash with local norms of male-female interaction. While such conditions clearly limit the ability of women to move into positions of political power in *municipios* and peasant organizations, potentially gender-segregated political organizations for women can also serve as a way to challenge male-run institutions. The exploration below of examples where women were able to make significant inroads into male-run institutions highlights the importance of gendered spheres and their potential as a positive factor in empowering women.

Finally, the case of Teotitlán suggests the importance of the heterogeneity of peasant women in terms of ethnicity, class, and generation. As seen in Teotitlán, in concrete terms these are often linked to differences in education and language ability, factors that can critically affect how well women are able to maintain a presence in male-dominated organizations, particularly if there is ongoing resistance to women's presence and participation.

Three Cases of Women's Participation in Peasant Movements

This section discusses three cases of peasant movements in which women's participation has moved beyond that of being faceless foot soldiers to establishing a formal women's presence within peasant organizations or communities. These cases cover distinct arenas, each at a higher level of organization, including an indigenous community, a regional-level *ejido* union, and a complex and diverse national coalition of regional independent peasant organizations. The details of each case are briefly compared with the situation of women in Teotitlán. I shall begin by exploring the formation of the Unión de Mujeres Yalatecas, an organization of Zapotec women in a town northeast of Teotitlán in the Sierra Juárez.

Unión de Mujeres Yalatecas, Oaxaca

Unlike Teotitlán, the Zapotec community of Yalálag has been controlled by *caciques* (political bosses) since the Mexican Revolution. This has had a major impact on local politics in Yalálag, where a community-level women's union (*unión de mujeres*) was formed in the town's third attempt to liberate its *municipio* from *cacique* rule. While political authority in Teotitlán continued to be mediated by ritual authority until quite recently, in Yalálag *cacique* rule directly linked economic and political power throughout this century. Women were most likely completely eliminated from having ritually based influence over politics. Recently, however, because of the extreme abuse of power by local *caciques* controlling the municipal government, women have joined in a broad community effort to oust *caciques* and in the process have won a space in the formal structure of the *municipio*. The relatively stable economic and political situation in Teotitlán has not produced that kind of opportunity for women.

The first attempts to liberate Yalálag from *cacique* rule were made in 1971, and again in 1974, when community members occupied the *municipio* building and had fraudulent elections annulled, and the popular candidates were installed in the *municipio* by the governor of Oaxaca. In 1975, however, a new governor annulled the previous results, calling for new elections, and the *cacique* faction that had been ousted once again came to dominate the *municipio* (Equipo Pueblo 1988:14–22; Ortigoza 1986:35–36).

In 1975, after the *cacique* was reinstalled, community members began to have ongoing discussions outside of the *municipio* concerning the meaning of *tequio*—unpaid community labor. They went on strike and refused to perform *tequio* for the *cacique* faction mayor. This was tantamount to a strike of all municipal workers and shut down the operation of the *municipio*. In 1980, members of the community approached the Oaxaca State Electoral Commission asking it to nullify the results of fraudulent elections and to hold new ones. During that time, the Unión de Mujeres Yalatecas was formed with the goal of participating in political negotiations to rid the community of *cacique* rule (Equipo Pueblo 1988:37). Women in Yalálag had previously participated in a few municipal committees, but the advent of community organizing outside the sphere of the *municipio* provided a new opening for women. Before that time, women from Yalálag exercised much of their political influence through informal networks, similar to the kin-*compadrazgo* networks through which women in Teotitlán continue to exercise political influence.

The successful formation of the Unión de Mujeres Yalatecas was related to the way in which political negotiations between the community and the Oaxaca state governor were carried out in 1980 and the fact that women participated in a spontaneous occupation of the *municipio*. In a series of meetings with the State Department and Justice Department of Oaxaca, the community commission sent from Yalálag demanded that all discussions be held in Zapotec. Women from a special women's commission were present at all of these meetings. They also held a special meeting with the governor's wife stressing their demands for due electoral process.

Documents describing the foundation of the Unión de Mujeres Yalatecas emphasize the importance of the nine-day occupation of the *municipio* in early 1981 by all sectors of the community. This was crucial in helping to solidify women's place in the political process. Because the occupation took place outside of the traditional all-male *municipio*, women's spontaneous participation became central and readily accepted. As the entire community acted to open up the closed political process controlled by the *cacique* faction, women were included, breaking the pattern of male-dominated politics still found in many indigenous communities such as Teotitlán.

Beginning in the 1980s, the Unión de Mujeres continued to hold its own meetings, but also actively participated in *municipio* assemblies. The Unión de Mujeres was reported to have about 300 members in 1986. That number has dwindled in recent years. Most of the women who regularly attend meetings are over thirty years of age and a significant number of elderly women are important participants. Many of the women are monolingual Zapotec speakers or speak little Spanish (Ortigoza 1986:50–51). The meetings provide women with a gender-separate space for advancing their view of community goals and for planning strategies to achieve these goals. The meetings are run informally, with several women talking at once. Decisions are made after all opinions have been heard (Ortigoza, personal communication). These meetings reflect many qualities of the informal political discussions in Zapotec that women held in female spaces in Teotitlán. The difference is that, in

Yalálag, these discussions are recognized as political and the meetings are known as political spaces for women.

Since 1980, the Unión de Mujeres Yalatecas has organized programs around rebuilding the *municipio*, construction of a technical secondary school and a bilingual education center, and installation of a community corn mill and store and continues watchdogging the political process in the *municipio*. Most of the group's time is spent running a community corn mill that operates under pressure from competing local mills aligned with *caciques*. In addition, women from the union run a communal store that stocks items unavailable in government CONASUPO (National Popular Subsistence Company) stores and often overpriced in other local businesses. The formation of a gender-specific political organization in Yalálag has given way to joint economic projects for women. This is almost the reverse of what is happening in Teotitlán, where women's joint participation in the artisans' market may encourage their political action as a group demanding formal representation on the municipal market committee.

Ethnographic descriptions of two women who actively participated in the Unión de Mujeres Yalatecas indicate that while the union may temporarily have secured a political position in the community, the legitimacy of women's participation may still be questioned within their households by their husbands. This is consistent with comments made by merchant women in Teotitlán, who stated that their business activities and politicking had to stay within the bounds of their roles as wives, daughters, and mothers. In Yalálag, women have to justify their political activity in terms of their responsibilities within the gendered division of labor. While women are permitted formally to participate in political decision making and in municipal meetings, their participation results in a double workload as they try to keep up their participation in household production as well as being political activists. For example, in 1984, the *presidenta* of the union had other women try to persuade her husband of the importance of her work after he complained that she was neglecting her work at home (Ortigoza 1986:67–73). A common complaint heard from women who participate in both rural and urban popular movements is that their political work is seen by their husbands as secondary to their household chores and child-care responsibilities. Often they must battle at home as well as within formal organizations to have their political participation validated and accepted, working to convert their husbands and fathers into supporters and promoters of their projects (Camarena 1988:18; Logan

1988:351, 1990; Magallón Cervantes 1988:412-415; Las Mujeres Tenemos la Palabra 1988).

In addition, while the Unión de Mujeres is allowed to function formally in Yalálag, structurally it does not seem to have the same legitimacy as male cargos. In 1985, the *presidenta* of the women's union gave up her cargo when her husband was also named to a municipal cargo. Because it was too hard for both of them to hold cargo positions and still have enough time left over to work in sandal-making and agriculture, Juana, the *presidenta*, quit her position, indicating the priority given to male cargos. While the Unión de Mujeres has been formally incorporated into the political structure of the *municipio* at the same level as committees for schools, running water, and the *ejido*, women serving in formal offices of the union do not get household credit for their cargo service. Usually only one household member is required to do cargo service at a time. Women's cargo service through their participation in the Unión de Mujeres does not carry the same weight as male cargo service, which entitles a household to a rest of one to three years between periods of service. The same *costumbre* of women's nonparticipation in *municipio* meetings as seen in Teotitlán is still subtly reflected in Yalálag, where it prevents women from receiving full recognition for their cargo service.

The case of the Unión de Mujeres Yalatecas underlines the importance of women having an autonomous space for political organizing before they can successfully participate in formal political groups that have a history of being run by men. As seen in Teotitlán, the fact that women perceived their attendance at municipal meetings as violating gender segregation norms was an important factor in inhibiting their participation. In Yalálag, the principle of gender separation, which structures many arenas of social life, has been recreated in political organizing. Women meet separately as a group and discuss local issues and projects in a manner that resembles the political discussions they engage in during fiestas or while marketing. Representatives from the Unión de Mujeres then go to *municipio* meetings and participate with men. As more women gain experience, they can express their viewpoints more successfully and in greater numbers in *municipio* meetings.

The inclusion of an ethnically based demand that state officials provide their own translators in dealing with community commissions in 1980 was also critical for the initial involvement of women in renegotiating fraudulent elections. As in Teotitlán and many other indigenous communities, indigenous languages—in this case

236   *Zapotec Women*

Zapotec—are spoken and used by most people in daily life, particularly women. In 1980, people from Yalálag consciously undermined a political system that assumes knowledge of Spanish and concentrates political authority in the hands of those who have the most outside experience and education. This demand allowed women as well as the elderly who were monolingual in Zapotec and who had ritually based authority to participate in the political process. The demand for respect for language and for those who hold authority by virtue of their age and ritual experience is an assertion of ethnic identity that has worked favorably for women in Yalálag and could work for women in other indigenous communities such as Teotitlán. In contrast to most indigenous monolingual women in Mexico, Yalálag women have not been excluded from dealing with state officials. They were able to conduct political discussions in their own language and style, not that of the state.

Within the community, however, the Unión de Mujeres Yalatecas is still not completely legitimate. On the one hand, it functions as part of the formal municipal structure. On the other hand, however, women's cargo service in the union does not count in the same way that male cargo service does. This signals an underlying layer of structural resistance to the incorporation of an autonomous women's organization into the *municipio*.

While the Unión de Mujeres Yalatecas provides an example of how women's informal political participation finds a legitimate expression in a formal organization, when the level of political organization moves beyond the community, the emergence of an autonomous women's presence becomes more difficult. In the case explored next, the constant presence of officials from the Agrarian Reform Ministry and its state-controlled union, the CNC, greatly complicated the formation of a women's organization within the Unión de Ejidos Lázaro Cárdenas (UELC) in southern Nayarit. Information about the emergence of a women's presence in the UELC is taken largely from an internal document written for a funding agency that supported several local women's economic projects (Camarena 1988), conversations with organizers of the women's union, and a brief field visit.

Unión de Mujeres, Unión de Ejidos Lázaro Cárdenas, Nayarit

While the community of Teotitlán never received *ejido* land under Lázaro Cárdenas in the 1930s, many communities did. As a result, an additional link to the state was created through local committees that oversee the use of *ejido* land grants and production and report to the Agrarian Reform Ministry. In an effort to have greater local control over their own production, some *ejidos* have formed unions to build a stronger regional presence, which challenges the domination of the government peasant union, the Coordinadora Nacional de Campesinos (CNC). Women have had a minimal role in the formation and ongoing operation of most *ejido* unions.

The Unión de Ejidos Lázaro Cárdenas (UELC) was formed in 1975, eventually bringing together fifteen agrarian reform communities in southern Nayarit. The formation of the union was catalyzed by successful efforts to broaden access to fertilizer and credit that culminated in the right to a major government fertilizer distributorship (Fox and Hernández 1990; Hernández 1988). Apart from the formation of the union itself, by the early 1980s there were several UAIMs (Agro-Industrial Units for Women) formed in three communities that participated in the union. These economic projects for women were state-initiated by the Agrarian Reform Ministry and did not emerge from internal demands from the *ejido* union. Because the UAIMs were not stimulated internally, their structure and the type of skills they were built on were not necessarily consistent with those women already had. In addition, the UAIMs were never assured of a secure place within the Unión de Ejidos Lázaro Cárdenas.

In 1987, with help from the DICONSA (Distribuidora CONASUPO S.A.), a government agency associated with the Agrarian Reform Ministry, women from the three UAIMs had meetings with women in all of the communities included in the UELC. In the meetings one female promoter from each community was chosen to support the formation of a women's organization that would operate within each *ejido* in the UELC. All of these female community promoters completed a training course, and in 1987 a regional meeting was held that included 170 women from the *ejido* communities. The goal of the meeting was to set up women's projects that would promote food self-sufficiency in conjunction with each of the *ejidal* enterprises. At this meeting women from four *municipios* formally created the *unión de mujeres* (women's union), pulling women from diverse communities into one organization. This was the first assertion of an extracommunity women's presence within the *ejido* union.

In 1987, after the women formed a growing *unión de mujeres*, their relations with the male directorate of the UELC temporarily broke down. Male reaction to women's assertion of autonomy with the *ejido* union was quick and clear, reflecting the difficulties women have had stepping into more active political roles in Yalálag. The UELC pulled out its support for the women's activities and began to question each transaction in which the women engaged. In addition to the problems that the larger Unión de Mujeres had in being recognized within the UELC, individual UAIMs also had problems being recognized within their respective *ejidos*. In one case, women who had one of the earliest UAIM projects tried for three years to be formally recognized within their *ejido*. They finally gave up and organized as a group outside of it. In other cases there were acts of sabotage against UAIMs, such as invading *ejidal* land assigned to women, prohibiting women from attending *ejido* meetings, and making fun of their internal disagreements and ignoring their successes (Camarena 1988:16–18). Unlike Teotitlán, where women conduct their politics informally and in a way that is probably less threatening to the social order, the open organization of a women's group in the UELC provoked severe reactions in some communities.

In response to these acts of sabotage directed against individual UAIMs as well as the bottling up of resources within the UELC, the Unión de Mujeres began to pressure the UELC to grant it a legal presence and to turn over the resources to which women were entitled. At one point, when the male directorate of the UELC was only providing information and resources selectively to some of the UAIMs, representatives from the Unión de Mujeres went to the Agrarian Reform Ministry and found out that resources for their projects were already available, but that the male directorate of the UELC had not passed along this information. In an effort to confront local male political authority, women invoked the superior authority of the Agrarian Reform Ministry to back their position. This is quite a different political strategy than that used by women and other community members in Yalálag, who pushed state officials to meet their demands according to local structures and language.

In 1988, with the backing of the Agrarian Reform Ministry, the Unión de Mujeres confronted the directorate of the UELC over the fact that it had frozen access to outside resources and funds for projects. In a stormy meeting, the president of the union changed his position, revised the statutes of the organization, and legally incorporated the Unión de Mujeres as one of the groups that formally constitutes the Unión de Ejidos Lázaro Cárdenas. With this step he agreed to cooperate fully in providing information regarding funding and resources for the productive projects, to coordinate the Unión de Mujeres activities with those of the Unión de Ejidos, and to support the women's participation (Camarena 1988; Fox 1990; Loubet 1988). Later the directorate threatened simply to turn all of the UAIMs over to the CNC, breaking their links with the independent *ejido* union. More recently, leaders from the Unión de Mujeres have themselves voted to affiliate with the CNC. It is unclear whether this action was a demonstration of their political autonomy from the UELC or an indication of the continual ability of the CNC to coopt independent organizations.

The most outstanding lesson of this example is the necessity for women to meet autonomously in order to pull together a political agenda before they can effectively participate on an equal level with men in a traditionally male political structure. Interestingly enough, according to Camarena (1988), the strongest impulse for independent organizing came from women in an indigenous community who had a fifteen-year history of working together on tasks that are similar to the work women do together for fiestas in Teotitlán. This may reflect a historical segmentation of gender spheres that makes these women more comfortable and effective in working with other women in decentralized projects. Because this type of gendered space did not exist naturally in all of the communities included in the UELC, it had to be developed. Unable to be taken seriously as individuals and even as members of UAIMs, women in the UELC were able to articulate a unified position only after they formed an autonomous women's group that first existed outside the domain of the UELC.

A second important ingredient in the formation of the Unión de Mujeres was the use of Agrarian Reform Ministry officials to sanction the existence of a women's organization. These state officials provided external legitimation for the group as it confronted the male leadership of the UELC. While communities such as Teotitlán do not have formal links to the Agrarian Reform Ministry through the existence of *ejidos*, communities in the UELC do. These links have provided women in the Unión de Mujeres with an alternate base of authority, but at a political cost. While state officials did provide important support for the union, other state offices periodically tried to coopt and absorb some of the UAIMs represented in the larger Unión de Mujeres in an effort to attack the UELC. State support for the autonomous women's union and the UAIMs was at best double-edged, providing them with legitimacy on the one hand, but also offering a ready avenue for coaptation by outside bureaucracies.

In this particular case, the president of the UELC was persuaded formally to recognize the Unión de Mujeres as a member group because the CNC, through the Agrarian Reform Ministry, was using the union as a way to try to gain control of the larger group, the UELC. Women were able to use the necessity to maintain internal unity and defend against an external threat as a way of gaining legitimacy for their group. This did not change the *machismo* that was the basis for their original exclusion, but did alter the balance of forces within the Unión de Ejidos Lázaro Cárdenas by formally incorporating women. Unfortunately, it appears that this strategy has only worked in the short run. The UELC directorate now seems poised to let the Unión de Mujeres become part of the CNC and to exclude it again from membership in the UELC.

In a discussion of UAIMs in the state of Oaxaca, Dalton (1990:14) notes that the most successful ones are monitored by political parties or include women participating directly in political parties, providing them with an outside source of legitimation. The two most successful UAIMs include one in Zimatlán that is linked to a left-wing party, and one in Guelatao, where a leader in the UAIM project is also a municipal authority affiliated with the PRI. Like the UAIMs in Nayarit, formal links to either the government or political parties provide both legitimization and an opening for coaptation. In communities such as Teotitlán, however, where there is a long history of resistance to involvement with state-run economic programs, government sources of legitimation for women's political projects are not available or necessarily desired.

Women in the Coordinadora Nacional "Plan de Ayala" (CNPA)

A history of independence from state institutions, particularly the CNC, and resistance to incorporation into state projects is highly evident in the last case explored here—not for economic reasons, as is the case in Teotitlán, but for the sake of maintaining an independent political identity. Just as Teotitlán's distance from state programs to develop craft production may have limited women's access to outside sources of political authority, the struggles of the CNPA (National Council of the Plan of Ayala) to maintain its identity as an independent peasant organization have also limited the possibilities for using outside authority to establish a women's presence within the organization.

Formed in 1979, the CNPA originally united more than twenty-one regional independent peasant organizations into a national coalition (Mejía Piñeros and Sarmiento Silva 1987:194). It is one of the most significant expressions of the independent peasant movement and because of its combativeness has been a target of state harassment and intervention. Because it operates on a national level and pulls together a tremendous diversity of groups, the unity of the CNPA has always been fragile and the state has made continual efforts to coopt regional members of the organization and to splinter it. Because of this pressure, efforts to establish autonomous presences within the organization at the national level have always been approached with extreme caution. Having survived a difficult period in the mid-1980s, the CNPA now has twelve to fifteen regional member groups.

Since its first national meeting in 1979, the CNPA has dealt with the issue of ethnicity, discouraging divisions within communities and citing a commitment to fight for the "rescue, conservation, and development of all of the cultural manifestations of indigenous communities in all of their forms" (Mejía Piñeros and Sarmiento Silva 1987:199). The twenty-one regional peasant organizations originally incorporated into the CNPA included members from thirteen different ethnic groups (Flores Lúa, Paré, and Sarmiento Silva 1988). In many cases, more than one ethnic group joined together in the formation of a regional organization that was a CNPA member. Of the thirteen ethnic groups represented in the CNPA in 1985, however, only the Movimiento de Unificación y Lucha Triqui (MULT, Movement for Triqui Unification and Struggle) identified itself ethnically. While the CNPA has clearly focused on class issues, it has maintained a continual dialogue on issues of ethnicity, most strongly felt when there was a movement within the organization in 1981 to have a common policy for all of the indigenous groups represented. This process never reached the level of an autonomous indigenous presence within the organization, however, because of fears of divisions within the CNPA. This is also the case for women.

The difficulty of establishing a formal women's presence at the national level is not surprising given the position of women in many of the regional organizations and communities represented in the CNPA. Like the women in Teotitlán, women in many of the indigenous communities represented within the CNPA have been eliminated from participating in formal municipal politics. Where they did maintain a position of ritual authority through *mayordomías* linked to civil offices, this authority eroded with the establishment of all-male *ejido* committees and independent peasant organizations that were often modeled on *municipio* committees, with a hierarchy of command and an emphasis on rhetorical Spanish skills. The few existing discussions of women's participation in organizations that are a part of the CNPA create a picture of women carrying out a great deal of work, but not receiving formal recognition for their participation. As described by Carbajal Ríos (1988:426–427; my translation), "When the fight is in its most intense moments, women go to the occupations of lands and offices, to marches and meetings. They confront the police and armed guards of the *caciques* because it is often argued that such guards are more violent with men. As a consequence women are beaten and mistreated. . . . Women are absent in decision making in local and regional meetings and also in training and educational meetings." Indicative of other descriptions, Neil Harvey (1990) notes that in the community of Venustiano Carranza, which is part of Organización Campesina Emiliano Zapata (OCEZ), also a CNPA member, women still play a supportive role and do not reach positions of decision making. When the gendered dynamics of politics in indigenous communities such as Teotitlán are pushed to a higher level of organization, the historical marginalization of women from politics has clear consequences.

In a description of women's participation in the OPA (Organización de Pueblos del Altiplano), a regional organization that is a CNPA member, María del Carmen Magallón Cervantes (1988) states that most women who participate act as the wives, mothers, and daughters of mobilized men, underlining the difficulties peasant women have in redefining their social roles as political activists. Of the 1,300 peasants organized in the OPA, only 100 women are formal members. Only one of the twenty or more groups formally included in the OPA is constituted primarily of women. Other women are provisionary members in a few other organizations. If the historical marginalization of women from local politics is so prevalent, then how can women overcome their traditional roles as supporters and be acknowledged as active members and leaders in peasant organizations? The recent history of the women's movement within the CNPA offers some clues.

The year 1981 marks the first movement at the national level within the CNPA to organize a women's presence. This effort was unsuccessful, however, primarily due to internal politics (CONAMUP, CNPA, et al. 1987:119). The national organization decided that an autonomous women's presence within the organization would be divisive, just as it did in relation to an autonomous indigenous presence the same year.

A second attempt in 1984 produced more concrete results for women in the CNPA. During the second CNPA congress, a women's commission was created that worked toward a national meeting of peasant women in 1986. The women's commission also tried to make the member organizations of the CNPA aware of the importance of women's work within their organizations and pushed to establish a direct relationship with women in all the organizations that are a part of the CNPA (CONAMUP, CNPA, et al. 1987:119). The formation of the women's commission also revealed emerging links among feminists, peasant women within the CNPA, and women from popular urban organizations such as the CONAMUP in Mexico City. While women from Teotitlán have created links with outsiders primarily through commercial contacts, women in the CNPA forged outside links through political organizing.

The official report from the 1984 CNPA meeting reflects extensive discussion by the women's commission, including a detailed recapitulation of all of the work that women do both inside and outside of the organization. The commission stated that women have had little participation in official negotiations with the state, few have received political training, and they have not participated in choosing authorities or reached positions of authority themselves within the CNPA. The commission enumerated particular problems related to women and asked for financial support, child care, and other resources that would help them to participate more fully in the CNPA. The official report also encouraged the inclusion of women's specific demands as part of those adopted by the organization, requested that women be given *ejidal* plots regardless of their marital status, and urged that the CNPA include at least one woman in its directorate (Documentos del Movimiento Campesino 1984: 123–126).

In preparation for a national meeting of peasant women in 1986, the women's commission held four regional meetings in Jalisco, Morelos, México, and Sonora. These regional meetings were organized differently from ordinary CNPA meetings. There was little emphasis on formal public speaking and the meetings were relaxed, with a focus on informal discussion. Women spoke with each other about the problems they had in trying to organize production cooperatives and their roles within the CNPA (Canabal Cristiáni 1985).

In 1986, 150 women from eleven states came to a national meeting of CNPA women with intentions of trying to start a national *coordinadora* (coordinating body) of women. They concluded, however, that they were not ready to do so. Instead, they decided that they needed to continue to build regional women's organizations before uniting at the national level (CONAMUP, CNPA, et al. 1987: 120). The CNPA was also having major difficulties during this time trying to survive as a unified political entity.

One of the notable outcomes of efforts to organize an autonomous women's presence within the CNPA has been the beginning of horizontal linkages between a few women from the CNPA and those from other popular movements such as the CONAMUP, with women from other peasant movements, and with feminist organizations working on projects with popular organizations. In Teotitlán, where few real links exist to popular organizations, women have no avenue for gaining access to these types of networks. In 1986, a few representatives from the CNPA participated with women from the

CONAMUP, the Sindicato "19 de Septiembre" (Women's Garment Workers' Union), and the Organización de Trabajadores Domésticas (Organization of Domestic Workers) in an international meeting of women from organizations in nine Latin countries to discuss women's roles in popular movements (Comisión Organizadora del Encuentro de Mujeres de los Sectores Populares de México, Centroamérica y el Caribe et al. 1987).[3] In 1987, women from the CNPA and from three other independent peasant organizations went to the third national meeting of women from the CONAMUP, which included 850 women and men from thirty-four organizations, both urban and rural. This meeting focused on a wide range of issues, including the exploitation of women, exchanges of experiences, the pros and cons of organizing women autonomously in mixed organizations, developing coordinated plans of action, and men's positions on women's oppression (Las Mujeres Tenemos la Palabra 1988). Participation in these meetings clearly can help peasant women to build links and gain political experience at a national level. Such forums also connected feminists, who attend such meetings in the capacity of invited supporters, with indigenous peasant women.

Unfortunately, because so few peasant women attend meetings outside their communities, the connections between urban and rural women activists remain quite tenuous. Meetings like the 1987 CONAMUP gathering have since led to the formation of an urban coalition of women's groups including feminist organizations, popular urban organizations, unions, political parties, and student organizations (Correspondencia 1989:19–22). The coalition, La Coordinadora de Mujeres "Benita Galeana," and the continued occurrence of meetings that bring women together to discuss survival issues suggest the possibility of a new popular feminism in Mexico with broad participation from many sectors.[4]

These meetings also emphasize conflicts between those who feel that women should organize autonomously within wider organizations and those who feel that they should not. This appears to be the pivotal issue for women within the CNPA, where efforts at organizing autonomous presences in relation to questions of both ethnicity and gender at a national level within the organization have been discouraged. The organization of autonomous women's groups appears to be easiest at the community level, where a certain degree of local ethnic unity already exists, as in Yalálag. With a major emphasis on class and the position of peasants in the national relations of production, large independent peasant organizations such as the CNPA do not provide a natural context for the autonomous organization of women. As the level of organization becomes more complex, the factors of outside cooptation and an increased potential for internal divisions discourage the development of an autonomous women's presence within peasant organizations, particularly at the national level.

Comparative Conclusions: Redefining Politics

The three cases of women's political participation discussed here and ethnographic material on women's political participation in Teotitlán suggest a broadened vision of the "political." The actions of peasant women have pushed so-called domestic issues such as lower prices for production materials, more efficient production, nutrition, and access to land and agricultural resources into the forefront of the political arena, moving the definition of political participation far beyond voting and membership in political parties (Jelin 1990). In some cases, as women organize in opposition to individuals and bureaucracies that inhibit them from carrying out their traditionally defined domestic roles (Kaplan 1982), they become transformed in the process into political actors participating in a group effort to achieve goals related to their daily needs. Once they have achieved representation as a group, they continue to press for economic demands as well as recognition of their own rights to participate fully in any organizational process. In other cases, women may find a political voice as part of a community movement to choose their own leaders and representatives. Having won a legitimate place in the community political arena through a common democratization struggle, women then begin to push their own agendas within the community, construing those issues that they have discussed among themselves relating to survival, raising children, and taking care of their homes as shared political concerns.

When peasant women join together as a group to push for demands they consider their own, the arena of social reproduction becomes politicized and a central focus of the political process. The more material aspects of social reproduction such as low prices for household goods and production materials are often the focus of women's initial political efforts. Later the more abstract and cultural elements of social reproduction are represented in women's organizing efforts as they demand to participate in the selection of community leaders and push for representation within community institutions such as the market committee in Teotitlán.

Women's political activity also enters the household as a gendered issue between men and women when it is questioned by their husbands or fathers. In some cases this questioning remains verbal, but is often associated with threats, intimidation, and sometimes physical beatings. When women's political activity begins to compete with their domestic duties, they often try to renegotiate the household division of labor, using each other to try to convince husbands, fathers, and children to be flexible. If such efforts are unsuccessful, women's political participation takes place under duress and they end up carrying at least a double or sometimes triple workload, engaging in wage labor, carrying out domestic work, and participating in political organizations (Dalton 1990).

Another issue of importance in broadening our understanding of the "political" has to do with what constitutes participation and leadership. As noted, the most salient feature of both outside descriptions of and organizational documents on peasant women's roles in political organizations focuses on their marginalization from decision making and leadership. At one level, the discussion centers on how leadership is defined. As seen in the ethnographic material on Teotitlán and Yalálag, indigenous peasant women clearly have leadership roles within their communities. Such roles are traditionally often tied to ritual authority and age. When systems of political authority become based on education, wealth, and experience in dealing with state functionaries, indigenous women leaders are usually marginalized from the political decision-making process. The basis of their leadership skills is invalidated. In addition, because of the prominence of segregation by gender on many occasions (both secular and ritual) in indigenous communities such as Teotitlán, women are accustomed to operating in a gendered political sphere. Their manner of speaking and leadership skills are not built on "public" speaking and maintaining control over large assemblies. Instead their skills are related to listening, consensus building, and persuasive discourse with the women to whom they are closest. They in turn use the women with whom they are connected through kinship and *compadrazgo* to build a group of political supporters.[5]

When political structures conserve some of the elements that allow female leadership to operate, then women are usually successful in asserting themselves. In Teotitlán, this has not yet happened. In Yalálag, however, the democratization of the *municipio* provided a chance for the creation of new political structures, resulting in a context where male, *cacique*-dominated institutions were partially torn down. Because the community insisted that all negotiations with the governor of Oaxaca be carried out in Zapotec, older Yalatecas with considerable political experience could be part of the process. In contrast, in Teotitlán, negotiations with the Oaxaca government continue to be in Spanish through male municipal authorities.

In Yalálag, the immediate establishment of the Unión de Mujeres Yalatecas as a separate female political space did not violate the principles of gender separation and allowed women of all ages and experience a place to air their opinions. Those women who felt most capable and prepared then went to the *municipio* meetings representing the group. Such a model is probably the most likely successfully to integrate women in Teotitlán into municipal politics as well. What is missing, however, is the political impetus for its introduction.

The establishment of autonomous women's groups at the community level seems to be critical as a means for letting the existing political and leadership skills of women emerge. If such groups are not formally constituted, then they surely exist informally, as in Teotitlán, where women continue their political discussions in their daily routines. The pivotal question of women's access to decision making and to leadership positions is not whether or not they have such skills, but whether or not a political arena exists in which they are allowed to express them.

While it is important to assert that indigenous, and in some cases mestiza, peasant women have always participated politically at some level and do possess leadership skills, it is equally important to address the reasons why they have often been structurally excluded from formal political organizations and to propose the steps that need to be taken to include them. Here I shall primarily address indigenous peasant women. The situation of mestiza peasant women can vary significantly from that of indigenous women.

As discussed in chapter 7, peasant women have been progressively marginalized from municipal political structures as religious hierarchies were divorced from the civil cargo systems that now are the backbone of local governments. As Borque and Warren note (1981 : 54, also cited in Nash 1986 : 15), when women are in a structurally disadvantaged position in relation to institutions that allocate community resources and make local policy decisions, their control is exercised through strategies that "attempt to limit or redirect the powers of those who are structurally superordinate." Women thus have developed strategies for participating informally in politics, whether it be at the level of *municipios, ejidos,* or other organizations.

The Mexican state began to pick up on the exclusion of women from formal political and economic structures in the 1970s. Updating national agrarian reform laws in 1971 formally to include women as *ejidatarios* with the same rights as men, the state moved forward with the formulation of specific programs aimed at incorporating women into the agricultural productive process and providing them with resources. Women, particularly peasant women, were viewed as unexploited political capital by the state. This can also be seen currently in the PRI's efforts to integrate women into higher-level functionary positions.[6]

As seen in the case of the Unión de Mujeres in southern Nayarit, state recognition of the importance of women and support for autonomous women's groups is double-edged. While legal recognition provides women with an institutional defense in *ejidos* and *uniones de ejidos,* when they have to use state allies actually to occupy those positions they risk coaptation from without. While the state can and has worked in a limited way to change the structural position of women within peasant organizations, such a process has clear costs to both the autonomy of women's groups and the position of independent peasant organizations in relation to the state. Women in Yalálag and Teotitlán who do not currently have recourse to the state as an alternate source of legitimacy must struggle for formal political recognition solely within their communities. In Teotitlán, the lack of any formal women's organizations and class divisions make it more difficult for women to forge an autonomous political presence within the community.

The four cases of Teotitlán, Yalálag, Nayarit, and the CNPA suggest an internal strategy for decreasing the structural marginalization of women. In Yalálag and Nayarit, where women were able to achieve a strong presence within a larger organization, they first began to meet autonomously. As pointed out above, the presence of autonomous women's groups within larger organizations, whether periodically or permanently constituted, allows women of varying ages and class backgrounds (which translates into different types of political skills) to discuss their ideas and problems in a manner to which they are accustomed. While such women's groups clearly also reflect power differences between women based on age and class experience as seen in Teotitlán, they nonetheless provide a more open space for political participation than larger organizations or *municipios,* which only allow women to act as supporters and informal participants. If and when the positions of such autonomous women's groups solidify, then women are more prepared to participate as a group in mixed-gender organizations.

Autonomous women's groups within regional peasant organizations and communities can also allow women to learn how to do national-level organizing if they participate in regional and national meetings with women from popular movements and feminists. These links between women's groups in different popular movements are important for preparing women to take up leadership at higher levels within their respective organizations. The interactions among women at larger meetings give them training and ideas on how to push from inside of their organizations for structural and process changes that will facilitate the further incorporation of women.

A final important question here concerns the factors that promote an autonomous women's presence in *municipios* and in peasant organizations. The limited literature points to a number of factors, which include, but are not limited to, the unintended consequences of the politicization of peasant women in state programs mandating the active economic participation of women (Dalton 1990); the presence of church, labor, or feminist organizers who specifically target women as a group; and the formation of ethnically based political demands and organizations that allow the existing political skills and experience of indigenous women to be utilized (Ortigoza 1986; Rubin 1987). A related question unanswered here, but an object for future study, is how the different origins of an autonomous women's presence within peasant organizations affect the kinds of opportunities opened up for women.

The 1980s in Mexico were marked by an increasing awareness of the importance of gender in present politics. Both the state and independent peasant organizations recognized the pivotal position of women in struggles for local autonomy and self-sufficiency. Historically marginalized from formal political institutions since the colonial era, women themselves nevertheless continued to participate in local politics on their own terms, working around the many structural limitations they encountered, as described in detail in Teotitlán. The current political process sees women working formally to assert their presence in *municipios, ejidos,* and independent organizations, often with the subtle backing of the state. As women in peasant movements work to move closer to center stage, the domestic politics of women as wives, mothers, and daughters as well as the political aspects of simply being female in rural Mexico are enriching the popular movements emanating from Mexico's countryside and transforming women's perceptions of themselves as political actors. As women join together to push for their agendas, the very act of participating in a group demanding services as simple as a health clinic transforms women from simply "mothers" and "wives" to political actors with a greater sense of purpose and collective power. In larger terms, the politics of social reproduction are emerging as a vital part in the wider political scene as well as revitalizing the not-so-obvious political struggles that take place between men and women in their own homes.

Chapter 11. Insights from Teotitlán: Traditional Domains of Female Power and Rural Women's Political and Economic Futures

> *My mother used to say that through her life, through her living testimony, she tried to tell women that they too had to participate, so that when the repression comes and with it a lot of suffering, it's not only the men who suffer. Women must join the struggle in their own way. My mother's words told that any evolution, any change, in which women had not participated, would not be a change, and therefore would not be victory. She was as clear about this as if she were a woman with all sorts of theories and a lot of practice. (Rigoberta Menchú, Quiché peasant activist, in Burgos-Debray 1984:196)*

THE EXPERIENCES of Zapotec women documented here as they have gossiped, woven, cooked, organized, mothered, farmed, fought, and migrated since the Mexican Revolution suggest that it is not possible to talk about the life experience of the "Zapotec woman." What is possible is a diversity of experiences of being female, a diversity shaped by age, local ethnic identity, and class relations. The commercialization of the weaving industry, changes in the local civil-religious cargo system, state campaigns to promote economic development and "Indian" cultures, changes in community evaluations of respect, shifts in local class relations, changes in the division of labor, and increasing educational levels—all of these factors influenced what it meant to be a Zapotec female in Teotitlán. Being female in Teotitlán today could mean being a sixteen-year-old student studying accounting to go into business or a seventy-five-year-old widow eking out a daily living by weaving a little, selling handspun yarn in the local market, and living from hand to mouth. The lives of Julia, Cristina, Angela, Alicia, and Imelda outlined in chapter 3 are all testimonies to the diversity of experience found among Zapotec women. We cannot capture the complexity of their lives by only describing them as women.

The ethnographic material from Teotitlán suggests that the job of future feminist anthropologists and practitioners is to look at the specifics of how gender is constituted and reconstituted in relation to other social, cultural, economic, and historical arrangements. This is not a call to abandon gender as an important lens for analysis. Gender must be seen as a real yet fluid category, an arbitrary social construct shaped by specific institutions and relations. Rather than deconstruct gender to the point of denying the political and economic marginalization of rural women on the basis of their femaleness, poverty, and indigenous identity, we must clarify the institutional, cultural, and ideological threads that tie femininity to marginality, break these, and encourage the broadening of women's bases of power. In the process much can be learned from the ways in which women have used traditional domains of female power such as the kin and *compadrazgo* networks described in Teotitlán.

Dynamic Interaction: Class, Ethnicity, and Gender

In analyzing the changing position of Teotiteco women in ritual, economics, and politics since the Mexican Revolution, it is apparent that the concepts of class, ethnicity, and gender are dynamic. Teotiteco women and men resisted definitions of "Indian," "peasant," "male," and "female" imposed by state agencies such as the census bureau, the Ministry of Economics, national tourist planners, development planners, tourists, and importers, elaborating their own versions in their own interest. Often they used and reworked these definitions in unpredictable ways that subverted the aims of the state or other outside forces. In the history of the community, we see repeated evidence of what Gramsci (1971) called counterhegemonic activity: people reclaiming and reordering imposed definitions of their identity through the process of social reproduction.

In Teotitlán, the primary focus of this counterhegemonic activity has been economic, ensuring the community's continued ethnic claim to its weaving products. The concerted efforts of Teotiteco merchants and weavers to control distribution within Mexico are an assertion of their ethnically based claim to their own textiles. The importance of asserting Teotiteco ethnic identity vis-à-vis other Mexicans and North Americans is clearly a struggle for economic control, but also invokes the construction and defense of a particular ethnicity—which lays claim to the rugs, blankets, pillow cases, and wall hangings that are now largely produced for U.S. consumers. Relative to the profits that U.S. importers make from their business dealings (300 percent and up) the 20–40 percent profit rates made by Teotiteco merchants are on a smaller scale. While the use of an ethnic claim to keep their profits is far more beneficial to merchants than it is to weavers, higher prices do ensure that a larger amount of the money made in marketing the textiles flows into the community. And a considerable amount of that money continues to be spent within the community, on fiestas as well as on public works (see Stephen 1987b).

The brand of ethnic identity that merchants use to try to maintain an upper hand in the negotiating process with U.S. importers tends to project a vision of a kin-based community producing traditional crafts tied to a glorious past. This outwardly projected identity reflects some of the same stereotypical images that municipal authorities used in the 1930s to convince bureaucrats from the National Office of Statistics that they were all "humble Indians working at simple looms." When assertions of common ethnic identity are made within the community, however, the meaning of ethnicity tends to be much more contested, particularly in conjunction with the relations of production. While merchants may use their kinship and *compadrazgo* ties to manipulate pieceworkers, weavers use the same relations to try to improve their wages and to get wealthy merchants to make donations to community projects. Within the community, the contact point between class differences and ethnic similarities produces a lively discourse. As the reach of international capital moves into every household economy in the community and pushes forward socioeconomic differentiation, the ways in which Teotiteco ethnicity is represented both internally and externally become increasingly complex.

Representations of gender are also fluid and are constantly being reformed in relation to class, age, and the demands of commercial weaving production. As seen in chapters 5 and 6, treadle loom weaving, which had largely been done by men until the 1970s (with some notable exceptions), is now part of "female work" that young women are taught to do along with making tortillas, raising animals, and washing clothes. The fluidity of gender representations is also evidenced in ritual. Older women can run a ceremonial event because of their authority and experience, while younger women may do little more on the same occasion than serve as a cog in a tortilla-making operation. Class as well as age differentiates femaleness in the ritual context, particularly under the current conditions of commercial capitalism. For example, merchant women can get away with spending less time working at local fiestas than weaver women, unless they are very close relatives of the hostess. This is probably because they bring greater quantities of goods with them and draw on their class status as busy merchants to excuse themselves. In all of these situations, women are all behaving like women, yet there are clear differences in power between them. All say that they are acting according to local standards for the behavior of Teotiteco Zapotec women, yet they do not all have to behave the same way to meet these standards.

Just as gender is fluid over time, it is also fluid within different social situations. Individual women are aware of their multiple female identities and use them toward specific purposes. In some instances they may use them to separate themselves from other women or in others to create a common sense of unity, as occurred when all women in the community worked in their own ways to organize a boycott of the local yarn factory as described in chapter 9.

Social Reproduction

Simply isolating women and men as categories does not allow us to understand how gender works in indigenous peasant communities. Here the concept of social reproduction has been offered as a way of relating cultural and economic spheres to understand the multiple ways in which male and female roles are linked to specific social relationships and institutions. Rather than dichotomizing gender roles by their "public" or "private" social location, gender roles can be more accurately described through examining the ways in which locally constructed maleness and femaleness operate in conjunction with other social institutions to reproduce significant social relations, particularly those tied to productive and cultural functions.

In Teotitlán, the most significant social institutions tied to gender were found to be the relations of production between merchants and weavers, ritual institutions and the networks and relations that held them together (such as *guelaguetza, compadrazgo,* and *respet*), and the local political system. While there are particular female gender roles within each of these institutions, the specifics of how they are defined for each particular woman vary depending primarily, but not exclusively, on class and age. Class and age differences between women inform how they operate as socially constructed females within particular situations and relationships. But women are not simply cultural zombies acting out their predestined roles. Zapotec women are actively involved in the process of social reproduction through a conscious manipulation of relationships, strategies, and resources at their disposal because they are women. In this way, they have an active role in producing and reproducing gendered Zapotec culture and class relations. The notion that women are involved in reproducing both cultural and economic relations has been addressed by recent policy-oriented studies of Mexican and other Latin American women.

From Social Reproduction to Popular Movements

Case studies of women's participation in home assembly work, unionization, state-sponsored programs, and community politics point out the need simultaneously to address economic production, reproductive activities in the home, and the place of women in the wider cultural ideology if the overall social and economic status of Mexican women is to be improved. In their study of industrial homeworkers among the working classes of Mexico City, Benería and Roldán (1987) conclude that raising women's income did little to improve their autonomy because of the limitations imposed on them by the cultural ideology of marriage. Even in the context of labor relations in the formal economy, Carrillo (1988) emphasizes how gender ideology about women's place in the work force reinforces social relations of production that put women workers in a disadvantaged position in relation to unionization possibilities and improved working and living conditions.

Arizpe and Botey (1987:70–73, 75) and Aranda (1985) describe the problems Mexican women had in getting small, state-sponsored agroindustrial units to be economically viable. One of the major problems they cite is that the institutional structure of the Agro-Industrial Units for Women (UAIMs) does not take into consideration the heavy domestic responsibilities of rural Mexican women and the emphasis that gender ideology places on these activities. The need simultaneously to address women's position in the division of wage labor as well as cultural ideology about women's domestic roles has been a focal point in the revolutionary societies of Cuba and Nicaragua, where concern about women's roles in social reproduction has been—if not resolved—at least explicitly addressed by the state. The position of the new UNO (United Nicaraguan Opposition) government led by Violeta Chamorro on gender remains unclear.

In Cuba, the incorporation of women into the rural labor force created a double workload for women as they went home from the fields to perform domestic chores and raise children. This resulted in the creation of the Family Code (1975), which requires men to share equally in child rearing and domestic maintenance activities (Deere 1986). While legislation of the sharing of domestic duties may be a positive step, implementation of such laws depends on the strength of local women's organizations and a long-term struggle between men and women at the level of the household.

In Nicaragua, where initial efforts to incorporate women into the agrarian labor force were made under the Sandinistas, a lack of attention to domestic workloads has resulted in women being excluded from institutional decision making and their issues being relegated to the back burner, "especially those whose solutions require attacking male privilege within the family, in production, and in political life" (Padilla et al. 1987:137). Observers note that this problem as well as many others was exacerbated by the U.S.-funded Contra war until 1990, since most of the Sandinista government's financial resources and planning energies were channeled into the war effort (Padilla et al. 1987). The domestic arena remains primarily the province of Nicaraguan women; Padilla et al. (1987:137) argue that women value the benefits of the Sandinista revolution primarily in relation to their children, brothers, husbands, and relatives, not necessarily in relation to themselves.

In the revolutionary society of Cuba, as well as in Mexican peasant communities such as Teotitlán, gendered cultural ideology in its varied forms limits the participation of women in formal political institutions and organizations. The types of obstacles to participation that exist for women vary according to class, ethnicity, age, and geographical area. By looking at the range of roles that women have in social reproduction in particular situations we can see how women have been marginalized from formal politics and at the same time how they have used their traditional roles within social reproduction to redefine the "political" through their participation in popular movements. Joann Martin (1990:479–480) writes of peasant women in Morelos who viewed their motherhood as a source of strength and used the respect granted to mothers as a banner for political activity. Through linking images of redemption, motherhood, and self-sacrifice to a crisis in local politics, these women moved out of the informal political sphere and created a women's group in the late 1970s. They opposed a local PRI candidate for governor and pooled their money to help each other start businesses. Local movements such as the one Martin describes are currently the most dynamic arena for women's political participation in conjunction with a national movement to redefine the PRI-dominated government and political process.

Women's participation in the rural and urban popular movements of Mexico is usually initially motivated by what Kaplan (1982) calls female consciousness. Within a particular class and culture, a particular gendered division of labor results in certain rights and obligations for women. When women accept the gender system and the division of labor that goes with it, they have a sense of female consciousness. In Teotitlán, female consciousness revolves around women's roles in maintaining ritual, raising children, processing food, maintaining labor exchanges and networks of kin and *compadres*, and working in weaving production. The way in which this consciousness is expressed in daily life varies according to class and age. This is the case in other indigenous communities as well.

When social disorder endangers daily routines and access to resources or limits the rights and obligations that women perceive that they have as women, they will work to reestablish order. In indigenous communities female consciousness has often been mobilized in response to capitalist development and/or political conflict that threatens ethnically based traditions—particularly those related to land use. In such cases, women act according to their roles in the gendered division of labor to confront institutions and individuals that are limiting their ability to carry out their traditional roles (Kaplan 1982:550). The process of mobilization, however, involves a dynamic of change that not only alters female consciousness, but can also alter both men and women's ideas about what is a political issue. As documented in Kaplan's work (1982:551) on women's roles in popular insurrections in Barcelona in the early 1900s, women's defense of the rights accorded to them by the sexual division of labor, although fundamentally conservative, can have revolutionary consequences. When combined with a larger political movement on both the right and the left to open up the national political system and free access to resources and the ability to organize from association with a ruling political party, as is occurring in Mexico, women acting on their female consciousness can result in a new political dynamic among women and perhaps the birth of a yet unnamed popular feminism.

While women in Teotitlán are still confined to expressing their political agendas through informal means, women in other indigenous communities have found a potential outlet for expression in independent peasant organizations such as the CNPA. At the urban level, hundreds of thousands of women have been the backbone of organizations dedicated to tenants' rights, the establishment of neighborhood food and nutrition programs, land occupations, and securing basic services such as electricity and running water. Often motivated by their roles as mothers and wives dedicated to feeding, clothing, and caring for their families, women have pushed these issues into the public forum in independent peasant and urban organizations. By doing so they have turned issues such as the procurement of food, traditionally the responsibility of mothers, into issues taken up by larger organizations. Elizabeth Jelin (1990: 189–190) describes the social and political results of new forms of female organization such as collective kitchens. "They are characterized by bringing women together in a public activity replacing the private and almost intimate activity of the kitchen in the domestic sphere. . . . A new space is opened to women of the popular sectors enabling them to partake in social confrontation, decision-making and supervision as social and political subjects. . . . The widening of women's sphere of action and traditional roles, as much in the sexual division of labor as in the public and private arena, is coming about through necessity in popular daily practice and as a response to the needs of survival."

While urban popular movements and peasant organizations have not until recently allowed women to move into leadership positions or even formally to be members, as in the case of the Unión de Ejidos Lázaro Cárdenas in Nayarit, women continued to use their existing political skills, usually not recognized as such, to assert their agendas. When outside funding agencies, state agencies, feminists, and representatives from political parties recognize their efforts, a new dynamic is created in which different types of traditional female consciousness are harnessed toward a broader political identity. Within this dynamic the different roles of women within social reproduction can be critical.

The ways in which women, particularly indigenous women, are connected to traditional domains of power have often been dismissed or underemphasized. It has not been readily apparent how women's ritual authority, connections to broad networks of kin and *compadres,* reciprocal labor exchanges, and control over household budgets and child rearing can be used to subvert traditional areas of ruling class economic and political power. Women in Teotitlán use these institutions to organize politically in their community and to try to exert control over the spheres in which they have influence. Women in Yalálag have been able to use their traditional domains of power to secure a place in community politics and also to participate in negotiations with Oaxaca state officials. While indigenous women such as those in Teotitlán and Yalálag have always had a sense of the limits and possibilities of such sources of power, they seldom have opportunities to share this knowledge with people outside their communities. The incorporation of large numbers of women in independent peasant and urban organizations in Mexico may offer them an opportunity to demonstrate the traditional power of females in different cultural and class contexts as well as to learn how to negotiate outside the traditional spheres to which they have been confined within their communities.

The larger question for indigenous women such as those living in Teotitlán is: how does their varied sense of themselves as female become converted into a broader political consciousness? What circumstances facilitate this process? Chapter 10 suggests various possible ways in which women can achieve a more independent political identity, including contact with feminist organizers, through programs offered by the state such as those in Oaxaca, through participation in independent organizations, and through projects supported by nongovernmental organizations or within indigenous movements. While no one prescription emerges for reformulating indigenous women's various identities into ones that permit political mobilization, such a process seems to be facilitated by projects and modes of organization that draw on a group of women who are already bonded by other modes of interaction, such as work or ritual, and push them in a new direction by offering them an exit from their usual roles within their community. In the case of Teotitlán, this might be women already bonded through years of working together in fiestas or the group of young women in the artisan market who pass long afternoons together waiting for the arrival of tourists and importers. With no impending economic or political crisis pushing them to action, however, these networks of Teotiteco women are unlikely to be politically activated as they have been in Yalálag or other areas of Oaxaca and Chiapas where armed confrontations over land have resulted in the highest numbers of human rights abuses in the entire country (Amnesty International 1986).

Conclusions

The varied realities of women's lives in Teotitlán since the Mexican Revolution offer insight into how economics, culture, and history have influenced all indigenous women. As Mexico rounds the corner into the twenty-first century, indigenous women remain the most marginalized sector of the population, as a whole appearing to have progressed little or perhaps even declined in their standard of living since Cortés and his band first set foot in Tenochtitlán in 1519. As Mexico liberalizes its economic policy to encourage increased foreign investment and struggles to make a dent in its huge international debt while still experiencing economic growth, the daily struggles of peasant and indigenous women get pushed further from the central political agenda being formulated in the bureaucratic halls of Mexico City. Yet the very basis of indigenous and peasant women's political and economic marginalization has also proved to be a resource as they use traditional bases of female power to make their voices heard within their communities and in larger organizations. In concert with the majority of the population, which has not benefited from over sixty years of PRI rule, indigenous and peasant women are now pushing Mexico toward a new political era from below. The future agenda for research on Mexican women will undoubtedly include a heavy focus on the role of women in reshaping Mexican politics and the changes in self-perception that political participation brings.

Appendix A. Research Methodology

Yesterday I heard some people talking in the mountains when
I went to gather wood. They said that the mayor was really
stupid for letting outsiders into our town to ask questions—
the kinds of questions anthropologists ask. What kinds of
questions are you going to ask? (Martín, age 35)

I CARRIED out fieldwork for this book beginning in the summer of
1983 as a second-year graduate student. Since that time I have spent
at least part of every year in Teotitlán del Valle. My field time in the
community includes June–August 1983; November 1984–January
1986; June 1986–August 1986; January 1987; one week in April
1987; two weeks in June 1987; two weeks in July 1988; and two
weeks in July 1989.

Language and Living Situation

During the first summer of fieldwork I lived with an extended family in which the senior adults were monolingual in Zapotec. Although this was a difficult beginning, it forced me to begin to learn
conversational Zapotec. Upon returning in November 1984, I resided with another family and began to learn Zapotec in earnest
through exchanging lessons in Zapotec for English. After about
eight months, my conversational Zapotec was sufficient to conduct
interviews and carry out detailed, regular conversation. The pa-
tience of elderly monolingual speakers in the community was a
great help in eventually feeling comfortable conversing in the language. My relationships with people in the community tended to be
structured in either Zapotec or Spanish, although some used both
languages, and as I became more proficient people preferred to speak
Zapotec.

Participant Observation

Participant observation was a critical part of my fieldwork methodology. After seeing the difference between information elicited

through conversation and that gathered simply by watching, I eventually developed a network of about forty families I kept in regular touch with, visiting them every two or three weeks, and often attended fiestas with them. Through these regular visits as well as extended time spent observing ritual events, political discussions, community meetings, and other nonhousehold-based events, I collected much of the information that served as the basis for in-depth work with case-study households, questions for a survey administered to 154 households, oral history interviews, structured interviews, and archival work.

After seven years of working in the community I became thoroughly integrated into many ongoing activities through the relationships I formed there and the four godchildren and sets of *compadres* I have. How well integrated I had become was illustrated in 1989 when I was on a postdoctoral fellowship at the Center for U.S.-Mexican Studies in San Diego, California. Two days after I arrived, I began to receive telephone calls from friends or *compadres* who were in neighboring Tijuana. The entire time I lived in southern California I had extended contact with people from Teotitlán living in Tijuana and in the greater Los Angeles area.

Interviews

I eventually interviewed over 250 households in the community. Once I began attending fiestas in the community, I made contact at least once with almost everyone who lived in Teotitlán. Attending a ritual event would often set up new relationships and result in additional interview opportunities. I used interviews to explore particular concepts and topics such as *respet, guelaguetza,* and *compadrazgo* as well as to discuss merchant-weaver relations, gender roles, history, and controversial issues in the community. Most of the interviews and discussions involved either detailed notetaking that was transcribed no more than eight hours later or tape recording. During the last four months of fieldwork in 1985–1986, many interviews were tape recorded.

Case-Study Households

To collect systematic data on household expenditures and labor allocations, I focused on a sample of twelve case-study households. These included six merchant and six weaver households. Because of the difficulty in collecting accurate budget data, I decided to collect data on expenditures rather than income. Such information is very sensitive in Teotitlán and can only be solicited from trusted informants. When I initially wanted to begin my case-study project, members of one family turned me down because they were convinced that I would lose my shoulder bag and their household expenditure data would be seen by all. I therefore opted to collect data more intensively from a smaller number of households I knew well, rather than extensively from a larger number of households. While the sample of households is not random, I feel that it accurately represents the real differences found between weaver and merchant households. The range of households included merchants with varying sizes of enterprises as well as weaver households with different numbers of laborers in them. Case-study household members were extremely cooperative in keeping track of daily labor allocations and expenditures. It was a time-consuming and tedious task that they did for me, not because they got anything out of it.

Data on expenses and labor allocation were collected from case-study households in two ways. First, I collected household data on reproduction and weaving expenses and adult labor allocated to household reproduction and weaving activities for a six-week baseline period. Because they appeared to be stable throughout the study period, they were not measured daily, but projected for the ten-month period. I checked the six-week baseline figures periodically throughout the ten-month period for representativeness. Data that would vary seasonally such as agricultural inputs and ceremonial expenditures were collected throughout the ten-month study period. I also counted ritual and farming expenses and amounts of adult labor allocated to ritual events and farming on a daily basis for ten months.

My case-study households helped me to collect data by recording them on daily log sheets that included space for all expenditures and labor according to category (household, weaving, farming, cargo, ritual, other) and listed the names of each household member. Labor was recorded in terms of twelve-hour days or fractions thereof. A literate member of each household was in charge of recording the daily data. I discussed these data with the record keepers and collected them at least once a week.

Questionnaire Used with Random Stratified Sample

In order to supplement local census information on population, land holdings, and literacy and systematically to gather more information on many issues I had discussed with people in the community, I decided to administer a detailed questionnaire to a random stratified sample of 154 households, which included merchants, weavers, farmers, service workers, and musicians. In tables 19 and 24 in this book where the number of weaving households is recorded as 100, farmers, service workers, and musicians are also included in the category "weavers." In most cases members of these 26 households devoted almost half or more of their adult labor time to weaving, in spite of the fact that they identified themselves as holding another occupation.

Selection of Weaver, Farmer, and Service Worker Households

I chose 100 weaver, farmer, and service worker (i.e., nonmerchant) households by first numbering all the doorways in the community on a detailed map and choosing random numbers from a random number chart to represent them. Households associated with the doorways assigned the selected random numbers were then interviewed. If more than one household resided in the area associated with a randomly chosen doorway, each household was assigned a number (usually one to four) and a die was thrown to determine which household would be included in the survey. Fortunately, this occurred in only about seven cases. If the randomly selected doorway belonged to a merchant household, the following doorway was used.

Selection of Merchant Households

The names of all merchant household heads in Teotitlán were collected through tax and census records and through lists compiled by six informants. The lists were then cross-checked and combined into a master list. Each pair of household heads was assigned a number. Fifty-four households were chosen through use of a random number chart. These households were then interviewed. The random sample included a high proportion of merchant households in order to ensure statistical significance. About half of the merchant households in the community were included in the survey.

The questionnaire given to households included in the random stratified sample provided data on each household member for gender, primary and secondary occupation, migration, position in the relations of production, language spoken, and years in school. Each household was evaluated for house construction, number of rooms, amount and type of land owned, and ownership of trucks, cars, looms, tractors, and various consumer goods such as televisions and stoves. Information was also collected about people employed by households, number of *guelaguetza* debts owed and paid out, history of fiesta sponsorship, cargos served, number of godchildren, and expenditures on rituals for the past year, as well as attitudinal questions directed at men and women about women's participation in politics, control of business decision making, household money, and feelings about the concept of *respet*, future ritual sponsorship, and going into business.

Data for the questionnaires were collected during three months of fieldwork. I collected the data for each household in conjunction with a male and a female research assistant who helped with translation difficulties and assurances about the confidentiality of information and also worked with informants of the same gender to solicit further information. Participation was voluntary and we were refused by only one household when we ran a pilot of the questionnaire on ten households. In retrospect, doing the household survey last during my field study was a wise decision; by the time we carried it out, I already knew most of the people in the community. I do not think they would have answered most of the questions in it without knowing me.

This questionnaire served as the basis for some statistical information in this book, including numbers of people in particular occupations, landholding patterns, education, migration patterns, linguistic abilities, patterns of *compadrazgo* sponsorship, ownership of consumer goods, attitudes toward women's political participation, and male-female control over decision making regarding cash and labor allocation for weaving production, merchant business, and ritual events. The households included in the random stratified sample were also used in the informant ranking exercises described below.

Informant Ranking Exercises

In Teotitlán, I conducted three different sets of stratifying exercises with informants following the methodology of Silverman (1966). The first set of ranking exercises elicited two different ways of ranking people, by wealth and occupation and by *respet*. Three male and three female informants who were representative of the age and economic divisions in the community participated in the exercise. I gave them slips of paper with the names of forty household heads on them. If the household was headed by a married couple, both male and female names were included. I then asked the informants to categorize them according to "differences." While at first reluctant to perform the categorizations, most informants soon set about putting the names into distinct groupings. Usually they began with two contrasting households, using these as reference points for building groups. When they had decided on the number of groups, each one was headed by a specific household, which was the point of reference for others that would be put into the same group. When informants finished their first categorization, we discussed what the groupings meant.

Most informants began by sorting the names of households into groups structured by wealth and by merchant or weaver status. When asked if there was yet another way to organize the households, all informants mentioned that they could also be organized by respect. They then proceeded to reshuffle the groups, explaining that wealth or occupational position was not the same as respect.

In addition to asking informants to rank households, I also asked them to rank individuals. This was done by presenting the names of male and female household heads on individual slips of paper. Informants insisted that they could not rank male or female household heads independently of their spouses or other household members. All refused to rank individuals, pointing to the importance of the household as a basic unit in the ranking system of Teotitecos.

The first ranking exercise, to solicit the basic dimensions of the stratification system, and two other exercises, in which informants ranked specifically according to wealth and respect, were done in Zapotec. All household heads in Teotitlán have Zapotec names. While the slips of paper used in the exercises originally had only Spanish names on them, informants would not proceed with the exercise until all Zapotec nicknames were accurately recorded. In the place of Juan Acosta, for example, the Zapotec nickname *Sed* meaning "salt" had to be used. In many cases, Teotitecos could not identify household heads by their Spanish surnames, knowing them only by their Zapotec nicknames.

A second set of ranking exercises was performed with another six informants (three male and three female) representative of age and socioeconomic differences in the community. These six informants ranked the names of household heads from the stratified random sample into groups according to wealth. The process was similar to that described above. Each informant decided how many groups were necessary accurately to rank all of the households in the sample by wealth.

The final ranking exercises involved the same informants who did the wealth rankings. They ranked the names of household heads from the random stratified sample by respect as well.

Ranking exercises were used to elicit information used in the discussion of wealth, respect, and the potential overlap between the two. The methodology is further described in chapter 9.

Oral Histories

Perhaps the most interesting and educational data I gathered were oral histories. I carried these out with ten elderly men and ten elderly women in the community, both merchants and weavers. The interviews lasted an average of two hours and were tape recorded and transcribed. Following these interviews, many of the people interviewed provided follow-up information on changes in the political and economic system of Teotitlán. They provided detailed information on the numbers of merchants in the community, naming them at certain dates as well as describing particular legal and political battles that were then checked for documentation in local archives. These interviews provided me with many clues and insights into the economic, political, and social history of Teotitlán since the Mexican Revolution.

Women's Life Histories

I also collected life histories of the five women included in chapter 3. These life histories were collected at different times. Because I had developed close relationships with these women, they were quite willing to share their life stories, often talking nonstop for ten or fifteen minutes at a time. More detail is provided in chapter 3.

Use of Archival Material

Teotitlán has municipal archives that are an ethnohistorian's dream. *Copiadores de oficios* for every year dating back to the 1600s document all incoming correspondence from state officials and the community's reply as penned by municipal authorities and scribes. Written in Spanish with healthy sprinklings of phoneticized Zapotec, these archives document one level of the community's history as formulated by those holding municipal political power. The archives contain detailed census and voting lists as well as birth and death records.

I was initially denied access to these records until the summer of 1986, when I returned to the community after having lived there for fourteen months. During the summer of 1986 I spent at least five hours per day copying things from the archive under the watchful eye of at least one *topil* or local policeman. After I had worked in the archives for two weeks, more of the *topiles* became interested in what I was doing and I began to talk with them and show them what I was reading in the archives. This process generated interest in a community history and language project that was initiated in 1987 with funding from Cultural Survival (see Stephen 1990b). While the outcome of the project is uncertain, a group of about five to six young men became aware of the extent of archival information held in the *municipio.*

Archival information from Teotitlán was used to check many historical details that came up in oral history interviews and to provide data on the changing economic relations in the community.

I also used data from the Oaxaca state archives, including yearly documents written by the governors of Oaxaca, state censuses, and the official newspaper of the state political apparatus.

Appendix B. Total Cash Outflow and Percentages Invested in Weaving, Household, Ritual, and Other Expenses

Case No.	Total	Weaving	Household	Fiesta	Other
Merchants					
1	1,564,564	800,669	456,485	107,010	200,400
	100%	51%	29%	7%	13%
2	1,772,237	433,806	1,237,061	101,470	
	100%	24%	70%	6%	
3	2,159,863	1,545,435	478,443	135,985	
	100%	72%	22%	6%	
4	3,150,538	2,513,926	488,392	148,220	
	101%	80%	16%	5%	
5	4,114,840	3,042,450	967,920	104,470	
	101%	74%	24%	3%	
6	9,134,634	5,496,830	2,938,784	435,390	263,630
	100%	60%	32%	5%	3%
Weavers					
1	264,140	45,033	184,862	34,245	
	100%	17%	70%	13%	
2	315,504		253,669	61,835	
	100%		80%	20%	
3	538,678	198,646	296,492	43,540	
	100%	37%	55%	8%	
4	553,878	112,480	394,813	46,585	
	99%	20%	71%	8%	
5	782,525	390,879	286,616	105,030	
	100%	50%	37%	13%	
6	1,093,965	50,000	554,640	489,325	
	101%	5%	51%	45%	

Notes

2. Ethnicity, Class, and Social Reproduction: The Frames of Women's Daily Lives

1. In the *Prison Notebooks* (1971:242, as cited in Buci-Glucksman 1980:92–93) Gramsci wrote: "Educative and formative role of the state. Its aim is always that of creating new and higher types of civilization [*civiltà*]; of adapting 'civilization' and the morality of the broadest masses to the necessities of the continuous development of the economic apparatus of production."

2. The words "Indian" and "Indianness" are used here to be consistent with use of the word in Spanish by various state offices and officials. In Spanish, the word *indio* usually has a derogatory meaning. Few people refer to themselves as *indios*. Wherever possible, the ethnic name of a particular people is used.

3. Absolute delineations are difficult because there are always some households that may be involved in reselling weavings while also engaging in piecework production for someone else. At a different time, the same household may be involved in independent production. Most households, however, categorize themselves as weavers, merchants, or independent weavers given what they view as their primary economic activity.

4. *Mayordomías* are sponsorships of ceremonial activities for local saints and virgins. These activities are explained in detail in chapters 7 and 8.

5. See Beals 1970:234; Cook and Diskin 1976:11; de la Fuente 1949: 120–123; Diskin 1986:34–39; Leslie 1960; Martínez Ríos 1964; Nader 1964; Parsons 1936; Vargas-Barón 1968:80–82.

6. In her further discussion of social reproduction Benería (1979:205) defines it as "structures that have to be reproduced in order that social reproduction as a whole can take place." She offers as an example structures such as inheritance that control the transmission of resources from one generation to another.

3. Julia, Cristina, Angela, Alicia, and Imelda: Five Women's Stories

1. Cristina is referring to a ceremony in which a young man's family formally asks for a young woman's hand in marriage—*contentar* in Spanish. The request is accompanied by a gift of candles, fruit, and chocolate. While formerly the gifts were quite limited, as in Cristina's experience, now such ceremonies involve up to sixty candles and truckloads of fruit, chocolate, and bread.

2. Angela is referring to a cave that was declared to be the site of a miracle about 400 years ago. Since the appearance of a virgin there, locals have gone to ask for miracles and things that they want in life. On New Year's Day, most of the community goes there. People signal their requests by producing small models of what they want—such as a house or a horse.

3. Alicia is referring to a checkpoint on a California highway that is usually staffed by immigration officers. All cars are stopped; if passengers look like they might be undocumented (i.e., if they look Mexican), they are asked for identification.

4. Setting the Scene: The Zapotecs of Teotitlán del Valle, Oaxaca

1. The 570 *municipios* in Oaxaca are grouped together in 30 districts or *distritos*. The *distrito* is an administrative unit of federal and state tax collection and the lowest level of the national court system. Each *municipio* unit is made up of a municipal seat and municipal agencies and police agencies.

2. These include ritual systems and civil-religious cargo systems (El Guindi 1986; Mathews 1985; Peterson Royce 1975); participation in local market systems (Cook and Diskin 1976; Malinowski and de la Fuente 1982); peasant economics (Benítez Zenteno 1980; Clements 1988b; Cook 1982b, 1984b; Cook and Binford 1986; Turkenik 1976); values (Selby 1974); legal systems and dispute settlement (Nader 1964; Parnell 1988); aggression (Fry 1988; O'Nell 1979, 1986); intercommunity conflict (Dennis 1987); general ethnography (de la Fuente 1949; Kearney 1972; Parsons 1936); ethnohistory (Chance 1978; Chance and Taylor 1985; Taylor 1972, 1979); history (Whitecotton 1977); *compadrazgo* (Sault 1985b); and women (Chiñas 1973). This is not a comprehensive list, but represents some of the richness of Zapotec ethnography.

3. One hectare is equal to 2.47 acres.

4. *Ejidos* are plots of land that were redistributed primarily in the 1930s under Cárdenas. The land was given to a group of households, called an *ejido*, which held use rights to the land. *Ejido* land cannot be sold and ultimate legal title is held by the state.

5. Contested Histories: Women, Men, and the Relations of Production in Teotitlán, 1920–1950s

1. While the restructuring of local governments as "free" *municipios* was supposed to increase the autonomy of indigenous communities, in reality it severely limited their control over local political and economic decisions (see Greenberg 1990; Stephen 1990a).

2. The documents known as *copiadores de oficios* contain copies of all official correspondence received from the government and the community's response as written by municipal authorities. The archives of Teotitlán

have a complete set of this correspondence for the entire twentieth century and before.

3. Teotitecos were adamant in their insistence that there were no factories in Teotitlán. While homes with more than several looms might have been considered factories by the state, they were never reported as such. Factories were required to pay taxes on their production. Textile manufacturers fought throughout the late 1920s and early 1930s to reduce federal taxes on production (Secretaría de la Economía Nacional 1934).

4. The recorded Spanish reads ". . . adornados con grecas y hídolos [*sic*] significación histórica de Mitla y Monte Albán incluyendo figuras Zapotecas y Toltecas. . . ."

5. Borque and Warren (1981:118–119) also found in their work with peasants in Peru that women and men had different perceptions of women's work in relation to community ritual and production activities. Men had more limited perceptions of what women did.

6. It is unclear exactly when Macuilxóchitl dropped out of weaving and shifted into full-time subsistence production. Census data suggest it may have been shortly after the Mexican Revolution in the 1920s. In the late 1980s, however, increasing numbers of households in the community took up weaving again to take advantage of the booming commercial market.

7. Oral histories collected from informants roughly corroborate census data from 1945 on. Informants were asked to name all merchants in Teotitlán during a particular year. Local informants also recalled *viajeros*.

8. These included the Dirección de Asuntos Trabajadores Migratorios (DATUM) of the Secretaría de Relaciones Exteriores and officials of the Secretaría de Gobernación and the Secretaría del Trabajo y Previsión Social.

6. Weaving in the Fast Lane: Ethnicity, Class, and Gender Relations under Commercial Capitalism

1. In a detailed economic history of *obrajes* in Mexico, Richard Salvucci (1987:61) maintains that the *obrajes* did not represent protoindustry or protofactories. He instead refers to them as rational, if inefficient, textile manufactures that responded well to the needs and limitations of the colonial economy. One of the key reasons he declines to call them factories is that the workers resided in the *obraje* (1987:32–33).

2. It should be noted, however, that electric blenders are now used by most women to supplement their metates. No Teotitlán kitchen is complete without one, as indicated by the high numbers given as wedding presents.

3. See Nagengast (1990) for a discussion of how prosperous households benefit from unequal nonmonetary and monetary exchanges with "relatives" utilizing the language of kinship among Polish farmers.

4. The Zapotec geometrics that weavers prefer are taken from the friezes on the ruins in Mitla, Oaxaca.

5. The three government agencies that funded the Lanera de Oaxaca included the Secretaría de Industria y Comercio (Secretariat of Industry and Commerce), the Secretaría de Programas Estatales de Oaxaca (Secretariat of Oaxaca State Programs), and La Financiera Nacional (National Financing Secretariat).

6. This figure came from a random stratified sample of 154 households carried out in 1986. The percentage is probably higher now, as younger girls continue to enter weaving production as early as age ten or eleven.

7. This is not to be confused with advocating that women be treated as economistic individuals engaged in rational choice theory.

7. One Man, One Vote: Changes in the Civil-Religious Hierarchy and Their Impact on Women

1. See Cancian (1965) for a thorough and sophisticated discussion of civil-religious cargo systems. Cancian's work was one of the first to raise questions about the relationship between social and economic stratification and cargo sponsorship.

2. See Segura (1979, 1980) for a more detailed description of the cargo system of Teotitlán.

3. *Ščäη* is a ritual greeting that connotes a great deal of respect. It is used ceremonially on all occasions when people enter ritual space. It is also used on the street in order to demonstrate respect to someone. It implies a subordinate relationship between the person who initiates the greeting and the one who receives it. When the word is spoken, the initiator offers his or her hands face up to the person receiving the greeting. The person receiving the greeting touches the initiator's hands with his or her own hands face down, connoting a superior position. The greeting is always offered by children and young adults to an older person and by others to people to whom they want to demonstrate respect.

4. This figure should be compared with average annual cash outflows for merchants and weavers. In 1985, the average annual cash outflow for six merchants of different sizes was US$7,857. For six weaver households measured the same year, it was US$1,600. The family sponsoring the *mayordomía* in 1989 was a small-scale merchant household.

5. The original Spanish read: "vé con satisfacción los propósitos que tienen de rectificar todas las costumbres que en nuestros pueblos producen la ruina o el estancamiento de su patrimonio moral y económico."

6. Tlacolula is the district head for the judicial and political district to which Teotitlán belongs. The district capital was moved from Teotitlán to Tlacolula after Mexican independence.

7. The Zapotec word *nän* is used as a title for both virgins and *mayordomas*, invoked when speaking to them.

8. Fiesta: The Contemporary Dynamics of Women's Ritual Participation

1. See Volkman (1984, 1985) for discussion of a similar process in Toroja, Indonesia.

2. See El Guindi (1986) for rich, detailed descriptions of Zapotec ritual space and ritual speech and their symbolic meanings.

3. The term "ritual kin" is used here instead of the more commonly used "fictive kin" in order to emphasize the genuine equality of this kin relationship—as real as blood kinship. The ritual kinship of *compadrazgo*, as well as adoptive forms of kinship, and those connections derived through marriage can all be seen as kin relations. As Gailey (1985b: 12) notes, the content of kinship can be seen as broadly reciprocal claims to labor and products, mutual responsibility, and balanced or generalized sharing.

9. Hidden Voices: Women's Political Participation in Teotitlán

1. Among others, see Borque and Warren (1981), Browner (1986a), Carillo (1988), Deere and León de Leal (1986), Harvey (1988), Nash and Safa (1986), Radcliffe (1988), Salinas (1986), and Siebold (1987).

2. Increasingly, analyses of the economic position of women in Latin America use class relations and culture as backdrops for analyzing gender roles. Such analyses also integrate "values, beliefs and expectations conditioning behavior and society in relation to the structural constraints of a given mode of production and level of capital accumulation" (Nash 1986:15).

3. As documented by Browner (1986a), local political authorities are often not responsive to the interests of women in structuring their agendas. Browner describes how a small group of Chinanteco women repeatedly confronted local authorities on issues ranging from bilingual education to support for a local health center. Although these women were chastised by local authorities for dividing the community, Browner believes that they represented an important emergent faction.

10. Creating New Political Spaces: Mexican Peasant Women in Local Politics

1. In using the term "popular" in conjunction with "movement," as in *movimientos populares*, I am referring to the idea of common marginalization and using it to link a wide range of disenfranchised groups in the Mexican political and economic system (García Canclini 1982; Higgins 1990). These "popular" groups include indigenous populations, peasants, the urban poor, urban workers, and the marginally employed and unemployed. In contrast to "social movements," which may emerge from any sector of the population in relation to a particular social issue or perspective, "popular

movements" emerge from the marginalized sectors of a population and have definite links to class identity. Their form in urban areas often involves strong residential or neighborhood ties. In the countryside such groups are often tied to specific pieces of land or resource tracts to which they are trying to gain access. Popular movements usually involve organizational forms and strategies that include both legal and extralegal tactics and focus on issues of reproduction and consumption (see Carlsen 1989; Cook 1990; Harvey 1990; Jelin 1990; Rubin 1990).

2. "Peasant" is one of the most slippery analytical terms in existence. It loosely refers to an agrarian-based individual who—while unavoidably participating in wider social, economic, and political relationships—is simultaneously active in local political, economic, and religious institutions. These institutions maintain an internal dynamic that is responsive to yet not solely determined by the state and national and international economies. Economically, we cannot define a peasant as an individual who participates solely in agriculture, for either subsistence or commercial purposes. In reality, most peasant individuals and households engage in multistranded strategies of employment, mixing wage labor, subsistence agriculture, craft production, migration, and other forms of work in order to make a living. Peasants manipulate labor and resources for the purposes of economic and social mobility in both class and nonclass relations (Stephen and Dow 1990).

3. The CONAMUP is one of many neighborhood-based popular organizations in Mexico that organizes for housing and urban services. The Sindicato "19 de Septiembre" was born during the 1985 earthquake and became the central organization for hundreds of female textile workers who lost their jobs as a result of the earthquake. It is the only independent women's union in Mexico (see Carillo 1988, 1990).

4. On June 22–24, 1989, the National Women's Axis of Equipo Pueblo, a national group of religious-based communities that supports independent worker and peasant organizations, organized a national meeting for women on survival strategies. The meeting included representatives from over thirty-five organizations involved in urban and rural popular movements. The group has decided to keep meeting in order to coordinate further activities.

5. Karen Brodkin Sacks (1988) provides a fascinating account of women's differing style of leadership as "center women" versus public male spokesmen in the organization of a union at Duke Medical Center.

6. In 1988, 11.5 percent of Mexico's legislators were female as compared with 5 percent in the United States (Rosenblum 1988). However, the Mexican legislature has little power compared to the office of the presidency, so the clout of women legislators is also limited.

Glossary of Spanish and Zapotec Terms

(Zapotec words are spelled using the International Phonetic Alphabet)

agencia: official government designation of population center under the control of a particular *municipio*

agricultores: agriculturalists (usually with land)

ahijadas/hijadas: female godchildren

ahijados/hijados: godchildren in general or male godchildren

alcaldes: judges

alcaldes mayores: regional administrative offices of the crown during the colonial period

almud: dry measure that when filled with corn is equivalent to two kilos

artesanía: artisanry, crafts

artes populares indígenas: indigenous folk arts

atole: corn-based drink

ayuntamiento: town council

BANFOCO (Banco de Fomento de Cooperativas): Bank for the Initiation of Cooperatives

bɛngul: an elderly person

bɛnguna: women

bɛ:n(i) loʔgetš: people of Teotitlán

biscochos: companions of *mayordomos*

biu: cochineal-dyed wool cloth worn as a skirt

bracería: working in the United States as a contracted laborer *bracero:* contracted worker under official U.S.-sponsored program for Mexican workers; also refers generally to those who migrate to the United States to work

cacique: political boss

cargo: civil or religious office within the community government or church committee

cliente: foreign buyer

CNC (Coordinadora Nacional de Campesinos): state-controlled peasant union

CNPA (Coordinadora Nacional "Plan de Ayala"): National Coordinator of the Ayala Plan, opposition peasant organization

cofradía: religious corporation founded to pay for cult ceremonies of local saints

comadre: relationship between a child's biological parents and godmother

comité de la iglesia: church committee

compadrazgo: ritual kinship

compadre: relationship between a child's biological parents and godfather

CONAMUP (Coordinadora Nacional del Movimiento Urbano Popular): National Council of the Urban Popular Movement

concuño: sister-in-law's brother

contentar: ceremony for marriage proposal

coordinadora: coordinating body

copiador de oficios: official record of document received and responded to by municipal officials

corregimientos: local administrative units of the crown, later called *alcaldes mayores*

costumbre: custom

cruz: cross

cultura: culture

dad: honorific title for men who are elderly or have been *mayordomos*, indicative of respect, also used as honorific for male saints *daɣn:* mountain

danzante: literally, dancer; refers to members of Teotitlán's ritual dance troop, which is a religious cargo of community service

DICONSA (Distribuidora CONASUPO S.A.): CONASUPO Distributor, Mexican food distribution program

diputados: former high-ranking *mayordomos*

distrito: district administrative unit that ranks above *municipio*

ejidatarios: members of *ejidos*

ejido: unit of land given to communities at the time of agrarian reform, often called agrarian reform communities, whose ultimate domain is the state

escribano: scribe

familia: literally, family; meaning related by blood, marriage, or ritual kinship

fiscal: top religious cargo rank

FONART (Fondo Nacional de Artesanía): National Fund for Artisanry

a la fuerza: obligatory

gañanes: migrant laborers paid by the day's work

ɣolbats: hand ax

guelaguetza: see *xɛlgɛz*

historia: history

(h)lats: flat farming land, countryside

huaraches: sandals

huehuete: ritual specialist

hurɛšlat(ši): merchant or seller of textiles

indio: Indian

industria de alimentación: food production

invitados: people invited to a party to share in the work and celebration, not equivalent of guests

jaɣ: wood

jarabe: traditional Zapotec dance to brass band music

jefe de sección: neighborhood sectional chief

jornalero: day laborer, wage laborer paid by the day's work

junta: assembly or community gathering

juntas vecinales: neighborhood committees

juzgado mayor: judicial office

La Lanera de Oaxaca: Oaxaca Wool Yarn Factory

madrina: godmother

manta: traditional cochineal-dyed wool cloth worn by women; can also mean cotton

mayor de vara: police captain

mayordoma: female sponsor of cult celebrations

mayordomía: sponsorship of cult celebrations for local saints and virgins

mayordomo: male sponsor of cult celebrations

a medios: going halves with another farmer in a sharecropping arrangement

mescal: strong alcoholic beverage made from the maguey cactus plant

mestizo: mixed ethnic category referring generally to Indian and white Spanish offspring; may also include black parentage (no longer used to designate a precise type)

metate: mortar and pestle for grinding

molenderas: female corn grinders

monte: mountain, mountainside

mozos: literally, servants; often refers to hired laborers in agriculture and weaving

muchacha: girl

municipio: administrative unit equivalent to a county seat

nān: honorific term of respect for women who are elderly or have been *mayordomas* and for female saints (virgins) *novia:* sweetheart, girlfriend

novio: sweetheart, boyfriend

Nuestro Señor de la Preciosa Sangre: Our Lord of the Precious Blood, patron saint of Teotitlán del Valle

padres del pueblo: town fathers, symbolic religious cargo

padrino: godfather

pelusa: blanket woven of animal hair and cotton

petate: mat

posada: religious celebration before Christmas commemorating Mary and Joseph's search for shelter

Presa Azul: Blue Dam, local dam construction in Teotitlán

presidenta: female president or committee chair

presidente: town mayor or any male chair of a group

PRI (Partido Revolucionario Institucional): Institutionalized Revolutionary Party, ruling political party in Mexico

promesa: literally, promise; promise to sponsor a cult celebration for a local saint or virgin

quehaceres de la casa: housework

rap⁽ᵃ⁾daŋ kos: they have things

rap⁽ᵃ⁾daŋ ṁed(ʒ): they have money

la raza cósmica: the cosmic race, referring to indigenous blood

regatones: merchants or resellers

regidor: town councillor in charge of specific areas or resources such as water or forest

respet: respect

ricos: the rich

rúnčilàt(ši): literally, maker of textiles; weaver

ruʔór̃(n): oven mouth river

sa(Pa)ɣúil(i): fiesta with music, extensive five-day ceremony

sa(Pa)tɛr(t)síl: fiesta in the morning, denoting a small-scale fiesta

SARH (Secretaría de Agricultura y Recursos Hidráulicos): Secretariat of Agriculture and Hydraulic Resources

ščāŋ: ritual greeting denoting respect

serranos: literally, people from the mountains; people from the surrounding communities in the Sierra Juárez mountains

Sindicato "19 de Septiembre": Women's Garment Workers' Union

síndico: advisor, legal counsel to town mayor

škalbao: clever, clever you

šruɛz: servant to the town mayor

šudao: bearer of religious symbols, a religious cargo title

suplente: alternate

šxía: literally, under the rock; Zapotec name for Teotitlán

tejate: refreshing drink made from corn, cacao, and sugar

tejedoras: female weavers

tejedores: male weavers or weavers in general

temporal: unirrigated farmland

tɛŋgjuwɛ²ɛñī(ŋ): is it a boy?

težapɛ²ɛ̃(nɛŋ): it's a girl.

lo típico: the typical

topil: policeman

UAIMs: Agro-Industrial Units for Women

UELC (Unión de Ejidos Lázaro Cárdenas): Lázaro Cárdenas Ejido Union, regional organization of fifteen agrarian reform communities

unión de ejidos: ejidal union

unión de mujeres: women's union

valles centrales: five central valleys in the central region of the state of Oaxaca

viajero: trader, traveling merchant

vocal: committee member

xɛlgɛz: guelaguetza, reciprocal goods and labor exchanges

xɛlgɛz štɛ majŕdō: reciprocal labor and goods exchanges for the *mayordomos* of a fiesta

xɛlgɛz xed jaγ: reciprocal exchange to gather wood

x́iabets: brother rock, mountain above Teotitlán

zacate: dried cornstalks

Bibliography

Acuña, René (ed.)
  1984   *Relaciones geográficas del siglo xvi, Antequera.* Vol. 1. Mexico
         City: Universidad Nacional Autónoma de México, Instituto de
         Investigaciones Antropológicas.
Adams, Richard
  1967   Nationalization. In *Handbook of Middle American Indians.*
         Vol. 6, *Social Anthropology,* ed. M. Nash. Austin: University of
         Texas Press.
  1988   Ethnic Images and Strategies in 1944. Prepublication working
         paper of the Institute of Latin American Studies, University of
         Texas at Austin, Paper no. 88-06. Austin: University of Texas,
         Center for Latin American Studies.
Aguirre Beltrán, Gonzalo
  1975   *Obra polémica.* Mexico City: SEP-INAH.
Amnesty International
  1986   *Mexico Human Rights in Rural Areas: Exchange of Documents
         with the Mexican Government on Human Rights Violations
         in Oaxaca and Chiapas.* London: Amnesty International Pub-
         lications.
Appel, Jill
  1982   A Summary of the Ethnohistoric Information Relevant to the
         Interpretation of Late Postclassic Settlement Patterns Data, the
         Central and Valle Grande Survey Zone. In *Monte Albán's Hinter-
         land.* Part 1, *The Prehispanic Settlement Patterns of the Central
         and Southern Parts of the Valley of Oaxaca, Mexico,* ed. R. Blan-
         ton, S. Kowalewski, G. Feinman, and J. Appel. Memoirs of the
         Museum of Anthropology, University of Michigan, no. 15. Ann
         Arbor: University of Michigan Press.
Aranda, Chepa
  1985   Las trabajadoras de agroindustrias y de la unidades agricolas-
         industriales para la mujer campesina. Mimeograph.
Archivo General del Estado de Oaxaca
  1890   Padrón general de población, Teotitlán del Valle.
  1926a Sección de gobernación, *Diario oficial,* vol. 34, no. 2:1–4.
  1926b Sección de gobernación, *Periódico oficial,* vol. 8, no. 4:27–28.
Archivo Municipal de Teotitlán del Valle
  1863–1984   Registro de difunciones.
  1868   Padrón general de población.

1890   Padrón electoral.
1900   Padrón general de población.
1914   Copiador de oficios.
1918   Copiador de oficios, no. 48.
1920   Padrón general de población.
1925   Noticia mensual de la casa del pueblo de Teotitlán del Valle (February–April).
1927   Copiador de oficios, no. 17.
1928   Copiador de circulares, no. 14.
1930–1939 Copiadores de oficios.
1931a   Copiador de oficios, July 13.
1931b   Copiador de oficios, August 31.
1932   Copiador de oficios, no. 113, February 17.
1938   Copiador de oficios.
1981   Censo del pueblo.
Arizpe, Lourdes
1985   *Campesinado y migración.* Mexico City: Secretaría de Educación Pública.
Arizpe, Lourdes, and Josefina Aranda
1981   The "Comparative Advantage" of Women's Disadvantages: Women Workers in the Strawberry Export Agribusiness in Mexico. *Signs* 7(2):453–473.
Arizpe, Lourdes, and Carlota Botey
1987   Mexican Agricultural Development Policy and Its Impact on Rural Women. In Deere and Léon 1987.
Atl, Dr. (Gerardo Murillo)
1922   *Las artes populares en México.* Mexico City: Secretaría de Industria y Comercio.
Babb, Florence E.
1986   Producers and Reproducers: Andean Market Women in the Economy. In Nash and Safa 1986.
1989   *Between Field and Cooking Pot: The Political Economy of Marketwomen in Peru.* Austin: University of Texas Press.
Baizerman, Suzanne
1988   Tourist Art, Ethnicity, and Economic Development: Hispanic Weavers in Northern New Mexico. Paper prepared for the Latin American Studies Association 14th International Congress, New Orleans, Louisiana, March 17–19, 1988.
Forthcoming Textile Tourist Art: Can We Call It Traditional? In *Mesoamerican and Andean Cloth and Costume,* ed. M. Schevill, J. Berlo, and E. Dwyer. San Francisco: Garland Press.
Barabas, Alicia, and Miguel Bartolomé
1986   La pluralidad desigual en Oaxaca. In *Ethnicidad y pluralismo cultural: La dinámica étnica en Oaxaca,* ed. A. Barabas and M. Bartolomé. Mexico City: Instituto Nacional de Antropología e Historia.

Barlow, Robert H.
1949   *The Extent of the Empire of the Culhua Mexica.* Ibero Americana no. 28. Berkeley: University of California Press.
Barth, Fredrick
1969   Introduction. In *Ethnic Groups and Boundaries,* ed. F. Barth. London: Allen and Unwin.
Bartolomé, Miguel Alberto
1979   Conciencia étnica y autogestión indígena. In *Indianidad y descolonización en América Latina: Documentos de la Segunda Reunión de Barbados.* Mexico City: Editorial Nueva Imagen.
Beals, Ralph
1970   Gifting, Reciprocity, Savings and Credit in Peasant Oaxaca. *Southeastern Journal of Anthropology* 26(3):231–241.
Benería, Lourdes
1979   Reproduction, Production and the Sexual Division of Labour. *Cambridge Journal of Economics* 3:203–225.
Benería, Lourdes, and Martha Roldán
1987   *The Crossroads of Class and Gender.* Chicago: University of Chicago Press.
Benería, Lourdes, and Gita Sen
1986   Accumulation, Reproduction and Women's Role in Economic Development: Boserup Revisited. In *Women's Work: Development and the Division of Labor by Gender,* ed. E. Leacock and H. Safa. South Hadley, Mass.: Bergin and Garvey Publishers.
Benítez Zenteno, Raúl (ed.)
1980   *Sociedad y política en Oaxaca 1980: Quince estudios de caso.* Oaxaca: Instituto de Investigaciones Sociológicas, UABJO.
Bennet, Vivienne
1988   Women and Class Struggle in the Sphere of Reproduction: Social Conflict over Urban Water Services in Monterrey, Mexico, 1973–1985. Paper presented at the 46th International Congress of Americanists, Amsterdam, the Netherlands, July 4–8, 1988.
Bennholdt-Thomsen, Veronika
1980   Toward a Class Analysis of Agrarian Sectors: Mexico. *Latin American Perspectives* 7(4):100–114.
Blanton, Richard E.
1978   *Monte Albán: Settlement Patterns at the Ancient Zapotec Capital.* New York: Academic Press.
Bonfil Batalla, Guillermo
1981   Utopía y revolución: El pensamiento político contemporáneo de los indios en América Latina. In *Utopía y Revolución,* ed. Guillermo Bonfil Batalla. Mexico City: Editorial Nueva Imagen.
Borque, Susan C., and Kay B. Warren
1981   *Women of the Andes.* Ann Arbor: University of Michigan Press.
Bossen, Laurel Herbenar
1984   *The Redivision of Labor.* Albany: State University of New York Press.

Bourgois, Phillip
  1988   Conjugated Oppression: Class and Ethnicity among Guaymi and Kuna Banana Workers. *American Ethnologist* 15(2):328–348.
Brandes, Stanley
  1981   Cargos versus Cost Sharing in Mesoamerican Fiestas with Special Reference to Tzintzuntzan. *Journal of Anthropological Research* 37(3):209–225.
  1988   *Power and Persuasion: Fiestas and Social Control in Rural Mexico.* Philadelphia: University of Pennsylvania Press.
Brintnall, Douglas
  1979   *Revolt against the Dead: The Modernization of a Mayan Community in the Highlands of Guatemala.* New York: Gordon and Breach.
Brito de Martí, José
  1982   *Almanaque de Oaxaca.* Oaxaca: Gobernador del Estado.
Browner, Carol
  1986a   Gender Roles and Social Change: A Mexican Case Study. *Ethnology* 25(2):89–105.
  1986b   The Politics of Reproduction in a Mexican Village. *Signs* 11(4):710–724.
Buci-Glucksman, Christine
  1980   *Gramsci and the State.* Trans. David Fernbach. London: Lawrence and Wishart.
Buechler, Judith Maria
  1986   Women in Petty Commodity Production in La Paz, Bolivia. In Nash and Safa 1986.
Bukh, Jette
  1979   *The Village Woman in Ghana.* Uppsala: Scandinavian Institute of African Studies.
Bunster-Burotto, Ximena
  1986   Surviving beyond Fear: Women and Torture in Latin America. In Nash and Safa 1986.
Burgoa, Fray Francisco de
  1934   *Geográfica descripción.* 2 vols. Mexico City: Archivo General de la Nación (1st ed. 1674).
Burgos-Debray, Elizabeth (ed.)
  1984   *I, Rigoberta Menchú: An Indian Woman in Guatemala.* London: Verso.
Camarena, Milagros
  1988   Cronología del proceso organizativo de las mujeres en el sur del estado de Nayarit. Unpublished manuscript.
Canabal Cristiáni, Beatriz
  1985   Un grito de rebeldía. *Que sí, que no México.* November 1985.
Cancian, Frank
  1965   *Economics and Prestige in a Mayan Community.* Stanford: Stanford University Press.
  1990   The Zinacantán Cargo Waiting Lists as a Reflection of Social,

Political, and Economic Changes, 1952–1987. In Stephen and Dow 1990.

Carbajal Ríos, Carola

1988 Una experiencia de participación de las campesinas en el movimiento popular. In *Las mujeres en el campo*, ed. Josefina Aranda Bezaury. Oaxaca: Instituto de Investigaciones Sociológicas de la Universidad Autónoma Benito Juárez de Oaxaca.

Cardoso, F. H., and E. Faletto

1969 *Dependencia y desarrollo en América Latina.* Mexico City: Siglo Veintiuno Editores.

Carlsen, Laura

1989 Mexican Grassroots Social Movements. *Radical America* 22 (4): 35–52.

Carrillo, Teresa

1988 *Working Women and the "19th of September Mexican Garment Workers Union": The Significance of Gender.* Cambridge, Mass.: Harvard/MIT Women in Development Group Papers.

1990 Women and Independent Unionism in the Garment Industry. In Foweraker and Craig 1990.

Castile, George P.

1981 Issues in the Analysis of Enduring Cultural Systems. In *Persistent Peoples: Cultural Enclaves in Perspective*, ed. George P. Castile and Gilbert Kushner. Tucson: University of Arizona Press.

Chance, John

1978 *Race and Class in Colonial Oaxaca.* Stanford: Stanford University Press.

1990 Changes in Twentieth-Century Mesoamerican Cargo Systems. In Stephen and Dow 1990.

Chance, John K., and William B. Taylor

1985 Cofradías and Cargos: An Historical Perspective on the Mesoamerican Civil-Religious Hierarchy. *American Ethnologist* 12(1): 1–26.

Chávez, Leo R., Esteban Flores, and Marta López Garza

1989 Migrants and Settlers: A Comparison of Undocumented Mexicans and Central Americans in the United States. *Frontera Norte* 1(1): 49–75.

Chayanov, A. V.

1966 *The Theory of Peasant Economy.* Homewood, Ill.: Irwin.

Chiñas, Beverly

1973 *The Isthmus Zapotecs: Women's Roles in Cultural Context.* New York: Holt, Rinehart and Winston.

1987 Women: The Heart of Isthmus Zapotec Ceremonial Exchange. Paper presented at the 1987 Annual Meeting of the American Anthropological Association, November 18–22, Chicago, Illinois, 1987.

Clements, Helen
1988a Mujeres, trabajo y cambio social: Los casos de dos comunidades oaxaqueños. In *Las mujeres en el campo,* ed. Josefina Aranda Bezaury. Oaxaca: Instituto de Investigaciones Sociológicas de la Universidad Autónoma Benito Juárez de Oaxaca.
1988b Buscando la Forma: Self-Reorganization in Craft Commercialization. Paper presented at the 16th International Congress of Americanists, Amsterdam, the Netherlands, July 4–8, 1988.
Cohen, Jeffrey
1988 Zapotec Weaving: Performance Theory, from Verbal to Visual Art. Paper prepared for the American Ethnological Society Annual Meeting, St. Louis, Missouri, March 24–27, 1988.
Collier, Jane Fishburne, and Sylvia Junko Yanagisako (eds.)
1987 *Gender and Kinship: Essays toward a Unified Analysis.* Stanford: Stanford University Press.
Comisión Organizadora del Encuentro de Mujeres de los Sectores Populares de México, Centroamérica y el Caribe, et al.
1987 *Las mujeres del pueblo avanzan hacia la unidad.* Mexico City: Red de Mujeres del Consejo de Educación de Adultos de America Latina.
Cook, María Lorena
1990 Organizing Opposition in the Teachers' Movement in Oaxaca. In Foweraker and Craig 1990.
Cook, Scott
1982a Craft Production in Oaxaca, Mexico. *Cultural Survival Quarterly* 6(4): 18–20.
1982b *Zapotec Stoneworkers.* New York: University Press of America.
1984a Peasant Economy and the Dynamics of Rural, Industrial Commodity Production in the Oaxaca Valley, Mexico. *Journal of Peasant Studies* 12(1): 3–40.
1984b *Peasant Capitalist Industry.* New York: University Press of America.
1988 Crafts and Class: Thoughts about How the Production and Exchange of Craft Commodities Differentiates Society. Paper Presented at the 46th International Congress of Americanists, Amsterdam, the Netherlands, July 4–8, 1988.
Cook, Scott, and Leigh Binford
1986 Petty Commodity Production, Capital Accumulation, and Peasant Differentiation: Lenin vs. Chayanov in Rural Mexico. *Review of Radical Political Economics* 18(4): 1–31.
1988 Industrial Commodity Production and Agriculture in the Oaxaca Valley. Paper presented at the 46th International Congress of Americanists, Amsterdam, the Netherlands, July 4–8, 1988.
Cook, Scott, and Martin Diskin
1976 The Peasant Market Economy of the Valley of Oaxaca in Analysis and History. In *Markets of Oaxaca,* ed. S. Cook and M. Diskin. Austin: University of Texas Press.

Coordinadora Nacional del Movimiento Urbano, Coordinadora Nacional "Plan de Ayala," et al.
1987 México: La situación del país y la organización de la mujer del pueblo. In Comisión Organizadora del Encuentro de Mujeres de los Sectores Populares de México, Centroamérica y el Caribe, et al. 1987.
Correspondencia
1989 Women's Coalition Building: La Coordinadora de Mujeres Benita Galeana. *Correspondencia*, June 1989:19–20. San Antonio: Interchange/Woman to Woman.
Crummet, María de los Angeles
1987 Rural Women and Migration in Latin America. In Deere and León 1987.
Dalton, Margarita
1990 La organización política de las mujeres y el estado: El caso de Oaxaca. *Cuadernos mujeres en solidaridad, serie nuestra voz,* No. 1. Oaxaca: Apoyo a la Mujer Oaxaqueña, Serie de Desarrollos Económico y Social.
da Silva Ruiz, Gilberto
1980 *Examenen de una economía artesenal en Oaxaca.* Estudios de Antropología e Historia 21. Oaxaca: Centro Regional de Oaxaca, Instituto Nacional de Antropología e Historia.
Deere, Carmen Diana
1978 The Differentiation of the Peasantry and Family Structure: A Peruvian Case Study. *Journal of Family History* 3:422–438.
1979 Changing Relations of Production and Peruvian Peasant Women's Work. In *Women in Latin America*. Riverside, Cal.: Latin American Perspectives.
1986 Rural Women and Agrarian Reform in Peru, Chile, and Cuba. In Nash and Safa 1986.
1987 The Latin American Agrarian Reform Experience. In Deere and León 1987.
Deere, Carmen Diana, and Alain de Janvry
1979 A Conceptual Framework for the Empirical Analysis of Peasants. *American Journal of Agricultural Economics* 61:601–611.
1981 Demographic and Social Differentiation among Northern Peruvian Peasants. *Journal of Peasant Studies* 8(3):335–366.
Deere, Carmen Diana, and Magdalena León (de Leal)
1986 Rural Women and Agrarian Reform in Peru, Chile, and Cuba. In Nash and Safa 1986.
1987 (eds.) *Rural Women and State Policy: Feminist Perspectives on Latin American Agricultural Development.* Boulder: Westview Press.
de Janvry, Alain
1981 *The Agrarian Question and Reformism in Latin America.* Baltimore: Johns Hopkins University Press.

de la Fuente, Julio
  1949   *Yalálag: Una villa zapoteca serrana.* Serie Científica. Mexico City: Museo Nacional de Antropología.
del Paso y Troncoso, Francisco
  1981   *Relaciones geográficas de Oaxaca: Manuscritos de la Real Academia de la Historia de Madrid y del Archivo de Indias en Sevilla, Años 1579–1581.* Mexico City: Editorial Innovación, S.A. (originally published in 1890).
Dennis, Philip
  1987   *Inter-Village Conflict in Oaxaca.* New Brunswick, N.J.: Rutgers University Press.
Departamento de la Estadística Nacional
  1925–1928   *Censo general de habitantes, 30 de Noviembre 1921.* Mexico City: Talleres Gráficos de la Nación.
Diamond, Stanley
  1951   Dahomey: A Proto-State in West Africa. Ph.D. dissertation. Columbia University. Ann Arbor: University Microfilms.
Díaz Polanco, Hector
  1981   La teoría indigenista y la integración. In *Indigenismo, modernización y marginalidad: Una revisión crítica,* ed. H. Díaz-Polanco, F. Javéri Guerrero, et al. Mexico City: Centro de Investigación para la Integración Social.
Dirección General de Estadística
  1897–1899   *Censo general de la República Mexicana verificado el 20 de octubre de 1895.* Mexico City: Oficina de la Secretaría de Fomento.
  1906   *Censo general de la República Mexicana verificado el 29 de octubre de 1900.* Mexico City: Secretaría de Fomento.
  1918–1920   *Tercer censo de población de los Estados Unidos Mexicanos verificado el 27 de octubre de 1910.* Mexico City: Secretaría de Hacienda, Departamento de Fomento.
  1936   *Quinto censo de población, 15 de Mayo 1930.* Mexico City: Secretaría de la Economía Nacional.
  1946   *Sexto censo de población, 1940.* Mexico City: Secretaría de Industria y Comercio.
  1954   *Séptimo censo de población, 1950.* Mexico City: Secretaría de Industria y Comercio.
  1963   *Octavo censo general de población, 1960.* Mexico City: Secretaría de Industria y Comercio.
  1973   *Novena censo general de población, 1970.* Mexico City: Secretaría de Industria y Comercio.
Diskin, Martin
  1986   La economía de la comunidad étnica en Oaxaca. In *Etnicidad y pluralismo cultural: La dinámica étnica en Oaxaca,* ed. A. Barabas and M. Bartolomé. Mexico City: Instituto Nacional de Antropología e Historia.

Documentos del Movimiento Campesino
1984   Acuerdos y resoluciones del II congreso nacional ordinario de la CNPA. *Textual* 5 (17): 115–127.
Dow, James
1977   Religion in the Organization of a Mexican Peasant Economy. In *Peasant Livelihood: Studies in Economic Anthropology and Cultural Ecology*, ed. Rhoda Halperin and James Dow. New York: St. Martin's Press.
Earle, Duncan
1990   Appropriating the Enemy: Maya Religious Organization and Community Survival. In Stephen and Dow 1990.
Edholm, Felicity, Olivia Harris, and Kate Young
1977   Conceptualizing Women. *Critique of Anthropology* 3: 101–130.
El Guindi, Fadwa
1986   *The Myth of Ritual.* Phoenix: University of Arizona Press.
Engels, Frederick
1972   *The Origin of the Family, Private Property, and the State,* ed. with an introduction by Eleanor B. Leacock. New York: International Publishers.
Equipo Pueblo
1987   La lucha de la mujer campesina: Porqué luchan los campesinos? *Cuadernos Campesinos* no. 3: 18–23.
1988   *Testimonios indígenas: Yalálag.* Mexico City: Equipo Pueblo.
Feijoo, Carmen, and Monica Gogna
1987   Mujeres, cotidianeidad y política. En *Ciudadanía e identidad: Las mujeres en los movimientos sociales latino-americanos,* ed. E. Jelin. Geneva: Instituto de Investigaciones de las Naciones Unidas para el Desarrollo Social (UNRISD).
Flannery, Kent, and Joyce Marcus
1983   The Changing Politics of A.D. 600–900. Editors' introduction in *The Cloud People,* ed. K. Flannery and J. Marcus. New York: Academic Press.
Flores Lúa, Luisa Parén, and Sergio Sarmiento Silva
1988   *Las voces del campo: Movimiento campesino y política agraria 1976–1984.* Mexico City: Siglo Veintiuno Editores.
Foster, George
1953   Cofradía and Compadrazgo in Spain and Spanish America. *Southwestern Journal of Anthropology* 9: 1–28.
1969   Godparents and Social Networks in Tzintzuntzan. *Southwestern Journal of Anthropology* 25: 261–278.
Foweraker, Joe, and Ann L. Craig
1990   *Popular Movements and Political Change in Mexico.* Boulder: Lynne Rienner Publishers.
Fox, Jonathan
1990   Democracy and the Development Process: Leadership Accountability in State-Structured Peasant Organizations. Unpublished manuscript.

Fox, Jonathan, and Luis Hernández
    1990   Offsetting the Iron Law of Oligarchy: The Ebb and Flow of Leadership Accountability in a Regional Peasant Organization. *Grassroots Development* 13 (2): 8–15.
Frank, Andre Gunther
    1967   *Capitalism and Underdevelopment in Latin America.* New York: Monthly Review Press.
Friedlander, Judith
    1975   *Being Indian in Hueyapan: A Study of Forced Identity in Contemporary Mexico.* New York: St. Martin's Press.
Fry, Douglas
    1988   Intercommunity Differences in Aggression among Zapotec Children. *Child Development* 59(4): 1008–1019.
Furtado, Celso
    1970   *Economic Development of Latin America.* Cambridge, England: Cambridge University Press.
Gailey, Christine Ward
    1985a   The State of the State in Anthropology. *Dialectical Anthropology* 9: 65–89.
    1985b   The Kindness of Strangers: Transformations of Kinship in Precapitalist Class and State Formation. *Culture* 5(2): 3–16.
    1987a   *Kinship to Kingship: Gender Hierarchy and State Formation in the Tongan Islands.* Austin: University of Texas Press.
    1987b   Culture Wars: Resistance to State Formation. In *Power Relations and State Formation,* ed. C. Gailey and T. Patterson. Washington, D.C.: Américan Anthropological Association.
Gamio, M.
    1946   La identificación del indio. *América Indígena* 6: 99–103.
García Canclini, Néstor
    1982   *Las culturas populares en el capitalismo.* Mexico City: Editorial Nueva Imagen.
García y Griego, Manuel
    1981   The Importation of Mexican Contract Laborers to the United States, 1942–1964: Antecedents, Operations and Legacy. La Jolla, Cal.: Center for U.S. Mexican Studies.
Gay, José Antonio
    1881   *Historia de Oaxaca.* Mexico City: Imprenta del Comercio de Dublán y Cía.
Gerhard, Peter
    1972   *A Guide to the Historical Geography of New Spain.* Cambridge, England: Cambridge University Press.
Good Eshelman, Catharine
    1988a   *Haciendo la lucha: Arte y comercio Nahua de Guerrero.* Mexico City: Fondo de la Cultura Económica.
    1988b   Crafts, Commerce, and Cultural Identity: A Case Study of Nahua Economic Enterprise in Guerrero, Mexico. Paper presented at the

Latin American Studies Association, 14th International Congress, New Orleans, Louisiana, March 17–19, 1988.

Graburn, Nelson
1982 The Dynamics of Change in Tourist Arts. *Cultural Survival Quarterly* 6(4):7–14.

Gramsci, Antonio
1971 *Selections from the Prison Notebooks*, ed. and trans. Quintin Hoare and Geoffrey Nowell Smith. London: Lawrence and Wishart.

Greenberg, James
1981 *Santiago's Sword*. Berkeley: University of California Press.
1989 *Blood Ties: Life and Violence in Rural Mexico*. Tucson: University of Arizona Press.
1990 Sanctity and Resistance in Closed Corporate Indian Communities. In Stephen and Dow 1990.

Griffin, K.
1969 *Underdevelopment and Spanish America*. London: Macmillan.

Hamilton, Nora
1982 *The Limits of State Autonomy: Post-Revolutionary Mexico*. Princeton: Princeton University Press.

Harris, Olivia, and Kate Young
1981 Engendered Structures: Some Problems in the Analysis of Reproduction. In *The Anthropology of Pre-Capitalist Societies*, ed. J. Karn and J. Lobera. London: Routledge and Kegan Paul.

Harvey, Neil
1989 Corporatist Strategies and Popular Responses in Rural Mexico: State and Unions in Chiapas, 1968–1988. Ph.D. thesis. Department of Political Science, Essex University, England.
1990 Peasant Strategies and Corporatism in Chiapas. In Foweraker and Craig 1990.

Harvey, Penelope
1988 Muted or Ignored? Questions of Gender and Ethnicity in the Politics of the Southern Peruvian Andes. Paper presented at the Latin American Studies Association, 14th International Conference, New Orleans, Louisiana, March 17–19, 1988.

Heath Constable, Maria Joy
1982 *Lucha de clases: La industria, textil en Tlaxcala*. Mexico City: Ediciones El Caballito.

Hernández, Luis
1988 La Unión de Ejidos Lázaro Cárdenas: Autonomía y liderazgo en una organización campesina regional. Unpublished manuscript.

Higgins, Michael
1990 Martyrs and Virgins: Popular Religion in Mexico and Nicaragua. In Stephen and Dow 1990.

Holloman, Regina Evans
1969 Developmental Change in San Blas. Ph.D. dissertation. Northwestern University. Ann Arbor: University Microfilms.

Howe, James
  1986   *The Kuna Gathering: Contemporary Village Politics in Panama.*
          Austin: University of Texas Press.
Instituto Nacional de Estadística, Geografía e Informática
  1984   *Décimo censo general de población y vivienda, 1980.* Estado de
          Oaxaca. 2 vols. Mexico City: Dirección General de Integración y
          Análisis de la Información.
  1986   *La industria textil y del vestido en México 1976–1985.* Mexico
          City: Secretario de Programación y Presupuesto.
Jelin, Elizabeth
  1990   Citizenship and Identity: Final Reflections. In *Women and
          Change in Latin America,* ed. Elizabeth Jelin. London: Zed Books.
Kaplan, Temma
  1982   Female Consciousness and Collective Action: The Case of Bar-
          celona, 1910–1918. *Signs* 7(3):545–560.
Kay, G.
  1975   *Development and Underdevelopment: A Marxist Analysis.* Lon-
          don: Macmillan.
Kearney, Michael
  1972   *The Winds of Ixtepeji: World View and Society in a Zapotec
          Town.* New York: Holt, Rinehart and Winston.
Kemper, Robert
  1982   The Compadrazgo in Urban Mexico. *Anthropological Quarterly*
          55:17–30.
Kirkby, Anne V. T.
  1973   *The Use of Land and Water Resources in the Past and Present
          Valley of Oaxaca, Mexico.* Memoirs of the Museum of Anthro-
          pology, University of Michigan, no. 5. Ann Arbor: University of
          Michigan Press.
Kiser, George, and Martha Woody Kiser
  1979   The Second Bracero Era (1942–1964). Editors' introduction in
          Mexican Workers in the United States. Albuquerque: University
          of New Mexico Press.
Kowalewski, Stephen A.
  1976   Prehispanic Settlement Patterns of the Central Part of the Valley
          of Oaxaca, Mexico. Unpublished Ph.D. dissertation. University
          of Arizona, Tucson.
Lenin, V. I.
  1967   *Selected Works.* 3 vols. Vol. 3. New York: International Pub-
          lishers.
  1974   *The Development of Capitalism in Russia.* Moscow: Progress
          Publishers.
Leslie, Charles
  1960   *Now We Are Civilized: A Study of the World View of the Zapotec
          Indians of Mitla, Oaxaca.* Detroit: Wayne State University.
Littlefield, Alice
  1978   Exploitation and the Expansion of Capitalism: The Case of the

Hammock Industry of Yucatan. *American Ethnologist* 5(3): 495–508.
1979   The Expansion of Capitalist Relations of Production in Mexican Crafts. *Journal of Peasant Studies* 6(4):471–488.

Logan, Kathleen
1988   Women's Political Activity and Empowerment in Latin American Urban Movements. In *Urban Life: Readings in Urban Anthropology*, ed. G. Grelch and W. Zenner. Prospect Heights, Ill.: Waveland Press.
1990   Women's Participation in Urban Protest. In Foweraker and Craig 1990.

Lomonitz, Larissa
1977   *Networks and Marginality: Life in a Mexican Shantytown.* Stanford: Stanford University Press.

Loubet, Rolando
1988   Historia campesina: El caso de la Unión de Ejidos Lázaro Cárdenas de Ahuacatlán, Nayarit. Jomulco, Nayarit: Centro de Investigación y Capacitación para el Desarrollo Regional A.C.

Lozano, Rafael Cruz, and María Teresa Vargas
1982   Análisis para la creación de un centro de convenciones en la ciudad de Oaxaca. B.A. thesis. Instituto Tecnológica de Oaxaca. Oaxaca, Oaxaca, Mexico.

Magallón Cervantes, María del Carmen
1988   Participación de la mujer en las organizaciones campesinas: Algunas limitaciones. In *Las mujeres en el campo*, ed. Josefina Aranda Bezaury. Oaxaca: Instituto de Investigaciones Sociológicas de la Universidad Autónoma Benito Juárez de Oaxaca.

Malinowski, Bronislaw, and Julio de la Fuente
1982   *Malinowski in Mexico: The Economics of a Mexican Market System.* Ed. and with an introduction by Susan Drucker-Brown. London: Routledge and Kegan Paul.

Margolis, J.
1979   El papel de la mujer en la agricultura del Bajío. *Iztapalapa* 1(1): 158–169.

Marroquín, Alejandro D.
1977   *Balance del indigenismo: Informe sobre la política indigenista en América.* Mexico City: Instituto Indigenista Interamericano.

Martin, Joann
1990   Motherhood and Power: The Reproduction of a Woman's Culture of Politics in a Mexican Community. *American Ethnologist* 17(3): 470–490.

Martínez del Campo, M.
1985   *Industrialización en México: Hacia un análisis crítico.* Mexico City: Colegio de México.

Martínez Ríos, Jorge
1964   Análisis funcional de la "Guelaguetza Agrícola." *Revista Mexicana de Sociología* 26(1):79–125.

Marx, Karl

1881/1967   *Capital.* 3 vols. New York: International Publishers.

Mathews, Holly F.

1982   Sexual Status in Oaxaca, Mexico: An Analysis of the Relationship between Extradomestic Participation and Ideological Constructs of Gender. Ph.D. dissertation. Duke University.

1985   "We Are Mayordomo": A Reinterpretation of Women's Roles in the Mexican Cargo System. *American Ethnologist* 17:285–301.

Medina Hernández, Andrés

1983   Los grupos étnicos y los sistemas tradicionales de poder en México. *Nueva Antropología* 5(20):5–29.

Meillassoux, Claude

1975   *Femmes, grenier et capitaux.* Paris: Libraire François Maspero.

Mejía Piñeros, María Consuelo, and Sergio Sarmiento Silva

1987   *La lucha indígena: Un reto a la ortodoxia.* Mexico City: Siglo Veintiuno Editores.

Mercado García, Alfonso

1980   *Estructura y dinamismo del mercado de tecnología industrial en México.* Mexico City: Colegio de México.

Mies, Maria

1982   *The Lace Makers of Narsapur: Indian Housewives Produce for the World Market.* London: Zed Press.

Mintz, Sidney W., and Eric Wolf

1950   An Analysis of Ritual Coparenthood (Compadrazgo). *Southwestern Journal of Anthropology* 6:341–365.

Morris, Walter F.

1986   Crafts, Crap and Art: The Marketing of Maya Textiles in Highland Chiapas, Mexico. Unpublished manuscript.

Las Mujeres Tenemos la Palabra . . .

1988   III Encuentro Nacional de Mujeres de la CONAMUP, Zacatecas, Zacatecas, November 20, 21, and 22, 1987. Mexico City: Ediciones Pueblo.

Munck, Ronaldo

1985   *Politics and Dependency in the Third World.* London: Zed Press.

Nader, Laura

1964   Talea and Juquila: A Comparison of Zapotec Social Organization. *University of California Publications in American Archaeology and Ethnology,* vol. 46, part 3:195–296.

Nagengast, Marian Carole

1990   *The Polish Paradox: Rural Class, Culture and the State.* Boulder: Westview Press.

Nash, June

1970   *In the Eyes of the Ancestors: Belief and Behavior in a Maya Community.* New Haven: Yale University Press.

1986   A Decade of Research on Women in Latin America. In Nash and Safa 1986.

Nash, June, and Helen Safa
1986   *Women and Change in Latin America.* South Hadley, Mass.: Bergin and Garvey Publishers.

Novelo, Victoria
1976   *Artesanías y capitalismo en México.* Mexico City: SEP-INAH.
1988   Las artesanías en México. Paper presented at the 46th International Congress of Americanists. Amsterdam, the Netherlands, July 4–8, 1988.

Novo, Salvador
1932   Nuestras artes populares. *Nuestro México* 1(5):56.

Nutini, Hugo
1984   *Ritual Kinship: Ideological and Structural Integration of the Compadrazgo System in Rural Tlaxcala.* Vol. 2. Princeton: Princeton University Press.

Nutini, Hugo G., and Betty Bell
1980   *Ritual Kinship: The Structure and Historical Development of the Compadrazgo System in Rural Tlaxcala.* Vol. 1. Princeton, N.J.: Princeton University Press.

Nutini, Hugo, and Timothy Murphy
1970   Labor Migration and Family Structure in the Tlaxcalan-Pueblan Area, Mexico. In *The Social Anthropology of Latin America*, ed. W. Goldschmidt and H. Hojier. Los Angeles: University of California Press.

O'Nell, Carl W.
1979   Nonviolence and Personality Dispositions among the Zapotec. *Journal of Psychological Anthropology* 2:301–322.
1981   Hostility Management and the Control of Aggression in a Zapotec Community. *Aggressive Behavior* 7:351–366.
1986   Primary and Secondary Effects of Violence Control among the Nonviolent Zapotec. *Anthropological Quarterly* 59(4):184–203.

Ortigoza, Gabriela
1986   Cambio y resistencia en la mujer Yalateca. B.A. thesis. Escuela Nacional de Antropología e Historia, Mexico City.

Padilla, Martha Luz, Clara Murguialday, and Ana Criquillon
1987   Impact of the Sandinista Agrarian Reform on Rural Women's Subordination. In Deere and León 1987.

Parnell, Phillip
1988   *Escalating Disputes: Social Participation and Change in the Oaxacan Highlands.* Tucson: University of Arizona Press.

Parrish, Timothy
1982   Class Structure and Social Reproduction in New Spain/Mexico. *Dialectical Anthropology* 7:115–136.

Parsons, Elsie Clews
1936   *Mitla: Town of Souls.* Chicago: University of Chicago Press.

Partido Feminista Revolucionario de Tabasco
1933   *Tabasco feminista* (March 1933). In the permanent collection of the Bancroft Library, University of California, Berkeley.

Peterson Royce, Anya
1975   *Prestigio y afiliación en una comunidad urbana: Juchitán, Oaxaca.* Mexico City: Instituto Nacional Indigenista.
1982   *Ethnic Identity: Strategies of Diversity.* Bloomington: Indiana University Press.
Portes, Alejando
1984   The Rise of Ethnicity. *American Sociological Review* 49(3): 383–397.
Primero Congreso Feminista de Yucatán
1917   *Primero congreso feminista de Yucatán convocado por el governador y comandante militar de Estado Gral. D. Salvador Alvarado, 13–16 enero de 1916.* Mérida, Yucatán: Talleres Tipográficos del "Ateno Peninsular." In permanent collection at the Bancroft Library, University of California, Berkeley.
Radcliffe, Sarah
1988   Así es una mujer del pueblo: Low-Income Women's Organizations under APRA 1985–87, The Case of the Domestic Servants. Paper presented at the Latin American Studies Association, 14th International Congress, New Orleans, Louisiana, March 17–19, 1988.
Raisz, Katherine
1986   Wooing Industry to Oaxaca: A Long Term Project. *Mexico City News,* January 13, 1986, p. 39.
Ramirez Saiz, Juan Manuel
1988   Para comprender el movimiento urbano popular (MUP). *Movimientos Sociales* 1:28–60. Guadalajara, Mexico: Centro de Investigaciones sobre los Movimientos Sociales.
Redfield, Robert, and Sol Tax
1952   General Characteristics of Present-Day Mesoamerican Indian Society. In *Heritage of Conquest,* ed. Sol Tax. Glencoe, Ill.: Free Press.
Robbins, Edward
1975   Ethnicity or Class? Social Relations in a Small Canadian Industrial Community. In *The New Ethnicity: Perspectives from Ethnology, 1973* Proceedings of the American Ethnological Society, ed. John W. Bennet. New York: West Publishing.
Rosaldo, Michelle Zimbalist
1974   Woman, Culture, and Society: A Theoretical Overview. In *Woman, Culture and Society,* ed. Michele Zimbalist Rosaldo and Louise Lamphere. Stanford: Stanford University Press.
Roseberry, William
1989   *Anthropologies and Histories: Essays in Culture, History, and Political Economy.* New Brunswick: Rutgers University Press.
Rosenblum, Keith
1988   More Mexican Women Achieving Prominence in Nation's Political Life. *Arizona Daily Star,* December 4, 1988, p. 3.

Rothstein, Frances
1982 *Three Different Worlds: Men, Women, and Children in an Indus-trializing Town.* Westport, Conn.: Greenwood Press.
Rubin, Jeffrey
1987 State Policies, Leftist Oppositions and Municipal Elections: The Case of the COCEI in Juchitán. In *Electoral Patterns and Perspective in Mexico,* ed. Arturo Alvarado. Monograph Series no. 22. San Diego: Center for U.S.-Mexican Studies.
1990 Popular Mobilization and the Myth of State Corporatism. In Foweraker and Craig 1990.
Sacks, Karen Brodkin
1988 *Caring by the Hour: Women, Work and Organizing at Duke Medical Center.* Urbana: University of Illinois Press.
Salinas, Gloria Ardaya
1986 Women's Equality and the Cuban Revolution. In Nash and Safa 1986.
Salomon, Frank
1981 Weavers of Otavalo. In *Cultural Transformations and Ethnicity in Modern Ecuador,* ed. Norman E. Whitten, Jr. Urbana: University of Illinois Press.
Salvucci, Richard J.
1987 *Textiles and Capitalism in Mexico: An Economic History of the Obrajes, 1539–1840.* Princeton: Princeton University Press.
Sapir, Edward
1956 Culture, Genuine and Spurious. In *Language, Culture and Personality,* ed. D. Mandelbaum. Berkeley: University of California Press.
Sault, Nicole
1985a Zapotec Godmothers: The Centrality of Women for Compadrazgo Groups in a Village of Oaxaca, Mexico. Ph.D. dissertation, University of California, Los Angeles.
1985b Baptismal Sponsorship as a Source of Power for Zapotec Women in Oaxaca, Mexico. *Journal of Latin American Lore* 11(2): 225–243.
1987 Godparenthood in Latin America, Joining Kinship and Gender. Paper presented at the Annual Meeting of the American Anthropological Association, Chicago, Illinois, November 18–22, 1987.
Secretaría de Agricultura y Recursos Hidráulicos, Oaxaca
1977, 1978, 1982, 1983 Datos definitivos de cultivos cíclicos. Dirección General de Economía Agrícola, Departamento de Estadística Agropecuaria Nacional Producción Cultivos. Oaxaca, Mexico.
Secretaría de la Economía Nacional
1934 *La industria textil en México: El problema obrero y los problemas económico.* Mexico City: Talleres Gráficos de la Nación.
Secretaría de Programación y Presupuesto
1979–1985 Cuestionario de inscripciones, inicio de cursos. Dirección General de Estadística. Oaxaca, Oaxaca.
1981 Carta de precipitación total anual. Mexico City.

Segura, Jaime Jesús

1979   Vinculación estado y sistema de cargos en una comunidad: Teoti-
        tlán del Valle. B.A. thesis. Centro de Sociología, Universidad Au-
        tónoma Benito Juárez de Oaxaca.

1980   El sistema de cargos en Teotitlán del Valle, Oaxaca. In *Sociedad y
        política en Oaxaca 1980.* Barcelona: ICARIA Editorial, S.A.

Selby, Henry

1974   *Zapotec Deviance: The Convergence of Folk and Modern Sociol-
        ogy.* Austin: University of Texas Press.

Sider, Gerald

1976   Lumbee Indian Cultural Nationalism and Ethnogenesis. *Dia-
        lectical Anthropology* 1(2): 161–171.

1986   *Culture and Class in Anthropology and History: A New-
        foundland Illustration.* Cambridge, England: Cambridge Univer-
        sity Press.

Siebold, Katharine

1987   Women's Networks in Choquecancha, Cuzco, Peru. Paper pre-
        sented at the Annual Meeting of the American Anthropological
        Association, Chicago, Illinois, November 18–22, 1987.

Silverblatt, Irene

1987   *Moon, Sun and Witches: Gender Ideologies and Class in Inca
        and Colonial Peru.* Princeton: Princeton University Press.

Silverman, Sydel

1966   An Ethnographic Approach to Social Stratification: Prestige in a
        Central Italian Community. *American Anthropologist* 68:
        899–921.

Smith, Carol

1984   Does a Commodity Economy Enrich the Few While Ruining the
        Masses? *Journal of Peasant Studies* 12(3): 60–95.

Smith, Richard Chase

1985   A Search for Unity within Diversity: Peasant Unions, Ethnic Fed-
        erations, and Indianist Movement in the Andean Republics. In
        Native Peoples and Economic Development, ed. Theodore Mac-
        Donald, Jr. Cambridge, Mass.: Cultural Survival.

Spicer, Edward

1971   Persistent Cultural Systems: A Comparative Study of Identity
        Systems That Can Adapt to Contrasting Environments. *Science*
        174: 795–800.

Spooner, Brian

1986   Weavers and Dealers: The Authenticity of an Oriental Carpet. In
        *The Social Life of Things: Commodities in Cultural Perspec-
        tives,* ed. A. Appadurai. Cambridge, England: Cambridge Univer-
        sity Press.

Stavenhagen, Rodolfo

1975   *Social Classes in Agrarian Societies.* Trans. Judith Adler Hellman.
        Garden City, N.Y.: Anchor Press/Doubleday.

Stephen, Lynn
  1987a Weaving Changes. Ph.D. dissertation. Department of Anthropology, Brandeis University. Ann Arbor: University Microfilms.
  1987b Zapotec Weavers of Oaxaca: Development and Community Control. *Cultural Survival Quarterly* 11(1):46–48.
  1988 Production, Social Reproduction, and Gender Roles in Zapotec Craft Production. Paper presented at the 46th International Congress of Americanists, Amsterdam, the Netherlands, July 4–8, 1988.
  1989a Anthropology and the Politics of Facts, Knowledge, and History. *Dialectical Anthropology* 14:259–269.
  1989b Popular Feminism in Mexico. *Z Magazine* 2(12):102–106.
  1990 The Politics of Ritual: The Mexican State and Zapotec Autonomy, 1926–1989. In Stephen and Dow 1990.
  1991a Culture as a Resource: Four Cases of Self-Managed Indigenous Craft Production. *Economic Development and Cultural Change* (July).
  1991b Zapotec Gender Politics: Gender and Class in the Political Participation of Indigenous Mexican Desert Women. Working Papers on Women in International Development, no. 216. East Lansing: Office of International Development, Michigan State University.
  1991c Export Markets and Their Effects on Indigenous Craft Production. In *Mesoamerican and Andean Cloth and Costume*, ed. M. Schevill, J. Berlo, and E. Dwyer. Oakland: Garland Press.
Stephen, Lynn, and James Dow (eds.)
  1990 *Class, Politics, and Popular Religion: Religious Change in Mexico and Central America.* Washington, D.C.: American Anthropological Association.
Stern, Steve J.
  1982 *Peru's Peoples and the Challenges of Spanish Conquest: Huamanga to 1640.* Madison: University of Madison Press.
  1987 New Approaches to the Study of Peasant Rebellion and Consciousness: Implications of the Andean Experience. In *Resistance, Rebellion, and Consciousness in the Andean Peasant World, 18th to 20th Centuries*, ed. S. Stern. Madison: University of Wisconsin Press.
Tamayo, Jorge L.
  1960 *Oaxaca: Breve monografía geográfica anexa a la carta municipal.* Mexico City: Instituto Panamericano de Geografía e Historia.
  1982 *Geografía de Oaxaca.* Mexico City: Comisión Editora de El Nacional, Cooperativa de Talleres Gráficos de la Nación.
Taylor, Robert B.
  1960 Teotitlán del Valle: A Typical Mesoamerican Community. Ph.D. dissertation. University of Oregon.
  1966 Conservative Factors in the Changing Culture of a Zapotec Town. *Human Organization* 25(2):116–121.

Taylor, William
  1972   *Landlord and Peasant in Colonial Oaxaca.* Stanford: Stanford University Press.
  1979   *Drinking, Homicide and Rebellion in Colonial Mexican Villages.* Stanford: Stanford University Press.
Turkenik, Carol
  1976   Agricultural Production Strategies in a Mexican Peasant Community. Ph.D. dissertation. University of California, Los Angeles.
UABJO. See Benítez Zenteno, Raúl
United Nations Secretariat
  1984   Population Distribution, Migration and Development: Highlights on the Issues in the Context of the World Population Plan of Action. In *Population Distribution, Migration and Development, International Conference on Population.* New York: United Nations.
van den Berghe, Pierre L.
  1981   *The Ethnic Phenomenon.* New York: Elsevier.
Varese, Stefano
  1982   Restoring Multiplicity: Indianities and the Civilizing Project in Latin America. *Latin American Perspectives* 9(2):29–41.
  1988   Multi-ethnicity and Hegemonic Construction: Indian Projects and the Global Future. In *Ethnicities and Nations: Processes of Interethnic Relations in Latin America, Southeast Asia, and the Pacific,* ed. Remo Guidieri, Francesco Pellizzi, and Stanley J. Tambiah. Austin: University of Texas Press.
Vargas-Barón, Emily
  1968   Development and Change of Rural Artisanry: Weaving Industries of the Oaxaca Valley, Mexico. Ph.D. dissertation. Stanford University.
Vogt, Evon A.
  1969   *Zinacantán: A Maya Community in the Highlands of Chiapas.* Cambridge, Mass.: Harvard University Press.
Volkman, Toby Alice
  1984   Great Performances: Toroja Cultural Identity in the 1970s. *American Ethnologist* 11(1):152–169.
  1985   *Fiestas of Honor: Ritual and Change in the Toroja Highlands.* Urbana: University of Illinois Press.
Walter, Lynn
  1981   Social Strategies and the Fiesta Complex in an Otavaleño Community. *American Ethnologist* 2:172–185.
Wasserstrom, Robert
  1983   *Class and Society in Central Chiapas.* Berkeley: University of California Press.
Weist, R. E.
  1973   Wage-Labour Migration and the Household in a Mexican Town. *Journal of Anthropological Research* 29(3):236–247.

Welte, Cecil
1965 *Mapa de las localidades del Valle de Oaxaca.* Oaxaca: Oficina de Estudios de Humanidad del Valle de Oaxaca.
Whitecotton, Joseph W.
1977 *The Zapotecs: Princes, Priests and Peasants.* Norman: University of Oklahoma Press.
Williams, Raymond
1977 *Marxism and Literature.* Oxford: Oxford University Press.
Winkler, Cathy
1987 Changing Power and Authority in Gender Roles, Ph.D. thesis. Indiana University. Ann Arbor: University Microfilms.
Wolf, Eric
1959 *Sons of the Shaking Earth.* Chicago: University of Chicago Press.
1986 The Vicissitudes of the Closed Corporate Peasant Community. *American Ethnologist* 13(2):320–325.
Wright, Erik Olin
1979 *Class Structure and Income Determination.* New York: Academic Press.
1985 *Classes.* London: Verso Editions.
Young, Kate
1976 The Social Setting of Migration. Ph.D. dissertation. London University.
1978 Modes of Appropriation and the Sexual Division of Labour: A Case Study from Oaxaca, Mexico. In *Feminism and Materialism: Women and Modes of Production,* ed. Annette Kuhn and Ann Marie Wolpe. London: Routledge and Kegan Paul.

Index

Subsistence Company), 234
Conquest. *See* Spanish colonial rule
constitution of 1917, 90, 171
Cook, Scott, 22, 23, 33, 82, 126,
    127, 149
Coordinadora de Mujeres "Benita
    Galeana," 244
Coordinadora Nacional de Campe-
    sinos (CNC), 91, 230, 236, 237,
    238–239, 240
Coordinadora Nacional del Movie-
    miento Urbano Popular
    (CONAMUP), 228, 242,
    243–244, 276n.3
Coordinadora Nacional "Plan de
    Ayala" (CNPA), 229, 240–245,
    256
    women in, 241–245
copiadores de oficios, 267
counterhegemonic activity, 100,
    251
Coyolapan, 107
Coyotepec, 123
Crummet, María de los Angeles,
    115, 116
Cuba, 254–255
Cuilapan, 81
cultural nationalism, 13–14
culture, social-scientific concep-
    tions of, 11, 14

dad, 156, 167–168, 215
dancing, 188
da Silva Ruiz, Gilberto, 67
Deere, Carmen Diana, 23, 115
Department of Education and Cul-
    ture for the Indian Race, 91–92
Department of General Statistics,
    93
Department of Indian Education, 92
Diamond, Stanley, 14
Díaz Ordaz, 87, 93, 107–108, 127
DICONSA (Distribuidora
    CONASUPO S.A.), 237
diseases, 67–69
Diskin, Martin, 22, 33–34, 82

domestic violence, 42, 43, 45, 53
dress, 40, 41, 46, 52
dyeing, 128, 131–132

Edholm, Felicity, 37, 38
education, 44–45, 49–50, 57–58,
    91, 149, 222, 224
    unequal, for women, 53, 56, 62,
    150–51
ejidos, 91, 230, 236–237, 272n.4
El Guindi, Fadwa, 32, 191
Engels, Frederick (Friedrich), 37, 39
Ensenada, 117
Escipulas, 46, 47, 170
ethnicity, 241, 251–252
    concepts of, 11–15
    intersection of, with class and
        gender, 11, 12, 154, 207,
        251–254
    in Mexico, 15–17; *see also* "In-
        dian" identity
    Teotitecos' construction of,
        12–13, 17, 19–21, 29
ethnographies of the Zapotecs, 22,
    29–31, 33–36, 66–67
Etla (Villa de Etla), 81
exchange, reciprocal. *See*
    guelaguetza

familia, 191–192
farming, 66, 70–78, 103–105, 111
    women's role in, 76–78, 104–105
feminists, 176, 243–244, 256
fieldwork, author's, 2–6, 261–268
fiestas
    animal production for, 78,
        196–199
    common occurrence of, in
        Teotitlán, 3, 64
    and *compadrazgo*, 191–194
    costs of, 192–193, 205–207
    differences between merchant
        and weaver households in re-
        gard to, 179, 197–198,
        201–202, 204–207, 252–253
    gendered division of labor in,

merchant class, 61, 118–119, 141,
154
women in, 154
merchant households, 209–216
class location of, 23, 24–25,
40–41
importance of women's and children's unpaid labor to, 124–127
proportion of, in Teotitlán, 80,
97, 124
and rituals, 183–184, 204–207
wealth of, 209–214
women's power within, 44–45,
48, 119, 202–203, 207
merchants, 20, 123–125, 144, 252
attitudes of, toward women's political participation, 218–221
defined, 24, 25, 118
as godparents, 123–124, 204–205
growing number of, 109, 110
and political authority, 141, 154,
216
recruitment of labor by, 21, 81,
119, 123–124
and rituals, 201, 215–216
see also merchant women
merchant/traders, 26
flourishing of, under system of
obligatory *mayordomías*, 26,
90, 106, 174–175
merchant women, 21, 40–45,
48–52
differences between, and weaver
women, 25, 204–205; in regard
to rituals, 179, 197–198,
201–202, 204–207, 252–253
and household decision making,
119, 149–150, 153, 202–203,
207
and politics, 209, 220–226, 234
Mexican government. *See* state,
Mexican
Mexican Revolution, 133, 175, 232
effects of, on Teotitlán, 26,
89–90, 100, 105, 163–164
Mexico, 119, 120
Mexico City, 112, 141, 228, 254

Mies, María, 115
migration to United States, 66, 146
effects of male, on women's roles,
27–28, 46–47, 109, 111, 113,
114–115, 126
use of savings generated by, 114,
115, 126
by women, 55, 56, 58–61, 151
see also *bracero* program
Mitla, 18–19, 20, 81, 93, 102, 107,
273n.4
Mixe, 19
Mixtecos, 59
monolingualism, Zapotec, 3, 40,
83–84, 151–152, 223
extent of, in Teotitlán, 83, 99
of older women, 3, 40
Monte Albán, 18, 20, 83, 102,
273n.4
Morelos, 16, 116, 255
Movimiento de Unificación y Lucha Triqui (MULT), 16–17, 241
municipio
functions of, 84–85
gradual separation of religious
and civil authority in,
171–173, 176, 208
offices in. *See* civil cargo system
relation of merchants to, 141,
154, 216
relations of, with federal and
state governments, 84–85,
99–103, 171, 175
Teotitlán as a long-standing, 19,
84
women in, 7, 176, 216–223; *see
also* civil cargo system, exclusion of women from most
offices in
municipios in other Oaxaca communities, 19; *See also* Yalálag

nán, 156, 167–168, 215, 274n.7
National Agrarian Commission, 90
National Commission of Roads, 90
National Indian Institute (INI), 91,
92

226 - social reproduction
256 - mothering motives
258 - of these organizations to NWAC
14. ethnicity & authentic culture
16 identity & grassroots politics
29 reproduction of legitimate social actors
32 ff. of ritual healing / potlatch
34 social reproduction / pit parties
3? social repro. defined
99. conversion of marginality to exotic
119. state/church moral orders + gender
157 political participation
248 struggle for legitimacy in community
175. self-determination ritual / of potlatch
177 9.5 self perceptions & the vote
177 ritual of potlatch + distance from
state (neo traditionalism)
179. class conflict of potlatch + strata in
Carrier - diff of economic, inherited
status mediated in ritual - class matter
ongoing construction of local identity

249. transformative nature of & political cult

387 historical periods
pol' econ of dev. + women
political culture
- special interest; health
education ?